Praise for
ONE
MORE
MOUNTAIN

For addressing a daunting and serious topic, *One More Mountain* was an entertaining page-turner! I became attached to the characters and could picture the lives they were living in Iran and on their journey. The intimate stories of family connections, traditions, and memories had you invested in their happiness and success. I loved learning about the beauty of the Baha'i faith as well as the rugged beauty of the Iranian landscape. This is the type of tale that should be read by all, so we can understand the value of freedom and never take it for granted.

Thank you for sharing your amazing and heroic story with us.

—Sabina Kilpatrick

As an American, I was hardly aware of the Baha'i faith at all, let alone understand the complicated relationship the Baha'i followers have with Muslim countries, especially Iran, where Baha'i's have been persecuted for decades. Mansur's story is one of a young man fleeing his homeland in search of religious freedom. It takes a tremendous amount of courage to leave everything behind for a future that is hopeful but uncertain. When his journey doesn't go according to plan, Mansur relies on instinct, sharp intellect, and perseverance to navigate his path to freedom. He details his treacherous voyage, trekking for days through the Iranian mountains in frigid temperatures, often at night, and always on alert for hidden dangers such as wolves and trackers.

As harrowing as his tale of escape may have been, it's ultimately a heartwarming story about a man who stayed true to his faith, made friends along the way, and ultimately achieved the American Dream.

—Sarah Moore

ONE MORE MOUNTAIN

Fleeing Iran for America

MANSUR NURDEL WITH JEANNETTE MONINGER

For information about this title or to order other books and/or electronic media, contact the publisher:

Del Mar Investments
www.OneMoreMountain.com
delmarbooks22@gmail.com

ISBNs:
979-8-9878086-0-3 (hardcover)
979-8-9878086-1-0 (softcover)
979-8-9878086-2-7 (eBook)

Printed in the United States of America

Cover and interior design: 1106 Design

In loving memory of my much-missed friend,
Tofigh Tabarmanaf

Since the Islamic Revolution began in 1979, millions of Iranians have fled to Turkey, seeking refuge from religious and political persecution. This is the story of one man's escape to freedom.

Contents

Foreword

by Mansur Nurdel

When I came to the United States at age twenty-five in 1989, fleeing religious persecution and certain death at the hands of my fellow countrymen in Iran, I counted myself among the tired, the poor, and the huddled masses yearning to breathe free. I collapsed into, and then thrived in, Lady Liberty's welcoming embrace.

Since my arrival, I have dedicated my life to caring for others—a promise I made during my perilous escape from an Islamic government that deemed my life unworthy. Today, as a doctor with thriving optometry practices throughout the metro-Denver area, I have protected and saved the vision of hundreds of people. I have helped other refugees fleeing religious persecution plant roots in their new homeland, just as I received help more than three decades ago. I consider it both an honor and a calling to help immigrants from all pockets of the world become productive American citizens. Regrettably, this mission has become almost impossible to achieve over the last several years.

A presidential executive order issued on January 27, 2017, titled "Protecting the Nation from Foreign Terrorist Entry into the United States" barred immigrants from predominantly Islamic countries—Iran, Iraq, Libya, Somalia, Sudan, Syria, and Yemen. Of course, not everyone who lives in these countries is a Muslim. And the vast majority of Muslims are peace-loving people, not terrorists, as the order implies. But when the executive order went into effect, it prevented all citizens from these countries from seeking asylum in the United States, regardless of their faith or life-and-death circumstances.

I am a follower of the Bahá'í Faith, a religion founded in Iran nearly 200 years ago that's now embraced and practiced all over the world. But in Iran, Bahá'í followers are continually marginalized, persecuted, and abused. A brief history of the Bahá'í Faith is necessary to truly understand the gravity of the story you're about to read. I hope it will also help you appreciate the enormous impact that a sweeping immigration ban has on people who are routinely terrorized in their homelands.

In the 1800s, followers of many faiths greatly anticipated the return of God's Promised One. Joseph Smith, founder of Mormonism, had a prophetic vision in 1820 in which he saw God returning with Jesus. William Miller, an American Baptist preacher, proclaimed that the Second Coming of Christ would happen in the 1840s. In the 1860s, Christoph Hoffmann convinced his Templer followers to leave Germany and build a settlement in the Holy Land of Palestine in anticipation of Christ's return. Around the same time, followers of the Islamic Shaykhi movement in the Middle East also prepared for the Qur'an's Promised One, the Twelfth Imam.

And then there was Siyyid Ali Muhammad.

In 1844, this young Iranian merchant proclaimed he was The Báb, which means "the gate." The Báb said he was like a gate to a divine messenger who would arrive soon to convey religious truths to the people. The Báb and this new messenger would assume their places in a line of prophets succeeding Moses, Jesus Christ, and Muhammad.

Muslims believe Muhammad was the last and final Prophet of God and that there will be no others. The Báb's teachings of future prophets were considered blasphemous and a threat to the very foundations of Islam. Islamic clergy implored the country's leaders to act. And they did. Within a decade, more than 20,000 Báb followers (Bábís) were tortured and slaughtered. Austrian Captain Alfred von Goumoens, who was employed by the Shah in the 1850s, left his post after witnessing the government's horrific treatment of Bábís. In the book *God Passes By*, a history of the Bahá'í Faith from 1844 to 1944, author Shoghi Effendi captures the captain's written observations: *"They will skin the soles of the Bábís' feet, soak the wounds in boiling oil, shoe the foot like the hoof of a horse, and compel the victim to run . . . As for the end itself, they hang the scorched and perforated bodies by their hands and feet to a tree head downwards, and now every Persian may try his marksmanship to his heart's content . . . I saw corpses torn by nearly one hundred and fifty bullets."*

After a firing squad executed The Báb in 1850, follower Mírzá Husayn Alí continued his teachings. He became known as Bahá'u'lláh, which means "the Glory of God." Building on The Báb's teachings, Bahá'u'lláh established the Bahá'í Faith in 1863. Bahá'ís consider The Báb and Bahá'u'lláh to be two of God's prophets, but they are certainly not the last.

Followers of Islam cite the Bahá'í belief in additional prophets after Muhammad as their main reason for mistreating Bahá'ís. I call this propaganda. It is a lie told to distract people from the real reason. They do not approve of the Bahá'í Faith's founding principles: equal rights for women and men; a blending of religions, cultures, and ethnicities to eliminate prejudices; and universal education for all. These teachings inherently challenge the Islamic clerical structure and the power and authority wielded by Muslim clergy.

History shows that the government's attempts at suppression became more ruthless as the number of Bahá'ís grew throughout Persia during the nineteenth and twentieth centuries. Homes of Bahá'í followers were pillaged and destroyed. Women and children were abducted and forced to become part of Muslim families. In cities across Iran, a great number of believers met gruesome deaths: beheaded, hanged, burned, and hacked into pieces. Bahá'u'lláh and other Bahá'í leaders were banished forever from their native land.

These atrocities continue today.

With the formation of the Islamic Republic of Iran in 1979, the government stripped Bahá'ís of all human rights. Over the past forty years, Bahá'ís have been routinely arrested, detained, tortured, imprisoned, and executed without cause. They are barred from higher education and unable to pursue careers in medicine, law, government, education, or any high-paying field. Their marriages are considered invalid and go unregistered. Their businesses face widespread discrimination, vandalism, and arson, resulting in financial ruin. Malicious acts against Bahá'ís go unpunished. Many Bahá'í holy sites have been plundered, destroyed, or taken over by Islamic factions. Despite this treatment, the Bahá'í Faith has grown to more than 5,000,000 followers throughout 200 countries and territories worldwide. You might be familiar with a few of them: actors Rainn Wilson from *The Office*, Eva La Rue from *CSI: Miami*, Justin Baldoni from *Jane the*

Virgin, legendary jazz trumpeter Dizzy Gillespie, painter Mark Tobey, the first African-American Rhodes Scholar Alain Locke, and singer Andy Grammer.

Of the 83 million people living in Iran today, almost all—99%—are Muslim. To be anything else is dangerous. Every year, Bahá'ís flee Iran in fear for their lives.

When the United States' immigration ban went into effect at the start of 2017, hundreds of hopeful Iranian Bahá'ís who had made their way to United Nations refugee camps in Turkey and other countries found themselves unexpectedly stuck in limbo. A refugee can apply for entry to only one country at a time, and it can take years for that country to grant or deny asylum. After receiving a denial, a refugee's only recourse is to start the long process over and apply for entry to a different country.

My cousin's son, Eman, was within weeks of boarding a flight from Istanbul to join his brother in America when the immigration ban went into effect. He has spent the last seven years living as a refugee in Turkey. When two of my oldest brother's children, Kamyar and Kiana, arrived in Turkey in 2019, they knew the ban would prevent them from joining my family and their older brother Hooman in America, despite the fact that Hooman, a naturalized citizen like me, is serving in the United States Air Force. Historically, a refugee has a much better chance of getting asylum if they have a family member living in a host country. When the U.S. immigration ban went into effect, this was no longer true for my family members and many others like them. Even with the lifting of the ban in January of 2021 (in the midst of a global pandemic), major obstacles to immigration remain.

Followers of the Bahá'í Faith in Iran are good people who seek basic, fundamental human rights that so many of us take for granted: freedom of religion and speech; protection from unreasonable searches and seizures; a right to live freely without degradation, discrimination, or punishment.

I give thanks every day that I was able to come to America and secure these freedoms for my sons, Ryan and Dustin. My children understand that their grandparents, uncles, aunts, and cousins who still live in Iran must fight every day to eke out a living, to avoid harassment, a beating, prison, or death. While my sons have the potential to become doctors, engineers, lawyers, teachers, or whatever they desire, Islamic law forbids their Persian Bahá'í cousins from attending a university. They must work in a family business or find jobs doing manual labor.

Over the years, I have shared bits and pieces of my life story with my children. It wasn't until I attended a 2007 theater production of *The Diary of Anne Frank* that it occurred to me that my story of religious persecution needed to be shared with a wider audience. I had never heard of Anne Frank, although I knew, of course, about the Holocaust and the horrors inflicted on the Jewish people. Anne Frank's story touched my soul so deeply that I fled the theater, unable to stifle my sobbing.

Like Anne Frank, I kept a diary throughout my childhood detailing the abuse my family endured because of our faith. Unfortunately, my journals were destroyed to protect my family from harm. This book is my attempt to recapture and preserve those memories for my sons, future generations, and all people. It is my hope that readers worldwide will come to know the strength, resiliency, and unwavering faith of Bahá'ís.

Foreword

The story you're about to read—my story—is true. I have done my best to recreate events and conversations from my memories as I recall them happening. To protect loved ones and friends in Iran who are still subjected to ongoing persecution, I have changed the names of certain individuals, as well as any identifying characteristics.

———

Acknowledgments

It's only fitting that we would meet on the sidelines of a soccer field while cheering on our sons, who started off as teammates and then became lifelong friends. Jeannette soon learned that Mansur was a doctor at their family's eye care clinic. It was during dinner after a soccer match that Jeannette first heard Mansur's life story for the first time. "What an inspiring and fascinating tale," she thought. "That would make a great book." But the story was so personal, too intimate, and nothing was spoken aloud about it.

It would be almost a decade until Mansur, now ready to share his story with the world, approached Jeannette about writing his memoir. The two spent hundreds of hours together at Mansur's dining room table as he recounted his life story, his family's stories, and stories about the Bahá'í Faith.

The final product—which you, dear readers, now hold in your hands—took almost four years. Like all of Mansur's endeavors, it was a labor of love, devotion, and perseverance.

This book wouldn't be possible without the steadfast support of our spouses, Roza Nurdel and David Spurlin, and our children, Ryan, Dustin, Campbell, and Chance. And of course, the love and encouragement of our parents: Aziz and Tahereh Nurdel, and Calvin and Lois Moninger.

Throughout his years as an optometrist, Mansur has shared parts of his life story with his patients who asked, "Where are you from?" Upon hearing just a fraction of his tale, patients often remarked, "You should write a book." And here it is. Thank you, optical patients, for giving Mansur the courage and the push to take this step.

We would also like to acknowledge the keen eyes, sharp editing talents, and sage advice of developmental editor and publishing consultant Anita Mumm of Mumm's the Word. Thank you for patiently guiding these literary novices through the labyrinth of book publishing.

So many friends, family members, and work colleagues took the time to read this book through all its myriad versions. Thank you, beta readers, for providing invaluable feedback that shaped and polished this memoir.

We are grateful to the dedicated staff at the Bahá'í National Review Office who checked this story for accuracy and offered helpful suggestions to truly capture the ongoing plight of persecuted Bahá'ís in Iran and around the world.

Finally, the life Mansur was able to create for himself and his families in America and Iran wouldn't be possible without the steadfast efforts of the United Nations Refugee Agency. Staff and volunteers at the United Nations continue to make a difference in the lives of refugees worldwide. We thank you for making such an impact on immigrants' lives and helping to reshape the fabric of society.

———

PART ONE

Harvan, IRAN

Chapter One

June 1967

I was four when I first understood that my family was different.

My cousin Arash Amjadi raced into my family's courtyard, grabbed my hand, and began pulling me along behind him. "Come on, Mansur!" he said excitedly. "*Baba* gave me money." He held out a dirt-encrusted palm that held several worn coins. "We can buy candy!"

My eyes widened in surprise. Candy was a rare treat. I looked at Arash, who had an inch of height and a year of life on me, and then looked at my *Maman*, who nodded and smiled. Arash and I took off down the dirt road, racing toward the village store, our bare feet kicking up clouds of dust.

"Hey! Hey! Why are you running?" a village kid asked as we hurried past. He and some other boys were lazily kicking a soccer ball against a courtyard wall.

"We're getting candy!" I told them, an ear-to-ear grin never leaving my face.

"I have money!" Arash said, thrusting his fist in the air, the coins safely nestled inside. He wanted the boys to know that we weren't little kids pulling their legs. Soon, we would be enjoying delicious sweets.

"Lucky! Bring us some!" they shouted as we skirted past them. Arash and I looked at each other and laughed. We were lucky.

"I'm getting taffy," Arash said as we caught sight of the village store, darkened by the shadow of the mosque next door.

"I want bubblegum," I said.

We were still giddily debating what treat to buy when we burst through the store's open doorway. Then our chatter quickly stopped. The store owner, Red Eye Mohammed, glowered at us from behind the checkout counter. All of the kids in the village were afraid of Red Eye, and I was certainly no braver than anyone else. His right eye had been permanently streaked with blood, and his unkempt beard couldn't mask his brown, rotted teeth. His thick and broad-shouldered form loomed menacingly over us.

Arash nervously approached the counter. Like a shadow, I followed a few paces behind. Arash pointed an unsteady finger at the wrapped pieces of pastel-pink bubblegum and looked back at me. I nodded my head. My heart jackhammered in my chest. I didn't care which candy Arash picked. I just wanted out of there.

"Two pieces of gum, please." Arash pried the coins from his sweaty palm and slid them onto the counter.

"Whose grandson are you?" Red Eye asked. His deep and gravelly voice vibrated through my ears down into my bare toes.

"Heydar Amjadi," Arash replied softly. Arash bowed his head and stared down at a stain on the scuffed wood floor.

Red Eye sniffed as if smelling something foul and made a low growling sound. "The gum's not for sale." His tongue flicked through a gaping hole in his teeth. He pressed his palms onto the counter and leaned forward as if challenging Arash to ask for gum again. The wood counter groaned under his weight.

I stared at the dark hairs spiraling out of Red Eye's knuckles, chewing on this surprising bit of news instead of the sugary treat I craved. Why did the store have gum if you couldn't buy it? Wasn't everything in the store for sale? I looked at my cousin to see what he thought, but Arash kept his head bowed. I didn't know what to do, so I looked down at the floor, too. The hem of my gray pajama bottoms was dusty with the chestnut brown earth of Iran; my yellowed t-shirt had been worn soft and thin by my two older brothers. I swallowed back tears and tasted salt. Arash and I must have done something very wrong to be denied the candy.

Arash scraped the coins off of the counter back into his hand. Dejected and confused, I followed him out of the store. We couldn't bear to pass the kids who were outside playing ball. They would laugh and call us liars when they saw we didn't have candy. We took a side route back to my house, which shared a stone courtyard wall and property with Arash's family home. I dragged my bare toes along the hard-packed dirt road, turning over small pebbles as I walked.

When I reached home, I threw myself into *Maman's* arms. Between sobs and hiccups, I told her what had happened. I worried that *Maman* might go to the store, angry, to talk to Red Eye. At five-feet two-inches, *Maman* was petite—but fierce. She was the family disciplinarian, doling out love and punishment with equal force.

Instead, a veil of sadness fell over *Maman's* face. "*Agha* will get you gum the next time he goes to Ajabshir," she said, as if that made everything okay. Ajabshir was the closest city to our village, Harvan. But it was four miles away, and nobody in Harvan owned a car. On foot, the round-trip trek took two hours, so my father went to the city only when it was essential. It would be forever before Arash and I got gum.

"But why can't we get candy here?" I whined, glancing at Arash for backup. Our tongues were primed for sweet gummy chewiness. We wanted our treats now. *Maman* sighed and looked away. "The storekeeper will not sell to our families," she said, bringing her attention back to me and looking into my eyes. "It is because we are Bahá'ís."

"Oh," I said, as if that bit of information explained everything. It didn't. I looked over at Arash to see if he understood, but he was once more fixated on the floor. My four-year-old brain couldn't see a connection between religion and gum. Still, I wasn't too young to have noticed how everyone in my village—all 700 Shi'a Muslims—faced Mecca and prayed five times a day.

Everyone except for my family and Arash's.

As followers of the Bahá'í Faith, we had no place of worship, no clergy, or sacraments. We were encouraged to pray once a day, but not in any formal fashion. We considered the act of helping others a form of worship.

We were different. And as the only non-Muslim families in Harvan, we were despised.

———

Chapter Two

1920s

M y father, Aziz Nurdel, was born to Muslim parents in
1926. When he was orphaned at age two, his mother's
brother, Khalil Zhian, and his wife, Sakinehe, took him into
their home in Harvan. They, too, were Muslims.

Perhaps Khalil's instant plunge into fatherhood triggered
a yearning for a greater purpose in life, for it was around this
same time that he and his cousin Heydar (my cousin Arash's
grandfather) secretly started attending Bahá'í gatherings
in Shishavan, a village nearly five miles north. The cousins
liked what they heard. Here was a religion that accepted
everyone, that viewed men and women as equals, and that
encouraged the mixing of races, beliefs, and social status.
It was a unifying, harmonious faith.

For two years, Khalil and Heydar went through the
motions of daily Islamic prayer rituals while sneaking off
to Shishavan to learn more about the Bahá'í Faith. They
fasted outwardly during the designated Islamic holy days
and surreptitiously during Bahá'í ones. Their stomachs and
their consciences gnawed at them constantly. Perhaps stress
and hunger were the final straws.

Family lore has it that Khalil's wife, Sakinehe, woke
him before sunrise on an Islamic holy day so the two
could partake in a meal before resuming their fast. Khalil
stunned his bride by stating that he was no longer a

Muslim. He was a Bahá'í, and he would eat when the sun came up.

Sakinehe pleaded with Khalil to reconsider. "You will be damned to hell!" she cried. "Is that what you want? To be separated for all eternity from me and everyone who loves you?" She acted out the Shi'a Muslim mourning ritual of flagellating, beating and whipping her chest, arms, legs, and face. In desperation, Sakinehe approached Heydar, who was both cousin and best friend to Khalil. "Please," she begged, "you must get Khalil to stop this foolishness."

Heydar shook his head. "I can't do that," he replied. "I am also a Bahá'í."

Khalil and Heydar's families were frantic. They begged the men to reconsider what they were doing, arguing that their souls, and their safety, were in peril. The Iranian people had a well-known history of persecuting, imprisoning, and even killing Bahá'ís, who they considered to be ungodly. Life would be very difficult for Khalil and Heydar if they chose this path. Their families would also pay a price for the men's desertion of Islam.

But Khalil and Heydar stayed true to their new religion.

It wasn't long before Khalil's absence at the village mosque was noticed, and the Mullah paid him a visit. Khalil was well respected in Harvan. Neighbors sought his advice on where and when to plant crops to reap the best harvest. His remedies healed ailing livestock, saving families' livelihoods. He couldn't read or write (most Iranians at that time couldn't), but he was known for his wisdom and generosity. It would reflect poorly on the Mullah if someone of Khalil's stature left Islam for a faith that most Iranians considered illegitimate and blasphemous.

The Mullah wasn't interested in listening to Khalil's reasons for embracing the Bahá'í Faith. "How can you understand their teachings when you can't read them?" the Mullah asked. Khalil pointed out that it was no different than believing in the Qur'an, another book he couldn't read.

"I have been exposed to the truth," Khalil explained to the Mullah. "I am an insignificant rock on the mountainside that nobody pays attention to. You are a diamond. You are wrapped in knowledge, but this knowledge keeps you in a box, insulated from truth. When the sun shines on the mountain, the rock is exposed, but the pretty diamond stays covered so no light can reach it."

The Mullah was enraged. He felt Khalil was making a mockery of Islam. When Khalil's uncle (Heydar's father) heard about the incident, he incited a mob to beat his nephew and son into submission. He wanted to end the shame the men's decisions had wrought on their families. After Khalil and Heydar recovered from the brutal beatings that nearly killed them, they resumed their weekly trips to Shishavan to learn more about their newfound faith.

– – –

Khalil's conversion put his wife in an unfortunate predicament. While there was no law like the one that exists in Iran today that makes marriage between a Muslim and non-Muslim illegal, their union was considered unholy. Even though Sakinehe remained dedicated to her Islamic upbringing, villagers shunned her. Even members of her own family treated her coldly, urging her to take the sinful step of divorce so she could marry a proper Muslim man. Sakinehe stood by Khalil. As she came to accept his decision, she began asking questions about the Bahá'í Faith. The more Sakinehe learned, the more intrigued she became.

My grandfather was a progressive man for his times. He adored my grandmother. He used to tell me that, while it was grandmother's beauty that first caught his eye, it was her brains and kind heart that won him over. In the privacy of their home, Khalil often sought Sakinehe's advice on everything from farming to land purchases to the best way to settle disputes among villagers. In stark contrast to Islamic beliefs that consider women to be subservient to men, Khalil viewed his wife—and all women—as equal. Parity among genders is a cornerstone of the Bahá'í Faith. My grandmother knew that her womanhood would always make her life less valuable than a Muslim man's. Nonetheless, she clung to her Islamic roots, too afraid to risk the possibility of being damned to hell.

One night, Sakinehe dreamt that she was locked in a dungeon. She screamed for help. She pounded her fists against the slick stone walls. When nobody came, she huddled against the cold, damp rocks and sobbed. She was certain everyone had deserted her because she had questioned her Islamic faith. Just then a holy man appeared. This holy figure reached out his hand to Sakinehe and pulled her gently up from the floor. A warm feeling flowed through her body. She felt loved and at peace.

When Sakinehe described her dream to Khalil the next morning, he showed her a picture of a Bahá'í holy man, 'Abdu'l-Bahá. Sakinehe immediately recognized him as the man in her dream who saved her when others turned away. She told Khalil she wanted to become a Bahá'í. Khalil rejoiced at this news, but Sakinehe's father and brothers threatened to disown her. Her mother and sisters acted out their grief, flagellating and beating themselves bloody. But Sakinehe and Khalil were steadfast in their new faith. Within the year, Sakinehe gave birth to the couple's first son. He died a few weeks later. A second son passed just shy of his first birthday. A third son lived for six years before succumbing to illness. The death of their sons, their families told Khalil and Sakinehe, was God's way of punishing them for turning their backs on Islam.

———

Chapter Three

1950s and 1960s

My orphaned father was raised as Khalil and Sakinehe's only son. He grew up in Harvan alongside the couple's three daughters, Tahereh, Nahid, and Faridehe. In keeping with the Bahá'í Faith, all three girls were educated as much as possible in the small village. They learned elementary reading and writing—skills their parents and their Muslim girlfriends in Harvan never mastered. Khalil and Sakinehe strongly believed that daughters should have the same educational opportunities as sons, even though the daughters were destined to become housewives and mothers.

Although he was immersed in the Bahá'í Faith, my father (*Agha* in Persian) had been born to Muslim parents. In contrast to many religions, Bahá'ís don't assume that their children will embrace their parents' religion. During the teen years, children are encouraged to examine their own beliefs and to make their own educated, informed decisions about their faith. For my father, there was never any question: Like the parents who raised him, he was a Bahá'í.

In remote Iranian villages like the one in which my father grew up, it was almost impossible for a Bahá'í to find a spouse. By the time *Agha* entered his mid-twenties, he was still a bachelor, a fact that greatly distressed my grandparents. It was not uncommon for cousins to marry, then or even now. So when *Agha* agreed that it was time to settle down, he looked no farther than his own house. He married Tahereh, his cousin and the eldest of Khalil and Sakinehe's daughters.

The woman who would become my *Maman* was fifteen, twelve years younger than *Agha*, when they wed in 1953. Two years later, they welcomed their first son, Behrouz. The only girl, Mahin, arrived four years later, followed by Javad, me, and Iraj. I share the same birthdate, September 23, with Behrouz, but we weren't actually born on that day. With no access to medical care, women in rural villages gave birth at home. Many infants didn't survive, so parents waited to register a birth until they felt confident the child would live. The day you took your first breath wasn't as important as the day your parents decided you had a chance at surviving. By the time my parents applied for my birth certificate, they had forgotten (or most likely, never bothered to notice) the date of my actual birth. My parents chose September 23 because it marks the start of a new school year and is therefore easy to remember.

For a while, all of us—my family, my grandparents, and aunts—lived in my grandparents' home in Harvan. In this small farming village, marriage prospects were bleak for my aunts Nahid and Faridehe. Although Bahá'ís don't arrange marriages, my grandparents had a hand in helping their two youngest daughters find Bahá'í husbands (distant relatives) in Tabriz and Tehran, respectively, when the time was right.

My family and Arash's family lived a few blocks apart. As the only Bahá'ís in Harvan, our homes were often subjected to vandalism and livestock and crop thefts. To boost security for both families, my great-uncle Heydar gave my parents land adjacent to his property. Here, my parents built a new place for my siblings and grandparents to call home.

– – –

Harvan is located in northwestern Iran, in the East Azerbaijan Province. At its northernmost reach, the area borders the countries of Armenia and Azerbaijan. East Azerbaijan Province is known for its historic capital city, Tabriz, majestic 12,000-foot mountain ranges that scrape the sky, and Lake Urmia, the second-largest saltwater lake in the Middle East.

When I was a child, my siblings and I joined throngs of people at Lake Urmia seeking relief from temperatures that often eclipsed one hundred degrees. We passed vast fields of watermelons and cantaloupes on our three-mile walk to the lake. There was one field in particular that we knew had the sweetest, juiciest watermelon. In the blazing heat, the temptation for that thirst-quenching fruit was simply too much. These melons were so good that the farmer hired young village boys to patrol his field and prevent thefts. But my brothers and I were stealthy and quick. We positioned my sister, Mahin, and younger brother, Iraj, as lookouts. No one would suspect a girl of being up to no good, and no matter Iraj's age, we always considered him too little to take part in big-brotherly exploits. When the coast looked clear, Behrouz, Javad, and I army-crawled on our bellies through the watermelon patch, thumping on the melons until we found the perfect one. We rolled that prized melon through the field until we reached the edge of the field. Then, we took off running with our bounty. The system worked almost flawlessly, except for one time when we heard Mahin loudly exclaim to Iraj, "I wonder how that farmer standing over

there is always able to grow such sweet, juicy watermelons."
As I peeked my head up, I noticed that he was holding the
cloth bag I had left at the side of the road to carry the melon.
The bag contained other snacks for the day, and we needed
to get it back. My brothers and I crawled as comfortably
close to a possible escape route as we could. With a nod of
his head, Behrouz gave the signal to run. He scooped up that
one perfect melon and, with Javad on his heels, booked it
toward Mahin and Iraj. Before the farmer could figure out
what was going on, I sprang up, ran past him, and snatched
the canvas bag out of his hands. The five of us took off, racing
down the dirt road, the farmer's threats roaring in our ears.

We were lucky that it was the older, slower farmer and
not one of the young, fast village boys guarding the field
that day. We easily outran him. When it was safe, Behrouz
used a rock to split open the crisp green rind. My siblings
and I grabbed chunks of the melon to suck on as we walked
the final stretch to the lake. We would arrive sticky with
melon juice and drenched in sweat. We jumped into the lake;
our eyes scrunched tight to keep the saltwater from setting
them on fire. Dried salt rings circled our legs, bellies, and
arms as we lounged on the sandy shore and watched ferries
shuttle passengers across the lake to Tabriz. At almost two
thousand square miles, Lake Urmia once nearly equaled
Utah's Great Salt Lake. Today, extreme droughts and crop
irrigation have sucked the lake dry. Ferries, swimmers, and
sunbathers are nothing but a memory.

— — —

Harvan doesn't have soaring mountains or a refreshing
lake; the village sits on a plateau. When I was born, in 1963,
one hundred homes made of clay bricks lined streets of dirt.

Most homes were hidden behind clay brick walls about four to five feet tall. The walls enclosed courtyards where families grew gardens or kept small livestock, like chickens and goats. To reach my home from the road, you had to open a solid wood door, cross a plank bridge straddling a creek, and pass through another wooden door onto the property. Apple, apricot, and sour-cherry trees lined the back of the courtyard.

Nine of us jostled for space in my family's small, 140-square foot house. My grandparents were the only ones who had any privacy. At night, they escaped to a small upstairs room where they slept on bedrolls, their heads and feet brushing against the walls. Outsiders might have considered my family poor: We had no indoor plumbing, no electricity, no heating system, and no car. But no one in Harvan had these comforts. We were no better or worse off than our neighbors—with a few exceptions.

Our neighbors could use the well that was located in the heart of the village. A gas-powered generator drew buckets of water up from the earth's belly. The water was then heated for use in the community bathhouse. My family wasn't allowed to use the well water or the bathhouse. These amenities were reserved for Muslims only. Bahá'ís were considered *najis*, spiritually unclean, and the villagers didn't want our sins tainting their pure water.

Fortunately, my family's property had a well. But we had to use a rope-and-pulley system to manually haul up the water-laden buckets. It was exhausting work. When I was little, I needed the muscle strength of another brother to retrieve just one bucket. The makeshift shower *Agha* crafted from an old steel drum required hauling up multiple buckets of water, which was a good enough reason for my brothers and me to skip bathing until *Maman* forced it upon us.

I was almost fifteen when the village got electricity in 1978. Until then, we spent our nights listening to a battery-powered radio. Kerosene lanterns provided just enough glow for reading. In winter, Siberian winds dropped temperatures to below freezing. To keep warm, we placed hot wood coals in a hole dug underneath a *korsi*, a low-sitting square table draped with blankets. Even though we would be shivering and cold, some of my best childhood memories are of my siblings and me gathering around the *korsi*, warming our bodies with the blankets, while my grandfather told stories. *Korsis* were not for cooking. *Maman* prepared meals on an outdoor kerosene stove or the clay tandoor oven, which sat inside a hole dug in a far corner of the house.

We raised goats, sheep, cows, and chickens, which we ate or sold at the market. One of my jobs was to protect the livestock from predators. When I was eight, I had a frightful encounter with a pack of wolves that attacked my family's sheep. With nothing more than shepherding poles and loud shouting, my brother Javad and I ran after the wolves as they tried to snatch up the lambs. We lost two lambs that day. One was carried off; the other was dropped but not before the wolf's razor-sharp teeth had punctured and mangled the lamb's soft body. I looked at the lamb, its wool tinged pink with blood, and shuddered at the destruction inflicted in such a short time.

Wolves weren't the only predators I had to watch out for. People from neighboring villages (and sometimes from within our own village) thought nothing of swiping a few of our sheep, goats, or cows. Even when *Agha* could identify the thieves, there was nothing he could do about it. The villagers always believed the word of a Muslim over a Bahá'í.

— — —

Most of my family's income came from a fruit-tree farm one mile away, outside the northeast village of Gurvan. My parents owned a small patch of an orchard and paid a fee to use the gas-generated pump that brought in water from a nearby spring. *Agha* had created a system of canals to irrigate the trees. When one row was watered, my brothers and I dug feverishly with our hands in the wet earth to form a dam that diverted the water to the next canal. My nails were permanently caked with dirt.

Tending to the orchard was hard work, but I looked forward to it for one reason: Every summer, my cousin Shahin came to stay with us and help with the harvest. Shahin was the second oldest of Aunt Nahid's three sons, who lived in Tabriz. While I was in awe of my cousin's imagined, sophisticated city life, Shahin longed to run wild in the country. Back at my home after a day under the scorching sun irrigating the crops or picking fruit, Shahin and I would form a two-man team and play soccer against my older brothers, Javad and Behrouz. We used the fruit trees inside the courtyard for the goals. When the soccer ball bruised or knocked off unripe fruit, *Agha* would come outside, yell at us, and threaten to ban the game. But he never did. Usually, after watching us do a few plays, he'd run onto our makeshift field, goofy smile plastered on his face, center the ball between the tree's fruit-laden boughs, and celebrate his goal.

At harvest time, *Agha* hired a driver and truck to transport the harvest—almonds, grapes, apples, peaches, and apricots—to Bonab, a midsized city fifteen miles south. Ajabshir was bigger and closer, but the people there often refused to buy goods from Bahá'ís. Our main crop was almonds. Unfortunately, almond trees are fickle. An early freeze could wipe out an entire harvest. I hated when that happened, because it meant *Agha* had to find work elsewhere as a mason to support the family. None of the communities near us would hire a Bahá'í, so *Agha* had to stay with his sisters in Tabriz or Tehran while he worked and saved money.

Months would sometimes go by before *Agha* returned, but he was always home for the Persian New Year celebration of *Nowruz*. In Persia, the start of a new year falls near the first day of spring, usually March 20 or 21. The entire country, regardless of faith, celebrates this national holiday. New Year's Day is the biggest day for parties and gatherings, but *Nowruz* festivities go on for weeks. On the eve of the last Wednesday before *Nowruz*, Iranians celebrate Chaharshanbe Suri. People jump over bonfires to purify their souls and cleanse away sins. Other celebrations mirror a mix of American customs. During Qashoq-Zani, children paint their faces, bang spoons against plates or bowls, and go door-to-door to collect sweets, fruits, and nuts in baskets, a tradition similar to trick-or-treating. Larger cities set off fireworks like it's Independence Day. But what I always loved best about *Nowruz* was the way that generations of families came together to reminisce, laugh, dance, and share meals. When I later learned about Thanksgiving gatherings and feasts in America, the holiday reminded me of *Nowruz*.

It's customary for families to visit their elders during *Nowruz*, even if it means traveling long distances. In keeping with this tradition, our Muslim relatives in Harvan and neighboring villages and cities would put aside their grievances and come to our homes to pay their respects to my grandfather, Khalil, and Arash's grandfather, Heydar. During these visits, scents of roasted lamb and decadent honeyed sweets wafted through the air. For two wonderful weeks, my siblings and I hung out with our Muslim cousins, who treated us as equals. We played games, kicked the soccer ball, climbed trees, and laughed a lot. It was a glimpse of how life could be if people accepted my family for who we were as individuals and not how we worshiped. I wished every day could be *Nowruz*.

———

Chapter Four
The 1960s

In 1963, the year I was born, the Shah, Mohammed Reza Pahlavi, launched the White Revolution to reform and revitalize the country. His decision to grant women the right to vote angered a lot of Iranians. Many of the Shah's initiatives were aimed at improving life for families like mine, who lived in isolated rural communities. His land reforms wrested power away from descendants of the Qajar dynasty. These Iranian royals had ruled over the country until the mid-1920s and still held onto property and assets that added to their wealth. The Shah angered the royals by forcefully taking back the land and offering farmers the opportunity to buy property from the government at prices significantly below market value. Downtrodden villagers celebrated. Nearly ninety percent of Iranian sharecroppers became landowners as a result.

Education was another key focus. In the 1960s, nearly two-thirds of the country couldn't read or write. Until the Shah introduced education reforms, children from rural areas were often taught by illiterate community members in makeshift classrooms inside people's homes—if they received any schooling at all. Only the wealthy could get a proper education. To address these problems, the government began building schools in remote villages. Arash's grandfather, Heydar, donated the land for the school in Harvan. For years, Heydar had watched as the village children chased, teased, and threw rocks and punches at his children, and then his grandchildren, all because of their faith. Heydar was a smart and generous man. By having the school on his property (which connected to my family's property), my cousins and I could get to school more easily without having to dodge rocks, run from our tormentors, or fight to defend ourselves.

Like the homes in Harvan, the one-story school was fashioned out of clay bricks. In many ways, the structure resembled a jail with a four-foot clay brick wall surrounding it and steel bars on the windows. The outside bathroom, a hole dug in the ground inside of a wooden structure, sat in the farthest corner adjacent to the school. We played soccer and volleyball on fields of packed dirt, while the Iranian flag fluttered on a metal pole planted at the school entrance.

Once villages had schools, they needed teachers—educated ones who knew how to read and write, and who could teach these skills to others. The Literacy Corps was created to fill this need. Every Iranian male is required to serve in the military for up to two years after he turns eighteen, unless he has a verifiable health condition, gets accepted into a university, or has a rich family who can buy his way out of the obligation. The Literacy Corps gave high-school-educated men the option of fighting illiteracy in rural areas instead of bearing arms in the service. Educated women could also teach.

Our school had two classrooms—one room for grades one through three and the other room for grades four through six—so we needed two teachers. They arrived in Harvan from the country's capital, Tehran. Iranians speak a number of dialects and languages, depending on where they live. These teachers spoke Farsi, or Persian, the country's official language. Unfortunately, people in Harvan spoke Azerbaijanian or Azeri, a language more Turkish than Persian. A conversation between an Azeri-speaking villager from Harvan and a Farsi-speaking city dweller from Tehran was like a Spaniard talking to a German—gibberish. Nonetheless, the teachers taught in Farsi, and students were expected to figure it out.

When it was time for my sister, Mahin, to start classes, *Agha* was concerned that the village school couldn't adequately meet the needs of his extremely bright and inquisitive daughter. Despite the distance, my parents decided Mahin would attend a bigger, more reputable school in Ajabshir. It wasn't long before her village teacher came knocking on my family's door. My father had picked up a little Farsi while doing masonry work in the capital. He was one of a few adults in Harvan who could communicate with the teacher, at least in simple terms. My brother Behrouz had learned Farsi during his schooling, so he helped translate the conversation between the two men.

Having grown up in a city with a large Bahá'í population, the teacher harbored fewer religious prejudices against my family. Still, he explained, a Bahá'í family's snub of the village school gave the impression that his teaching skills were subpar. He worried that Mahin's absence would encourage other families—Muslim families—to pull their kids from the school. Bahá'ís strongly believe in the importance of education for all. We also believe in taking actions to promote the common good. Mahin surely would have gotten a better education in Ajabshir, but *Agha* put the needs of the village before the needs of his daughter and moved Mahin to the Harvan school.

Javad was in third grade when I started first grade, so we were in the same classroom. As one of the youngest students, I sat at the front of the room, closest to the teacher and the blackboard, on a wood bench I shared with two classmates. There were about 15 students total in first through third grades. Like my siblings, I was advanced for my age. I remember being so excited to start school. I wanted the village kids who had always picked on me to see how smart I was. I could already read. I didn't know that class was taught in Farsi. Looking back, I'm not sure why my older siblings didn't teach me some Farsi before I started school. On that first day, as I sat perched on the edge of the bench, pencil in hand, ready to learn, my eager smile quickly slid from my face. I had no idea what the teacher was saying. I carefully printed the words from the blackboard into my notebook, pressing hard with my pencil in frustration. I couldn't read any of the words. I was no smarter than my peers. I snuck a look back at Javad, who sat a few rows behind me. He cut me a curt look and then stared straight ahead. He didn't want to get into trouble for not paying attention. The teacher smacked my desk with a ruler and said something, but the only part I understood was my name, Mansur. From his tone, I knew I was in trouble. He pointed at the blackboard, and I nodded my head. I kept my eyes forward from then on.

By the end of first grade, I was fluent in Farsi. But that first year was difficult. My classmates and I were constantly in trouble for not following the rules—rules that were explained to us in a language we didn't know. We often discovered that a rule had been broken only when one of us got into trouble. Our teachers ran the school in a military fashion. We marched single file when we entered and left the building. Getting out of line or acting up earned you a hard smack against the head. My teacher's favorite punishment was to sandwich a pencil between your index finger and middle finger and squeeze the digits together for what felt like several minutes. The pain traveled up your arm and into your skull.

Farsi wasn't the only subject I learned that first year. I quickly got a lesson from my classmates in all that was wrong with Bahá'ís. The village kids vacillated between being my friend and being my tormentors. "*Najis*," they would say to me, implying that my soul was too tainted for heaven. The daily verbal abuse often turned physical. I was small, but my older brothers taught me how to stand my ground and fight back. One time I saw another kid beating on my brother, Javad, in the dirt yard that served as the school's playground.

"*Najis* Bahá'í dog!" the kid shouted, his fists raining down on my brother. Being called a dog is the ultimate insult in Persia. Dogs are considered filthy animals. God won't accept prayers from anyone who keeps a filthy animal inside their house, and without prayer, you won't reach the Promised Land. The bully was getting the best of Javad, so I jumped on his back and bit his ear until I tasted blood. He stopped.

My great-uncle Heydar had hoped that the school's proximity to our homes would spare our families from abuse, but my siblings, cousins, and I frequently came home from school with bloody noses, ripped shirts, and bruises. When

I was eight, Arash's family packed up their belongings and moved to Ajabshir to be part of a larger Bahá'í community. Heydar had died a few years earlier, leaving Arash's family more vulnerable to verbal and physical threats. When Heydar was alive, his Muslim relatives in the village showed some small measure of respect to the family in deference to Heydar's senior status in the community. With Heydar gone, the family was seen as fair game. They'd had enough of the village's mistreatment.

Arash was my best friend, and I missed him terribly. His family's departure also meant my family was now the lone village scapegoat. My parents were determined to stay. Harvan was all they knew, and leaving would have broken my grandparents' hearts. But more than that, if we left, the all-Muslim community would make sure that no other Bahá'í family could ever set down roots in Harvan again. As long as my family had even a slight toehold on the land, there remained a remote possibility that other Bahá'ís (perhaps the families of our future spouses) would one day join us and grow the faith in the village. Harvan was our home, and we were not leaving.

– – –

With fewer Bahá'í kids to pick on in school, our classmates doubled up their assaults on my siblings and me. Despite having to learn in this traumatic environment, my siblings and I excelled in school. We were consistently the highest-scoring students throughout the province.

The Harvan school taught to fifth grade only. After that, my siblings and I walked or biked almost eight miles round trip to attend school in Ajabshir. The one-way trek should have taken about an hour on a bike, but we couldn't go the

most direct route through the village of Shishavan. The
village had changed since my grandfather and great-uncle
had traveled there for their introduction to the Bahá'í Faith
more than four decades ago. No Bahá'í families remained.
It was now comprised wholly of Shi'a Muslims, who were
intent on running off all Bahá'ís.

The longer route took us past another village, called
Guravan. One day when I was twelve and biking alone, I
was followed by a classmate who lobbed insults as I pedaled
furiously for home. "Bahá'í dog!" he shouted. "You're going
to hell! Your whole family is going to hell! That's where
filthy dogs belong!"

I snapped.

I can't explain it. I'd just had enough. I jumped from
my bike not bothering to brake. The bike rolled on without
me. The bully wasn't expecting me to fight back. Caught
off guard, I easily knocked him off of his bike and threw
him onto the ground. Fists of anger and fury battered his
face, arms, and chest. I felt something crunch as my hand
connected with his nose. I saw splatters of red. I heard
sobs. And then, suddenly, I was somersaulting, head over
heels, through the air. I landed hard on the dirt, the wind
rushing from my lungs, gravel burrowing painfully under
the skin on my palms. I looked up into the eyes of a very
angry man.

"What do you think you're doing, you filthy Bahá'í,"
the man roared. He yanked me up, slapped my face, and
threw me back to the ground. A thousand pinpricks stung
my cheeks. I felt something warm trickle down my face. I
tasted blood. The man lifted me up and slapped me back
down several more times. I knew he could kill me, and my

family would never get justice. There was no place to run, and nobody around who could save me. Eventually, the man's anger was spent. When he turned his attention to the injured boy, I raced to my bike. With head and hands throbbing, I pedaled for home.

Mansur's 5th-grade school-book picture,
the only picture from his childhood.

Chapter Five

1978

I was fifteen when everything in my world shifted. The year started with civil unrest in Tehran. Exiled political dissident Ayatollah Ruhollah Khomeini spoke out against the Shah's reform policies, stirring up feelings of anger and fear among thousands of Iranians. Khomeini preached to his followers that Iran was too closely aligned with the United States and Israel. The country, he warned, had moved too far away from its fundamental Islamic roots. Angry anti-Shah protests took place every day across the nation.

In Harvan, my family was engaged in its own battle. While walking home from the village, my ten-year-old brother Iraj came across a group of older boys throwing manure against a neighbor's courtyard wall and door. Everyone in the village knew that this neighbor had a temper. It was no secret that he beat his wife—whom he berated publicly for giving him four daughters and no sons. His daughters were also abused. Iraj stopped and watched as the boys plastered the man's property with barnyard waste. "I was shocked at what they were doing," Iraj later told my parents. "I was too scared to walk past them. I knew they would throw that stuff at me, too."

So Iraj stood glued to the spot, mouth agape, waiting for the boys to finish so he could continue on his way home. And that's when the neighbor came storming out of his courtyard gate. The teen boys took off running, laughing and shouting at the man. Iraj watched as the man surveyed the damage, and then stood frozen in fear as the man barreled toward him.

"How dare you destroy my property!" the man shouted. Iraj fervently shook his head and tried to explain. "No! It wasn't me. I didn't do it!"

Of course, the man had seen the group of teens run off. He could name each of the vandals. But those boys were members of Muslim families in the village. Iraj was not. The man brought his wrath down on Iraj. He slammed Iraj's slender ten-year-old frame against the wall causing the back of Iraj's skull to crash against the bricks. It would be weeks before the knot on Iraj's scalp went away and even longer before he stopped seeing double and having headaches. "*Najis* Bahá'í!" he spat in Iraj's face. The man—easily forty years older and more than one hundred pounds stronger—broke Iraj's nose and blackened his eyes. He repeatedly kicked Iraj in the groin and kidneys as he curled in a fetal position on the ground. For weeks after the assault, Iraj screamed out in pain as he urinated streams of blood.

The man likely would have beaten Iraj to death that day if his daughters hadn't managed to pull him away. One kind daughter helped Iraj to his feet and walked him home. When my grandfather saw what this man had done, he flew into a rage. He grabbed one of *Maman's* cooking knives and headed for the door. *Agha* blocked his way. He was seething, too, but he knew that if they went after the man, the village would take his side and perhaps use the opportunity to imprison or kill *Agha* and *Baba*. This incident pitted the word of a "dishonorable" Bahá'í boy against the word of a Muslim man. Even at my young age, I knew that we couldn't win.

Iraj was never the same carefree, playful boy after that day. That neighbor had robbed him of his innocence and his sense of security. He was scared to go anywhere alone. Even when I accompanied Iraj outside of our courtyard—the protective big brother who pretended not to be frightened of anything—I would catch him looking back over his shoulder, a look of terror constantly flashing in his eyes.

— — —

My grandfather's health was already failing when Iraj was beaten, but it was as if the assault happened to *Baba*, too. Like Iraj, he never quite recovered from the incident. Much to *Maman's* lament, she never got that knife back. *Baba* carried it with him everywhere until his dying days. I worried that he would one day plunge it into that wicked neighbor's blackened heart, and I would have to watch as they hung my beloved grandfather.

Baba and I shared a special love for stories. He would tell me tales from his youth, and in return, I read books to him. One of his most frequent requests was *The Dawn Breakers*, a compilation of true stories about the founding of the Bahá'í Faith. At the time, I thought I was doing my illiterate grandfather a favor by reading to him. It wasn't until I was older that I realized *Baba* knew all of the stories by heart. He wanted to make sure his grandson knew them, too.

Toward the end of *Baba's* life, our Muslim relatives came around to pay their final respects. My parents feared that these family members wanted to bury *Baba* in the village's Muslim cemetery. When *Baba* passed away in July, my family kept his death a secret for two days. *Agha* went to Ajabshir to send word of *Baba's* passing to our Bahá'í relatives. Soon, family members and friends arrived under cloak of darkness.

In the early morning hours, we carried *Baba* to the Bahá'í cemetery, which was situated on a small patch of land that was part of Heydar's homestead. When I was younger, Arash and I would climb the sour-cherry trees that bordered the cemetery, chasing away the birds so that we could fill our faces with the tangy red fruit. Now Arash and *Baba* were both gone. One by one, the village was ridding itself of Bahá'ís.

After the oak coffin was in the ground, *Agha* worried that someone would desecrate the grave or try to move *Baba's* body to the Muslim cemetery in the middle of the night. For months, *Agha* spent his nights standing guard at the cemetery protecting the grave of the man he called father.

— — —

Back in the nation's capital, there was turmoil. After months of anti-regime protests, the Shah imposed martial law. On September 8, hundreds of demonstrators were killed in Tehran when troops opened fire. Although Harvan was hundreds of miles away, my parents worried. I could hear their murmurings at night when they thought my siblings and I were asleep. My parents didn't have a particular allegiance to any leader, but unrest in the country was never a good thing for Bahá'ís. Even though we had nothing to do with the events taking place, people always seemed to find a way to take their anger and frustration out on us.

One early morning in September, Ajabshir police raided my family's home. We were rudely yanked from our dreams and were still rubbing the grit from our eyes when the police ushered us outside and into the courtyard. Officers lined the courtyard perimeter, guns poised and ready to fire. Everyone in my family was wearing the same mask of sheer terror. We didn't understand what was happening.

"You are selling drugs!" an officer shouted in my father's face. "Opioids!"

Agha adamantly shook his head. "No! There are no drugs here!" *Agha* glanced at *Maman* in disbelief and fear. Drugs?

The chief shook his head in disgust. "Ah, you lie," he chuckled. "Bahá'ís always lie. Filthy, lying Bahá'ís. Don't worry. We will find your drugs." Three officers stood less than a foot away with guns pointed at my family. Meanwhile, a swarm of what looked to be about a dozen more tore apart our home, looking for drugs that I knew did not exist.

Some of the strongest language in Bahá'í teachings centers around drug use. In the late 1800s, Bahá'í founder Bahá'u'lláh explicitly condemned the use of addictive substances like alcohol. In later writings, Bahá'u'lláh's son 'Abdu'l-Bahá specifically addressed opium: *"It turneth the living into the dead. It quencheth the natural heat. No greater harm can be conceived than that which opium inflicteth."*

I had never seen my father so much as take an aspirin for a headache. There was no way he was involved with dealing drugs. Still, police ransacked every square inch of our home. Every bedroll was flung open, every food canister inspected. Wood ashes from the tandoor oven and *korsi* were dug up and black streaks smeared across the floor. They even searched the latrine and barn, stirring the livestock into a frenzy. When the first search yielded nothing, they started over.

As I huddled and held hands in the courtyard with my family, my thoughts darkened: What if a villager had planted drugs in our home? If the police found illegal drugs, *Agha* could be executed or sent to prison. Iranian prisons were notorious for their deplorable, inhumane conditions. Inmates were routinely tortured, beaten, starved, and subjected to mock firing squads, as well as actual executions. Few people got out alive. Those who did were never the same.

My heart sank as an officer excitedly ran out of the house. "I found something!" he shouted, a big grin plastered on his face. In his hands was a small container of white powder. I knew that container. *Maman* used it when baking *naan* in the tandoor.

The commanding officer turned a knowing eye at my father. "We've got you now," his expression seemed to say. *Agha* remained calm, modeling for us children how to react. If one of us panicked, the entire family could be shot. We held our collective breaths as the officer licked his finger, dipped it into the crystalline powder, and tasted. Ground flour.

The commanding officer looked at his subordinate and tossed the flour into the man's face. White powder dusted his eyebrows and eyelashes and little snowballs trickled down his uniform. Both men looked like fools, but none of us dared to laugh. Finally, after three hours of searching, the police gave up their quest. Their raid had yielded nothing.

Nobody said a word as we restored order to the shambles the police had left behind. As I swept and scrubbed, my mind turned over the morning's events. Clearly, someone had made a false report about *Agha*. Someone was out to get my family. Now that this attempt had failed, what would they do next?

I wondered, for the millionth time, why can't they just leave us alone?

– – –

School started soon after. Even though Mahin finished Teacher Training College in Mahabad at the early age of sixteen, the law stated that you had to be eighteen and have

Summer 1978: In Harvan, at Mansur's childhood
home. Mansur is on the bottom right. The
house was destroyed in late 1978.

Haravan—Summer of 1978
Mansur with his siblings and cousins.

earned a high-school diploma before you could teach primary school. As backwards as it sounds, Mahin returned to high school to get her diploma and then secured a teaching job in Ajabshir.

My older brother, Javad, showed so much potential in school that he moved in with Aunt Nahid's family in Tabriz to attend one of the region's best high schools. I was happy for him but sad to see him go. I was also a bit jealous that he got to live with our "fun cousin" Shahin in the city, while Iraj and I were stuck doing chores in Harvan and attending school in Ajabshir. The family splintered even more when Behrouz left to fulfill his military obligation.

A few weeks after school started in late September, the political turmoil intensified. Across the country, workers walked off their jobs in protest of the Shah's leadership. Striking oilfield workers effectively shut down oil production, the country's biggest export. Teachers also walked out. Schools closed, forcing Javad and Mahin to return home. My family had no way of knowing that, by the time classes resumed in February 1979, our lives would be forever changed.

———

Chapter Six

December 1978
Muharram Holy Month

After the police raid, my family went about life as if the ground beneath us was made of eggshells. We cocooned ourselves inside our courtyard, rarely venturing outside the protective walls, fearful of drawing unwanted attention. I missed learning and going to school. Still, the closures made it easier for my siblings and me to lie low during a very tense time.

For two months, we were invisible. That changed with the start of Muharram, one of four Muslim holy months sanctified in the Qur'an. The dates for Muharram are based on the Islamic lunar calendar and change each year. In 1978, Muharram began on December 2.

The word *muharram* means "forbidden." The holy month is meant to be a time of mourning and peace, a time without violence or bloodshed. Nonetheless, Shiite men flagellate—whip, beat, and punish themselves to the point of drawing blood.

For my family, Muharram was anything but peaceful.

Every evening during the start of Muharram, men from our village would throw rocks at my family's home and shout slurs.

"Bahá'í dogs!"

"*Najis!*"

The tenth day of Muharram, the Day of Ashura, is the most sacred. It commemorates the martyrdom of Imam Husayn ibn Ali, the grandson of the Prophet Muhammad and the Third Imam to Shi'a Muslims. Imam Husayn was killed alongside his family in the Battle of Karbala in Iraq in the year 680.

Every year, after the Day of Ashura ended, the villagers left us alone. But for ten days prior, my family's home and safety were under nightly attack. We had endured this treatment for years and knew what to expect.

But this year was different.

Given the recent unrest in the country, we didn't know what our Muslim neighbors might do. Tensions were high, and we knew from the earlier police raid that the villagers had it out for us. My parents feared that this year's Muharram could be especially brutal. They decided that *Maman*, my grandmother, sister, Mahin, and my still traumatized brother Iraj would go to Tabriz to stay with *Maman's* sister Nahid until the holy month was over. The unspoken implication was clear: the women in my family were not safe in Harvan.

Although I was scared, I put on a brave face. At fifteen, I was proud to stay behind with *Agha* and Javad to safeguard the family home. There really was no other option. If the entire family fled to Tabriz, the villagers would take possession of our home. We would never be allowed to return. It wasn't our intention to fight back against the villagers. The Bahá'í Faith shuns violence. Besides, there were three of us and hundreds of villagers. We only hoped that our presence would stop our neighbors from destroying our home. And if things got too dicey, *Agha* had a plan.

During the first nine days of Muharram, we stayed within the confines of the courtyard, passing the time reading books and listening to the radio. Like clockwork, the sun set, and a group of villagers gathered outside our courtyard. A wall shielded the lower level of our house, but the second floor was exposed. The villagers knocked clay bricks from the walls, picked up stones from the road and creek, and hurled them at our home. They screamed until their throats were raw. They threw until their arms gave out, and my family's home was scarred with pockmarks.

When the home was under attack, *Agha*, Javad, and I holed up in the small bedroom upstairs. We remained fully clothed, boots on, around-the-clock, ready to take off at a moment's notice. Even though it was bitterly cold, sweat pooled inside my rubber boots and the wool socks knitted by *Maman*.

The upstairs room had a door that led outside to the flat roof. You couldn't see this part of the house from the road. Next to this door we stashed bags of food and clothing. If there was trouble, each of us would grab a bag, jump off the backside of the roof onto a pile of hay that we had moved there to cushion our landings, and make a break for it through the woods behind our home. While on the run, we would zig and then zag, avoiding any roads. The villagers would expect us to head northwest toward Ajabshir. Instead, we planned to go southeast to Shiraz, where we would catch a bus to join the rest of the family in Tabriz. Our home in Harvan would be lost forever.

Agha repeated this plan every day as the sun sank lower: Grab the bags and run. I made sure my yellow boots were fastened and ready.

On December 12, the Day of Ashura, the villagers made their big move. After gorging all day on a Muharram feast, they made their way to my family's home. They pelted the house with stones and bricks that hit with so much force I expected a gaping wound to open in the wall. Chants of "Bahá'í dogs" and *"Najis"* filled the air. The assault went on for a long time. It felt like hours.

And then things got quiet. Too quiet. The next sound we heard was a loud "Whoosh!" followed by a foul stench of smoke, and then shouts and cheers. The mob had doused the wooden entryway into our courtyard with kerosene and lit it on fire. The gate was far enough away from the main part of the house that we weren't too worried about the fire spreading. Still, it was unsettling to know that people despised our religious beliefs so much that they wanted to burn down our home while we were still in it. With a bag in each hand, Javad and I stood next to the door, prepared to flee. To our surprise, once the gate was engulfed in flames, the villagers took off back to their homes as if they were afraid of getting in trouble for pulling a childish prank.

Finally, the holy celebration was over, and we could rest. The next morning, I yanked off my yellow boots and lobbed them one by one across the room. I peeled the sweaty wool socks from my feet for the first time in more than a week. My toes reveled in the biting cold air. I donned clean socks and shoes, and headed outside to help *Agha* and Javad build a new gate.

When the holy month ended, *Maman*, Mahin, and Iraj returned. My grandmother's health had slowly deteriorated since losing *Baba*. Her advanced age, the frigid temperatures, and the stress of nonstop harassment in Harvan had taken a toll. At my aunt's home in Tabriz, she didn't have to cross a frozen courtyard to relieve herself in a hole in the ground. Plus, the home was heated. Grandmother was safer and more comfortable there. My brain understood this, yet my heart ached. My grandparents had been a part of my life since birth. Now, in a matter of months, both of them were gone.

———

Chapter Seven
1979

Life for Bahá'ís across the country went from bad to worse. The still-exiled Khomeini continued to stir up anti-regime sentiments from afar. On January 1, 1979, the Shah, who hadn't been seen in public for months, announced plans to leave the country on vacation with his family. Demonstrators cheered. They wanted the Shah to go away for good. On this same day, a string of Bahá'í persecutions took place.

Forty-five miles south of Harvan in a city called Miandoab, a mob surrounded the home of Bahá'í follower named Mir Parvis Afnani and his twenty-four-year-old son, Khosraw. The reason for the clash is unclear. It's possible that someone accused the elder Afnani, who owned a lumber business, of unfair business dealings. As an attacker began slaughtering the family's sheep, Khosraw, who had recently completed military training, fired a gun to scare away the crowd. Unfortunately, the bullet struck and killed a man. Father and son were dragged from their home and hacked to pieces with farming scythes. Their mutilated bodies were then set ablaze.

In Ajabshir, a riot broke out. To disperse the unruly crowd, an Islamic military soldier with the last name of Balai fired multiple rounds into the group. Four people died. Enraged community members wanted someone to pay for the loss of their loved ones. In an attempt to channel the public's anger away from the soldier (who was Muslim), authorities said that the shooter's last name was Bahai, not Balai. Hearing the word "Bahai" was enough to convince the mob that a Bahá'í soldier was responsible for the deaths. They stormed into Bahá'í neighborhoods, dragged followers into the streets, and mercilessly beat them.

In Harvan, my family once again felt too afraid to leave the courtyard.

– – –

Not everyone in my village harbored ill will against my family. Our next-door neighbor kept *Agha* informed of area happenings. To protect the neighbor from incurring the village's wrath for befriending a Bahá'í family, *Agha* would crouch on the roof of our home near the spot where we had planned to jump on the Day of Ashura. This section of the roof was near the corner of the neighbor's courtyard and wasn't easily seen from the street. The neighbor would stand on his side of the courtyard and indirectly talk to *Agha* while pretending to toil in his garden.

If one of us saw the neighbor standing in that corner of his courtyard, we knew he had something important to share. This particular January day brought nothing but bad news. *Agha* was stopped cold when he heard about the brutal, unprovoked deaths of fellow Bahá'ís throughout the country.

"They are coming for your family tonight," the neighbor warned. Men from nearby villages were already on their way to help the residents of Harvan get rid of their filthy Bahá'í dogs for good.

My stunned father tried to wrap his head around this sudden turn of events. He had to figure out a way to get the family safely out of Harvan. We had no car, and the sun was already starting to sink.

Agha tried to appear calm and confident when he broke the news to the family. "It will be like another Day of Ashura," he said. "We will stay here, and God willing, all will be okay." I wanted the family to head for the woods like we had planned for Muharram. But *Agha* said it wasn't possible: the temperature was hovering near freezing; there were six of us, including two women, and it would take hours to reach Shiraz walking through the dark, cold woods. He didn't say it, but I knew: The Harvan villagers just wanted us gone; the others were out for blood. If we tried to flee on foot, we would be chased and slaughtered, our bodies left for the forest animals to pick clean.

While my family waited for the unknown, our hearts in our throats, the mob assembled at the mosque. The air was thick with testosterone. There was much talk about exterminating the Bahá'í vermin that had polluted Harvan for too long. Outsiders goaded the crowd, trying to ease any lingering doubts villagers may have had about attacking a neighbor who had never done them any harm.

"Bahá'ís are unholy!" the men shouted. "You cannot have unholy people living amongst you. God will condemn you, too!"

My family still had Muslim relatives in the village, descendants of my great-grandfather Mustafa. We were a major source of embarrassment for them, yet we remained friendly. Their presence had always afforded my family a slim degree of protection against the worst violence. This time, they were up against an angry sea of strangers. There seemed to be little they could do to keep us safe.

- - -

In the end, I would owe my life to a man named Wolf.

My cousin's real name is Ahmad Taymouri. At six-feet, four-inches, Ahmad was unnaturally tall for a Persian man. He towered over everyone, casting a formidable shadow. Because of his great size, villagers feared Ahmad, almost as much as they feared wolves. Wolves are cunning and stealthy creatures. In an instant, they can steal away a lamb or wipe out an entire flock.

They attack humans, too.

As far as I know, my cousin Wolf had never done anything particularly wolf-like or frightening. His size alone was enough to earn him widespread respect and a nickname that made people tremble.

At the mosque, Wolf stood with a sharpened scythe in hand, looking, perhaps, a little like the Grim Reaper. Most farmers owned scythes to cut grass, wheat, and hay. As the Afnani family unfortunately discovered, these farming tools were also extremely effective at slicing through flesh and bone.

"No harm is to come to anyone in my family," Wolf declared to an instantly shocked and silenced crowd. "Do what you will to their home, but you will have to go through me to get to them, and I will take out thirty of you first."

Murmurs rippled through the crowd. This wasn't the plan. They had come for blood. They knew the police would never arrest anyone for wiping out a family of heretics. Yet Wolf, with more members of the Mustafa tribe standing by his side, had spoken.

– – –

Nearly four hours passed before we heard the sounds of the mob headed our way. We huddled in a corner of the house used for food storage. It was the area farthest from the front door. My father hoped to reason with the villagers, to remind them of the many times his father Khalil helped a family save their crops or how Khalil's brother Heydar generously donated the land for the village to build the school. *Agha* prayed the villagers would remember these things and be merciful. If this tactic didn't work, we were to flee the house and head for the woods. With any luck, one of us might make it out alive.

Maman corralled us kids into a circle facing inward, toward one another. I had a tight grip on Javad and Iraj, whose hands were latched on to *Maman* and Mahin. *Agha* was the lone sentinel, shielding his family as best he could. Silently, we prayed. As the voices grew louder and closer, *Maman* instructed us to look down toward our feet, not at the men.

But I could see. And I could hear.

Wolf was the first person through the door. I nearly lost control of my bladder when I saw his scythe. My family had no way of knowing what had transpired earlier at the mosque. Given our family's history—the brutal, near-fatal beating of my grandfather and great-uncle when they converted to the Bahá'í Faith—it was possible that Wolf and our relatives had gotten first dibs on taking us out. I was terrified as I saw Wolf's eyes land briefly on *Maman's* face and then skip over to lock eyes with *Agha*. I didn't think I could bear to see my parents killed. I prayed for Wolf to be swift and merciful. To my surprise, Wolf gave an almost imperceptible nod toward my father and turned his back to us. Three cousins joined him in forming a protective human barricade around my family.

And then, the rest of the mob poured in.

We would later learn that close to 400 men—from Ajabshir, Shishavan, and surrounding areas—took part in that night of destruction. They came brandishing sledgehammers, axes, and knives. They shattered windows, splintered the *korsi,* smashed what little furniture we owned. They pulverized the walls, shredded books and photos, ripped open our bedrolls. As they raged against our home, they screamed about our unholiness, our *najis,* our dog-like status. Our family, they proclaimed over and over, was damned.

The noise was thunderous. I wanted to cover my ears, but I didn't dare let go of my brothers' hands. Outside, more men took sledgehammers to the courtyard wall, the bathhouse, the latrine. They rounded up the frightened livestock and herded the animals away to distribute among themselves as part of their bounty.

With so many men, it should have taken just minutes to obliterate everything on our small property. But this mob was fueled by years of pent-up hatred for Bahá'ís. Even those who didn't know my family loathed us. They were furious that Wolf and our kin wouldn't let them have what they most wanted—our blood. And so they pounded and shouted; they battered and screeched; they threatened and got as close to us as they dared without incurring Wolf's wrath.

Time stopped. My parents say the attack lasted about an hour. It felt much longer. Eventually, the men were spent. There was nothing left to demolish. Our home and our belongings were in ruin. Thanks to God's grace and Wolf's protection, my family was shaken but physically unharmed. Before leaving, a person from another village approached my father, who was still partially blocked by Wolf. "*Najis* dogs," he said, as he spat on the floor in disgust. "You have until first prayer call tomorrow morning to come to the mosque and pledge loyalty to Islam. If you do not show, you'd better hope we don't find you." He looked up at Wolf and gave an almost imperceptible nod. The message was clear: If they needed to take out Wolf next time to get to us, they would.

As the men made their way out, I heard the bleating of sheep and the receding sound of hoofbeats as the last of our livestock were stolen away. I knew recanting was not an option. We believed in our faith. My family had less than twelve hours to get out.

Two of our Muslim cousins set off to Gurvan to hire a truck to take *Maman* and Mahin to Aunt Nahid's home in Tabriz. Javad would go along as the male protector. It was time for *Agha*, Iraj, and me to put the Day of Ashura plan into action. At the first light of dawn, we would set out on foot through the woods.

We scrambled to gather the remaining vestiges of our life in Harvan to take with us. There were scraps of photos and books to piece back together. Clothing and blankets to mend. Iraj and I stuffed food and extra clothes into bags to keep us going during our frigid journey. The night pulsed with fear and frenzy. There was no time to get nostalgic about leaving behind our home, the place where my siblings and I took our first breaths and Baba his last.

As I hustled to find the broken mementos of my childhood too precious to leave behind, I heard *Maman's* voice raised in anger. "I am not leaving my family!" She was staring heatedly at a cousin who had suggested that she should stay in Harvan, and go back to her Islamic roots, while the rest of us went to Tabriz.

Not having any luck with *Maman*, the cousin turned to my father. "You cannot take her! She belongs here!" he said. But *Maman* was having none of that nonsense. For a small woman, she commanded a large space. "I belong with my family," she said. "If you don't want to help us, then go."

The cousin stayed.

When the truck arrived, it fully hit me. I had taken a lot of punches to the gut over the years from classmates bent on making me suffer. But this was the ultimate blow. There would be no coming back to Harvan. I wouldn't see my childhood home again.

The pickup truck was held together by rust and string. Its driver was a reluctant chauffeur. As a Muslim, he could be killed if anyone found out about his role in our escape. It was a tight squeeze fitting *Maman*, Mahin, and Javad into the cab, but with temperatures hovering below freezing, riding in the back wasn't an option. We loaded the truck bed with as many of our belongings as we could salvage. The villagers hadn't left us much, but the broken and shredded items were all that we now owned.

It hurt to look at *Maman* and *Agha* as they hugged goodbye. Nobody had to say out loud what was haunting all of our thoughts: This could be the last time we saw each other. Our cousins had paid the driver handsomely to get our family safely to Tabriz. Still, the truck could be stopped at any point. What if it broke down? What if the driver's allegiance to his Muslim brothers was stronger than his fear of retribution from Wolf, and he killed our family to make himself a hero? We could only pray that God would keep each of us safe and that we would see one another again.

Maman and my siblings probably had similar dark thoughts as they drove away, the family divided. *Agha*, Iraj, and I would traverse dark woods in freezing temperatures. *Agha* had mapped out a circuitous route devised to throw trackers off of our trail. We would reach Shiraz in about three hours, nearly twice as long as the normal route would take. We would stay far away from the main road, which meant relying on memories of earlier times hunting rabbits and ducks to keep us from getting lost. More importantly, we had to get a far-enough head start to make it harder for the villagers to catch us.

After the cousins left, there was not much to do but wait for enough sun to peek through to light our way. There was no chance of sleep. I wandered through the wasteland that once was my home. Walking through the courtyard, I heard noises coming from the barn. Inside I found four terrified chickens that had taken refuge behind splintered feed troughs. They were the best things I laid eyes on all night. I could sell the chickens in Tabriz and give the money to *Agha*. Chickens are usually difficult to catch, but these fowl were so traumatized that I easily snatched them up and deposited them into a small wood crate that I nailed back together. When *Agha* saw what I had, he looked at me and nodded. *This was a start*, his nod said.

— — —

We set off at daybreak, slipping stealthily into the trees' shadows. I was so terrified of being exposed and so focused on getting safely camouflaged that it didn't occur to me to look back at my home until I was too far into the woods to see it anymore. But I can still close my eyes and see my family sitting around the *korsi*, laughing and telling stories, *Baba* picking apples in the courtyard, *Maman* and grandmother cooking meals in the tandoor oven, the home filled with dancing relatives during *Nowruz*, and cousin Shahin and I kicking the soccer ball.

As I walked through the woods, my ears strained for any sound of a pursuit. Iraj carried both of our bags so I could deal with the chickens. I was worried they would start squawking and give us away. To my relief, they still seemed to be in shock. I picked my way over fallen branches and leaves as quickly and quietly as I could. *Agha* had hunted in these woods for decades, so I relied on his internal compass to guide us first south and then east.

Surely, my hands and feet were painfully cold, but I don't remember. I think adrenaline kept me warm for the entire trek. Starting out, we often stopped in our tracks, growing a few inches taller as we swiveled left and then right, certain we'd heard a twig snap, footsteps, someone moving in the woods. But the manhunt never came. We had either outsmarted them, or more likely, the villagers didn't care what my family did as long as we were out of their sight forever.

The walk to Shiraz was long, exhausting, and mercifully uneventful. *Agha* purchased bus tickets to Tabriz with money Wolf had given him. What little savings my parents had was gone. We would start our new life in Tabriz with just the clothes on our backs.

———

PART TWO

Tabriz, IRAN

Chapter Eight
1979

The bus ride to Tabriz took more than fifteen hours. Every time the bus stopped—to let people on or off, or for food and bathroom breaks—my heart also stopped. I expected authorities to board the bus and drag us back to Harvan so the villagers could finish us off. *Agha*, Iraj, and I squeezed into one well-worn vinyl seat with *Agha* on the outside and Iraj pressed up against the window. I sat sandwiched between them with the crate of squawking chickens perched on my lap. This trip marked the first time I would see a city as large as Tabriz and the first time I would see my Aunt Nahid and Uncle Shoá Allah's house, the place that my cousin Shahin called home.

As the bus rolled into Tabriz, I was excited to see signs for the Iran Tractor Manufacturing Company in the city's west industrial area. The company sponsored East Azerbaijan's professional soccer team, the Tractor Sports Club. Now that I would be living in Tabriz, I hoped to see the team play. The bus and train station were at the same location. As the bus pulled in, I looked in wonder at the massive train sitting on the track. It was even bigger than the pictures of trains I had seen in books. I couldn't believe something so big could move effortlessly over those tracks.

Agha got us a taxi to take us to my aunt and uncle's home. I hadn't ridden in many cars, and I certainly hadn't ridden on streets that were packed with cars, trucks, and motorcycles. Vehicles weaved in and out of Azadi Boulevard. A cacophony of horns never stopped. Even though it was chilly, Agha cracked the window to let out some of the stench from the taxi driver's cigarette. This also let in the smell of diesel fumes. I had never seen so many buildings, so many people. I wondered where everyone was hurrying to go. The chickens clucked nervously in the wood crate on my lap. I knew how they felt. I was nervous, too.

– – –

Compared to the modest homes in Harvan, my aunt and uncle's place was massive. It rose two full stories and even had an apartment unit, with renters. Despite its big size, there was little room for my family along with my aunt, uncle, grandmother, and three cousins. I settled in with my family in the home's twelve-by-twelve-foot cellar. Shahin and I were happy to see each other, but I could tell he was as sad as I was, knowing that we would never again send a soccer ball soaring between the almond trees in Harvan. That part of our childhood was over.

In the cellar's dank confines, I slept on the dirt floor next to my parents and three siblings, a clanging furnace, and a water heater that hissed noisily off and on. *Maman* cooked meals over a small propane grill outside and washed dishes in a cement water trough in the backyard. For the first time in my fifteen years, I was in a home with indoor plumbing, but because the cellar didn't have an entryway into the house, I had to go outside and through the front door to access the bathroom. To minimize disrupting the household, I limited bathroom treks, developing a ten-gallon bladder that would come in handy later in life.

In Tabriz, I was one of hundreds of Bahá'ís, so my non-Muslim status didn't turn many heads. Discrimination persisted, but I didn't have any problem buying gum or anything else I wanted. Most of the time, people didn't care about my faith. It felt good to be so invisible, and I was excited to be living with Bahá'í relatives in a big city. I was reunited with my grandmother, who hadn't returned to Harvan after the village mob set fire to our property during Muharram. And I finally had a chance to get to know Shahin's brothers better. But with so many of us in the house, space felt tight. My parents decided that my sister Mahin and I would take grandmother to Tehran to live with Aunt Faridehe's family.

— — —

Bahá'ís don't have a mullah, priest, or any type of spiritual leader. Instead, we elect nine Local Spiritual Assembly members to oversee spiritual and educational development of the Bahá'í community. These local assemblies report to the National Spiritual Assembly in Tehran. Similar to churches, local assemblies help people in need regardless of faith. When my family arrived in Tabriz, we became the local assembly's charitable cause. It was a humbling experience. My family had never been rich, but our home, our crops, and our livestock in Harvan had been just that: *ours*. In Tabriz, we owned nothing. I ate meals prepared with food that other people gave to us and wore other children's castoff clothes. My family had always been among the first to give. While we were grateful for the support, none of us were comfortable being on the receiving end of these handouts.

Agha continued to search for steady work, picking up whatever odd jobs he could find. For a brief period, nineteen-year-old Mahin was the family's primary breadwinner. It pained *Agha* that he had to rely on his only daughter and handouts from strangers to support his family.

Unfortunately, Mahin's teaching job was still in Ajabshir, which was now more than sixty miles away. *Maman* fretted and prayed each day that Mahin boarded the bus for the four-hour round-trip journey. She couldn't relax until Mahin was home safely. *Maman* had good reason to be concerned. Plenty of people in Ajabshir knew that my family had been run out of Harvan. There was no guarantee that someone wouldn't try to harm Mahin for not recanting her faith.

It was during this time that Mahin received the first of several marriage proposals from lovestruck Bahá'í men. Mahin was not only beautiful, she was also smart and kind. Men were drawn to her. She turned them all down—not because she wasn't interested, but because our family relied on her wages. Once married, Mahin and her husband would need her earnings to support their home and family. Marriage would have to wait.

In Harvan, I spent my free time running around and playing soccer in open fields. It was the only life I knew. The backyard in Tabriz was much too small for soccer, the streets too busy. Uncle Shoá Allah was a military officer and very strict. I was expected to stand and say, "sir" whenever he entered a room. Horseplay and laughter were frowned upon. It's no surprise that my cousins preferred to hang out with my family in the cramped basement instead of upstairs in their more spacious home.

My parents reassured me that these sacrifices were all part of God's plan. Still, I struggled to make sense of the situation. I missed my home and my old life. As cruel as my village peers could be, I missed them, too. It pained me to know that another family—a Muslim family—was living in my family's home and making money from our crops.

"It's not fair. Why is God doing this to us?" I asked *Maman* one night. I immediately wanted to stuff the words back into my mouth and swallow them. It was selfish to complain. Other Bahá'í families had fared much worse. Nobody in my family had been maimed, raped, imprisoned, or executed. We were all still relatively happy, healthy, and forging a new life together.

"There is a plan for each of us," *Maman* assured me. "You must have faith that everything will work out."

I didn't know about God's plan, but I planned to attend a university and pursue my dream of becoming an architect. Every student in Iran had missed five months of school while the protests and strikes raged on. When classes finally resumed in February, I threw myself into my schoolwork with a fervor. I aced every subject, even outscoring Muslim classmates in an Islamic studies class.

As at all schools during my youth, bullies ruled the classrooms. But, in Tabriz, it was the teachers—not students—who instigated fights. It was no secret that I was the only Bahá'í among all of my classmates. But because I was smart and went out of my way to help others, my peers liked me and treated me fairly. Teachers, however, were so prejudiced against Bahá'í students that the Local Spiritual Assembly coached us on how to handle threatening situations.

On one particular school day, my history teacher informed the class that Bahá'ís were not to be trusted: We were all spies for the United States or Israel. This was a common, unfounded allegation used to fuel hatred against Bahá'ís. The assertion could be traced to the country's supreme religious leader, Ayatollah Ruhollah Khomeini, who claimed, "Bahá'í is not a religion, it is a political party. It is a party that was initially supported by the British and is now supported by America. They are spies . . ."

After the teacher made this accusation, I nervously raised my hand. Upon getting the teacher's okay to proceed, I stood up and recited the script that I had rehearsed numerous times with my Bahá'í youth leaders. "Excuse me, sir. This topic isn't part of our curriculum," I said, clearing my throat and trying to tap into a level of confidence I didn't possess. "I am a Bahá'í. If you have questions or concerns about this matter, I would be happy to speak with you after school."

Most teachers waved off this offer and moved on to another topic. But one Bahá'í high-school student was arrested for taking a similar stance. He was beaten and then imprisoned for more than a year. Every time I had to stand up to a teacher (it was at least a weekly occurrence), I did so knowing that I risked being sent to prison.

On this particular day, my teacher responded by digging in. He repeatedly stated that Bahá'ís were spies, and so I continued to offer to speak with him later. Finally, a class-mate raised his hand. My heart sank when I saw it was the president of the school's Islamic Club. To my shock, instead of agreeing with the teacher, the student stood, looked over at me, and said, "Mansur, why are you arguing? Everyone knows that Bahá'ís are not spies. That's absurd." The student's rebuke flustered the teacher, but he didn't dare discipline one of the most popular kids in school. The class returned to the lesson plan. I have never forgotten the courage it took for this classmate to speak up for me.

– – –

Things began to look up for my family when summer rolled around. In June, we got news that my brilliant older brother, Javad, had been accepted into the University of Tabriz medical school. The government paid for higher education, but in order to pursue a university degree in Iran, high-school students must score high marks on an extremely challenging national entrance exam. That year, the government admitted fewer than one percent of the more than two million students who took the exam. Out of those two million students, Javad's exceptionally high test results placed him in the top 420. This was an amazing accomplishment for a child born to illiterate parents and raised in a poor farming village. I was proud of Javad and excited to have a doctor in the family. I was also filled with hope. If Javad could get into a university, so could I. After a year of being beaten down in Harvan and then forcibly uprooted from my home, Javad's news sent me soaring.

My family's good fortune continued. *Agha* found steady masonry work helping to build a home for an affluent family in an all-Bahá'í community. Unfortunately, the work was one hundred miles away. I saw him occasionally on weekends. When school was out for the summer, Javad and I also got jobs at the construction site. I was fifteen, with arms like twigs. The work involved moving heavy cinder blocks and pushing wheelbarrows weighted with cement, bricks, dirt, and rock. My pubescent body was not built for this hard manual labor. Still, I gave it my all. One day, as I was struggling to move a wheelbarrow full of bricks, the owner of the home walked over and handed me a glass of water.

"Mansur, take a break," he said. I was afraid he was angry at my slow pace, perhaps questioning why he was paying this skinny kid who clearly wasn't cut out for the tasks. It would be humiliating to get fired. I didn't want to disappoint *Agha* and my family. I wiped the stream of sweat from my brow, drank the water in one gulp, thanked the owner as I handed back my glass, and proceeded to return to my job.

"That's not a break," he said. "Come, sit with me. Tell me what you have studied in school." The man was essentially my boss. It was his house we were building. If he said "sit," I sat. He kept me talking for almost an hour—long enough for others on the work crew to finish the job I'd abandoned.

For weeks, the homeowner sought me out, pulled me from the job, and then proceeded to share tips with me about how to become a successful businessman. He took a keen interest in my dream of becoming an architect. I wanted to be the person who designed buildings, not the person who physically built them. He saw how I struggled to do the construction work. He also saw how determined I was to do my share. Not once did he dock my pay for the time I spent sitting and talking. That was a blessing, because I needed my wages to contribute to the family fund.

When I wasn't working, I went to the library. I loved learning, and I loved to read. I devoured books about scientific discoveries, immersed myself in the philosophical teachings of Jean-Jacques Rousseau and Bertrand Russell, read every Jack London book translated to Farsi, and fell in love with *Anna Karenina*. I was trying to make up for missed school days, as well as struggling to understand the world around me and my place in it. I am still trying to figure out these things.

– – –

Eventually, *Agha* was able to use our collective family funds to move us out of the depressing cellar and into a place of our own. The house had two rooms: a bedroom and a family room. The kitchen and bathroom were outside in the courtyard. It also had electricity and plumbing. Despite how nice this house was, I still yearned for my home in Harvan.

In the fall, I started tenth grade at a different high school closer to home, Iraj began seventh grade, Javad went to medical school, and Mahin continued to teach and turn down her suitors. While I dedicated myself to my studies, tensions mounted in the nation's capital. On November 4, thousands of University of Tehran students and Islamic revolutionaries stormed the United States Embassy, taking sixty-six Americans hostage. They called the embassy a "den of spies." The hostage takers believed the United States was plotting to return the Shah to power. In reality, the Shah was in America, getting treatments for the cancer that would eventually take his life.

Even as a teenager, I was interested in politics. I tried to stay up to date on political happenings by reading books and newspapers at the library and by tuning into news segments on television and radio. I felt sorry for the Americans. I knew how it felt to be unjustly labeled a spy.

One week after the start of the hostage crisis, Islamic revolutionaries began to systematically target leaders of Bahá'í communities throughout the country. It began with the abduction of Ali Murad Davudi, a philosophy professor at the University of Tehran and secretary of the National Spiritual Assembly. The following month, Ruhi Roshani, author of many Bahá'í Faith books and secretary of Tehran's

Local Spiritual Assembly, disappeared. Neither man was ever heard from again.

The message to Bahá'ís was clear: You are disposable.

The hostage situation lasted for more than a year, ending in January 1981, months after the Shah had died in exile. During this time, the United States crippled the Iranian government's finances by refusing to purchase the country's oil and freezing billions of dollars of assets held overseas. Today, the former U.S. Embassy is home to an Islamic cultural center and museum. Every year on the anniversary of the embassy siege, throngs of Iranians take to the streets to celebrate the coup while chanting "Death to America."

Chapter Nine

1980

The newly formed Iranian government began breaking up monopolies to give the lower classes a chance to become business owners. *Agha* was able to purchase a home-appliance store at a fraction of its worth from a respected, well-to-do Bahá'í business owner. Yadalloh Astani was an affable man who let *Agha* pay off the shop's purchase price in installments. He even taught *Agha* the ins-and-outs of running a business. I chuckled at the notion of my father, a lifelong village farmer who'd lived without electricity for much of his life, selling stoves, refrigerators, and other appliances he was still learning how to use.

Thanks to steady income from the business and drastically low loan-interest rates, my parents were able to purchase a bigger house. This new place had three bedrooms, a living area, and an indoor kitchen and bathroom. It also had a basement, a room that became instrumental to the launch of my first business venture: plastic shopping bags.

I learned about the market for plastic bags from a friend whose parents were turning a profit on it. The setup looked like a relatively easy way to earn extra cash. I ordered sheets of plastic from a distributor, cut them into squares with scissors, and used a hot press to seal the top and bottom edges together. I then used scissors to cut a handle out of the top. I sold the bags back to the plastics distributor, who sold them to local merchants. Everyone except *Maman*, who was busy running the household, had a hand in making the bags. Anyone with a spare moment was expected to be in the basement cutting and sealing plastic shopping bags.

– – –

It wasn't long before acts of hostility against Bahá'ís hit home. A national volunteer militia called the *Basij* formed in response to Ayatollah Khomeini's call to create a "twenty-million-man army." The *basiji* were supposed to back up the Islamic Revolutionary Guards. But these lawless, gun-toting fanatics quickly established themselves as the country's morality police. They arrested women for not wearing hijabs, infiltrated the local police, recruited child soldiers to their cause, and harassed and arrested citizens—mostly Bahá'ís—without justification.

Soon after *Agha* started the appliance business, a *basiji* pulled over *Agha's* truck as he was hauling a refrigerator to the store. Appliances were a hot commodity in Iran's lucrative black market. Even though *Agha* had paperwork showing that he was doing legitimate business, he was taken to the police station for questioning. There, the captain badgered him to falsely confess to shady black-market sales.

"I legally sell appliances at my store. I have the paperwork to prove it," *Agha* insisted. Except by this point, he no longer had the paperwork. The *basiji* had taken it while searching the truck.

"You are Bahá'í?" the captain asked. With a nod, *Agha* replied, "What does my faith have to do with this?"

The captain shrugged. "Bahá'ís lie." He pulled a gun from his holster and motioned to the back wall. "Go, stand over there." *Agha* had no choice. He walked over and stood with his back to the wall. The captain raised his gun and pointed it at *Agha's* chest. *Agha* silently prayed. The captain looked around the room at his fellow comrades and burst out laughing. "You Bahá'ís are so quick to want to die," he chortled. "I wouldn't be so eager to go to hell." The captain grabbed the store paperwork from the *basiji* and looked it over.

It was around this time (after the mock execution) that I arrived to try to straighten things out. I was relieved to see *Agha* physically unharmed. "You can go," the captain said as he handed the paperwork back to *Agha*. "But I will shoot you for real if I catch you selling on the black market." *Agha* nodded his understanding.

As we turned to leave, the captain grabbed my arm. I looked at him, frightened of what he might do. "Your father is a foolish man. He has been misled," he said to me. "You are still young. There is still time to save your soul." He began to recite scripture from the Qur'an about Muhammad being the last prophet. I joined in, finishing the scripture with him, and then adding a different excerpt that supports the idea of additional prophets. The captain was taken back by my knowledge of Islam. His theory that I had been brainwashed didn't hold up. "Bahá'u'lláh is the Promised One," I said defiantly to the captain. It was a brave and foolish statement. The captain shook his head and wagged a finger at me. I thought, *He's either going to arrest me or shoot me.* Instead he chuckled and said, "You shouldn't say that to anyone." And with that, *Agha* and I were free to go.

– – –

In April, the police arrested Mr. Astani, the kind soul who'd helped *Agha* get his start with the appliance store.

They also arrested Faramarz Samandari, a medical doctor and professor of medicine at Tabriz University, who also served on the Local Spiritual Assembly. The men were falsely accused of working for the deposed Shah's secret police, giving money to Israel, and soliciting prostitutes. They spent three months in prison before a firing squad sent each man to an early grave. There was no trial. Twenty-two other Bahá'ís from Tehran and Tabriz were executed that same day for trumped-up charges ranging from adultery to gambling, drug trafficking, and solicitation.

At the time of Mr. Astani's execution, I had attended more funerals in my seventeen years than celebrations. Whenever a member of the local Bahá'í community died—and especially when the death was unjust—people came out in droves to pay their respects. The mostly Muslim cemetery in Tabriz had a small, separate area for people of other faiths. There was a morgue on the cemetery grounds, where workers cleansed the body before burial. After the cleansing, a member of the Bahá'í Local Spiritual Assembly placed a burial ring onto the deceased person's left forefinger. The ring's inscription read: "*I came forth from God, and return unto Him, detached from all save Him, holding fast to His Name, the Merciful, the Compassionate.*" The body was then wrapped in cloth before being placed in a wooden coffin and lowered into the ground.

Only a handful of people could fit inside the cold cinder-block morgue to bear witness to these burial rituals. With permission from grieving families, a small group of Bahá'ís—myself included—attended the sacraments of those who were executed. I was there to pay my respects, but I was also there to take photos of the bodies to document the tortures and killings. This was a life-risking endeavor for anyone caught holding the camera.

I remember the morgue workers peeling Mr. Astani's stiff, blood-soaked clothes from his body. I can still see the gaping wounds in his chest and abdomen where the bullets had done their damage. His brutalized body was hard to look at, but what really did me in were the loud sobs that echoed off the morgue walls. The cemetery's gravedigger, Omar Tabrizi, stood just inside the morgue's doorway, overcome with grief. Mr. Astani had been a friend to all. He'd made it a point to attend every Bahá'í funeral, which meant he and Mr. Tabrizi saw each other on an almost-daily basis up until Mr. Astani's arrest. Although he was Muslim, Mr. Tabrizi considered Mr. Astani his friend. After Mr. Astani's coffin was lowered into the ground, the gravedigger instructed us to gather rocks to place at the head of the grave to mark Mr. Astani's final resting place. Mr. Tabrizi was heartbroken at what his Muslim brothers had done to such a kind and generous man. Many years later, when the gravedigger died, I heard that his children honored his wishes to be buried in the non-Muslim section of the cemetery, near Mr. Astani. Mr. Tabrizi never openly admitted it, but I believe in his heart he considered himself to be a Bahá'í.

– – –

In August, all nine elected members of the National Spiritual Assembly in Tehran were arrested, along with two other Bahá'ís, while attending an assembly meeting. They were never heard from again. To this day, the government denies having any knowledge about the fates of these missing Bahá'ís.

The *basiji* and Revolutionary Guards were known for forcing their way into Bahá'í-owned homes to confiscate and destroy religious texts, pictures, symbols—anything they considered indecent. Their actions were disturbingly reminiscent of Nazi raids on Jewish families. The Spiritual Assemblies feared that it was only a matter of time before they seized and destroyed all Bahá'í sacred texts in the country.

To ensure the word of The Báb and Bahá'u'lláh would always be known in Iran, the assembly tasked certain youths with memorizing Bahá'í prayers, scriptures, and other critical writings. My peers and I became, in essence, living libraries. I was asked to memorize all 650 words of the Tablet of Ahmad and more than 1,000 words of the Fire Tablet. I also became an expert on the history of The Báb's ministry. Because no Bahá'í was safe from prison or death, several different youths memorized the same writings. With this approach, should anything happen to one of us, the knowledge would still be secured in the minds of others.

For weeks, I studied these texts alongside my friend Siamak Naeemi. Siamak was wearing a Persepolis Football Club shirt when we met for the first time at a youth committee. This professional soccer team was the rival of my beloved Esteghlal team. Siamak and I shared some good-natured banter as we walked back to our homes after the meeting. Siamak and I became fast friends, often meeting at five in the morning to jog a few miles at a nearby park before heading off to our respective high schools. Siamak had grown up in Tabriz, but his parents had been chased out of Miandoab, a city in West Azerbaijan Province, a decade before he was born. He was respectful when I talked longingly about Harvan and never questioned how I could miss a place that treated my family so poorly. As members of the youth assembly, Siamak and I spent hours mentoring younger children as they explored the Bahá'í Faith and other religions. Senior Bahá'í community members looked to us to protect the faith for future generations.

Siamak's father died when he was fifteen. His siblings were grown and married. Occasionally, his *Maman* would travel to Tehran to visit her sister, and I would spend those days and nights with Siamak, enjoying the quiet and freedom of a mostly empty house. It was the only time I spent away from my family, who were just a few blocks away.

Decades later, as a father to sixteen- and seventeen-year-old boys, the idea of leaving them unsupervised at home for a week or longer seemed inconceivable. But Siamak and I grew up in a different era in a different place. As Bahá'ís, we didn't touch alcohol. We were interested in girls, but girls didn't seem very interested in us. In Persian culture, teenagers and young adults don't casually date. Declaring an interest in a girl is essentially seen as declaring your intentions to marry. Marriage didn't interest me, nor was it a possibility at the time. Custom dictated that younger siblings didn't marry before their older siblings. My siblings were still single. A man was expected to provide for his bride, and that required money—something my family always seemed to lack. Mahin continued to turn down her suitors, using her wages to help support our family.

Siamak and I spent our time dreaming about the future. We both had big plans for earning university degrees and having successful careers that would allow us to support our future brides and children, as well as our parents. We wanted our families never to have to worry about money. In our hearts, we knew we might have to, one day, leave Iran to realize our dreams. With the current government in power, we had little chance of making a major mark in Iran as Bahá'ís.

For months, Siamak and I pored over Bahá'í texts. We spent hours reciting and memorizing lines together, encouraging and correcting each other as needed. My brothers and sister were also feverishly committing words to memory. Decades later, I can still recall every word of The Tablets. This passage from the Fire Tablet reminded me of my countrymen's treatment of Bahá'ís: *"Coldness hath gripped all mankind: Where is the warmth of Thy love, O Fire of the worlds?"*

Becoming so intimately familiar with these sacred texts should have bolstered my faith. Instead, I was angry and grieving over the way Bahá'ís had been persecuted since the religion's founding. I wanted to believe that this maltreatment was in the past, something that happened ages ago to a different people, living in a different world. I wanted the harassments and oppression to be a part of history, not the present, and certainly not the future, which was looking bleaker every day.

– – –

On September 22, Iraqi President Saddam Hussein ordered his troops to invade the western border of Iran. The attack was strategically timed to take advantage of the instability of the newly formed Iranian government, which was still getting its footing under Ayatollah Khomeini. There were many reasons for the invasion, one of them being that President Hussein, a Sunni Muslim, felt threatened by Shiite Muslims' continued rise to power in Iran following the Islamic Revolution. He sought to oust the new regime before the Shiites became too powerful and attempted to overthrow the Sunnis in Iraq.

When the war started, my eldest brother Behrouz had completed his time with the military. He worked as an accountant for a Bahá'í-owned construction company and lived with my family in Tabriz. Mahin's gender and Javad's university studies exempted them from serving. In two years, I would turn eighteen and graduate from high school. The war with Iraq was in its infancy. There was no telling how long it would last. More than ever, I needed to get a high score on the placement test to secure a spot at a university. Otherwise, I would be forced to take up arms.

I was relatively certain that I would do well on the test. Still, I worried. I had switched schools multiple times and missed months of classroom instruction due to school closures. The shopping-bag business was doing well, but I decided I needed a more secure backup plan for making a living in case a degree wasn't in my future. Through a family friend, I learned about stable job opportunities in the optical business. During my last two years of high school, I apprenticed at an optical lab, learning how to grind, shape, and surface eyeglass lenses. I introduced my friend Tofigh Tabarmanaf to the business. Tofigh was the younger brother of Javad's best friend from medical school. He also aspired to become a doctor. Until high school and the entrance exams were over, the two of us honed our skills at the optical lab. It wasn't a job that either of us wanted to do forever, but it helped support our families. And we knew it would bring in money if we didn't get into a university.

———

Chapter Ten

1981

The *basiji* continued to randomly pillage the homes of Bahá'ís across the country, destroying anything they considered *haram* ("forbidden by Islamic law") and hauling citizens off to jail for no justifiable reason. Most of those arrested never returned. I was at school in April when my parents received word that the *basiji* had taken a relative, Farnoosh, for questioning.

Farnoosh was in the wrong place at the wrong time. He had offered to pick up a friend's Bahá'í membership card at the home of Habibu'llah Tahqiqi. Membership cards are needed to vote in an assembly election and participate in other activities. When Farnoosh knocked on the courtyard door, he had no way of knowing that guards had seized Mr. Tahqiqi and were searching the premises.

Mr. Tahqiqi was a petroleum engineer who'd made his fortune setting up oil refineries. He and his family lived in an opulent home in the city's more affluent neighborhood. He was the only person I knew who had servants to answer the door, cook meals, and keep the place immaculate. Although Mr. Tahqiqi was an elected council member of the Local Spiritual Assembly, it's likely that the *basiji* were more interested in his wife, who maintained a record of all Bahá'ís living in Tabriz. Mrs. Tahqiqi wasn't home when the guards took away her husband. When her car pulled onto the street, a neighbor flagged her down and ushered her into the safety of their home. It was from this vantage point that Mrs. Tahqiqi watched as the *basiji* answered Farnoosh's knock at the door and led him into the courtyard.

At first, Farnoosh mistook the *basiji* for a servant. He grew nervous as several men went in and out of the house carrying boxes of books and documents. After learning that Mr. Tahqiqi wasn't home, Farnoosh said he would come back at another time.

"I felt a sharp, painful jab to my ribs and looked down to see a gun pointed at my side," Farnoosh later told me. In the eyes of authorities, Farnoosh's faith was enough to label him a criminal. From across the street, Mrs. Tahqiqi saw the guards, guns drawn and pointed, shove Farnoosh into the backseat of a car and drive off. She immediately called Farnoosh's father, who reached out to *Agha* for help.

Farnoosh arrived at a local police station around noon. For the remainder of the day and throughout the night, three men wearing hooded masks drilled him with questions about the Local Spiritual Assembly, its members, and what he knew about the Tahqiqi family. When Farnoosh couldn't answer the questions to their satisfaction, they threw him to the floor and kicked him in the ribs, shins, back, and stomach. They threatened to send him to prison, where Bahá'ís were routinely tortured and killed. But Farnoosh was a twenty-year-old college student. He truly didn't have the information they wanted.

Agha waited outside the station all night. When he was finally allowed to see Farnoosh more than twenty-four hours later, he didn't try to comfort him. Instead, *Agha* screamed at him. "Farnoosh, you have been told not to go

to that house! You are not to have anything to do with the
assembly! You will be severely punished for disobeying your
family!" It was all an act. To my father's great surprise, the
police released Farnoosh into his custody.

During this time, *Maman* had no way of knowing what
was happening at the police station. She fretted that the
basiji would arrest her husband, too. She was acutely aware
that guards could show up at any minute to search the
family home for whatever materials they deemed illicit.
They could put all of us in jail. Or worse. To protect us,
Maman and Mahin dashed through the house gathering
up Bahá'í scriptures, pictures, and books. Frantically, they
searched for a safe place to dispose of the contraband, a
place authorities wouldn't think to look or couldn't look.
They decided on the well.

At some previous point in history, former residents of our
home had hauled water from a well in the backyard. Indoor
plumbing pipes now snaked through the house delivering
water at the turn of a spigot. The well dried up long before
my family moved in. I have no idea of the well's depth, but
you could count off several seconds before hearing the dis-
tinct thud of a dropped object smacking dirt. Even with a
flashlight, it was impossible to make out the bottom. *Maman*
and Mahin pulled mightily to lift the heavy iron door that
covered the well's gaping mouth. And then they swiftly fed
everything down its black throat.

Some of the books *Maman* seized in her feverish purge
were my personal journals. Starting in my early teen years,
I poured my fears, anxieties, sadness, and happiness onto
those pages. My journals were a safe place to vent, to dream,
to weep, and to hope. Those scribbles contained memories of

my grandparents, my childhood in Harvan, happier times, and yes, the alarming "drug bust," and the frightening village mob that ultimately drove my family out of our home. To this day, I mourn the loss of those journals. By the time I got home from school and heard what was going on with Farnoosh, my journals were lost forever to the bowels of the earth.

I understood *Maman's* concerns. The *basiji* would have been incensed to read what I thought about the horrors visited upon my family in the name of Islam. The punishment would have been immediate and severe. Still, I was angry that she'd disposed of something so dear to me in such an irretrievable way. Had I been home, I could have buried the journals in the yard or hidden them behind loose stones in the courtyard wall, retrieving them when the threat passed. It broke my heart to think about the journals' plastic covers cracking, the pages yellowing, curling at the edges, and disintegrating into dust. What stabbed at my heart most: No one ever came to search our home. My memories had been lost for no reason. Whenever this thought made me sad, I had only to reflect on how differently the situation could have turned out. Mr. Tahqiqi was imprisoned for three months before being marched in front of a firing squad. He died along with seven other elected Local Spiritual Assembly members from Tabriz and one other unlucky Bahá'í.

A few weeks after these executions, a family acquaintance asked me to find a safe place to hide documents that held classified information about the assembly members' final days at the Tabriz Central Prison. I was caught off guard at the request and agreed without truly thinking through the risks. The acquaintance brought the documents to my home, a move that endangered my entire family. After he left, I hurried to the basement, the thick envelope hidden underneath my shirt. There, I turned off the lights in the hopes that nobody would come down the stairs looking for me. With a flashlight in one hand, I read through the papers. My hands shook. There were transcripts of each Bahá'í follower's interrogations. What I read made me gasp, and then weep. Although it didn't appear that these assembly members were tortured, they were subjected to horrific threats of broken bones, ripped-out fingernails, beatings, and floggings. In one instance, the assembly members were told that they could all disappear—just as the National Spiritual Assembly members had vanished in Tehran. Nobody would ever know what happened to them. Mr. Tahqiqi's only hope of staying alive—the only hope for any of the imprisoned Bahá'ís—was to recant their faith. This wasn't a falsehearted offer. Had Mr. Tahqiqi publicly denounced his faith through a paid newspaper or television advertisement and embraced Islam, he would have lived. In my hands, I also held Mr. Tahqiqi's hastily handwritten will, along with the wills of the other prisoners, composed moments before their deaths. All of them had remained true to their faith until the end.

I didn't ask how the acquaintance came to possess these documents. For his safety, and that of his family, I cannot name him. Whoever smuggled out the files from the prison did so at great personal peril. I hadn't realized the gravity of what I'd agreed to do until it was too late. I already possessed the documents; their contents were etched on my heart. The *basiji* were still randomly searching homes of Bahá'í families. If they discovered these documents, every member of my family could be tortured and killed. No doubt, my parents would have been furious at this person for asking so much of me. Or perhaps they would have been more shocked at how readily I'd said, "Yes."

As an eighteen-year-old high-school student, my brain coursed with the perfect combination of naiveté and invincibility to take on such a dangerous, reckless task. Although I was nervous and frightened, I considered it an honor to be entrusted with the job. It was becoming increasingly clear that it was up to my generation to do something to halt the atrocities befalling our people. I was tired of doing nothing while innocent lives were being lost. I itched to do something to push back against the authorities. I silenced any doubts and seized this chance.

I decided to stash the documents on the roof of my family's home. Thanks to the shopping-bag business, I had plenty of plastic on hand to tightly encase the papers to keep them dry. I stuffed this sealed plastic pouch into the waistband of my pants, filled a bucket with wet red clay, and climbed a ladder onto the flat asphalt roof. It was not unusual to see someone on the roof of a home. During hot summer months, families often congregated, and sometimes slept, on rooftops to catch a cooling breeze. In the winter, people climbed to the roof to shovel off snow. I held the package against the backside of the clay parapet wall that ran along the roof's edge and coated it with layer upon layer of fresh red earth. Once dry, that section of the clay wall looked no different from the rest.

A month passed before I was asked to deliver the documents to a designated location in Tehran. My source made sure I understood the risks. "If you are caught with these papers, they will peel the skin from your body." He wasn't being overly dramatic. The guards would torture me until I told them how I got the papers, and then they would kill me. This scenario gave me pause, yet I was committed to seeing the job through. I told my parents I was going to Tehran to meet with some people about the plastics business.

I freed the envelope from the clay wall and rewrapped it in clean plastic. I wedged this plastic bundle tightly in the crook of my left armpit underneath my clothes for the entire eight-hour bus ride. When a passenger sat next to me, I pressed my body up against the side of the bus and stared out the window. When a checkpoint guard boarded the bus as we left Tabriz, trickles of sweat ran down my side. The guards could yank anyone off the bus. As the guard walked down the aisle peering into passengers' faces, I did my best to look like any other sullen, annoyed teenage boy who would rather be anywhere but on a hot, crowded bus. Finally, the guard gave the okay for the driver to move on.

When the driver stopped for a dinner break, I had no choice but to get off the bus. Everyone was eating except me. I was too nervous. I didn't even consider using the bathroom for fear of dropping the package on the floor while unzipping my pants. By the time we reached Tehran, my arm was numb from squeezing the papers so tightly to my side, and my bladder was ready to burst.

From the bus station, I took a taxi to the designated location. A tall gentleman with gray hair and a mustache ushered me into the courtyard and closed the gate. After we exchanged information confirming our identities, I handed over the plastic bundle, still damp with my sweat. It wasn't until I climbed into the taxi that would take me to my aunt's house that my body started to shake. I stifled a sob. The taxi driver glanced in the mirror, his brow furrowed in concern and what I thought might be curiosity. I pretended to have a coughing spell and quickly pulled myself together. I wasn't safe yet. I didn't know if I would ever feel safe again. I called my source from my aunt's home to let him know that the drop-off was complete. The next morning, I boarded the bus and headed back to Tabriz. I hoped that the documents might someday prove the many injustices inflicted on innocent Bahá'ís. Unfortunately, to my knowledge, the documents have never surfaced.

Tabriz, 1984

— — —

Two years after the revolutionaries took over, the government began stripping away the few privileges Bahá'ís clung to. The new Islamic Constitution recognized four religions: Islam, Christianity, Judaism, and Zoroastrianism, an ancient pre-Islamic religion practiced in remote areas of Iran. Unlike the Bahá'í Faith, these religions share commonality in the sense that all of them are pre-Islam, thus, there is no dispute over their legitimacy. On the other hand, Bahá'ís believe in the idea of progressive revelation, which, put simply, is the idea that God's mission is progressively revealed, and God sends down his prophets at different times in history to preach a message He deems fit for that time. Bahá'ís believe that Bahá'u'lláh is God's messenger for this time and age. In the eyes of the Islamic government, who believed that Muhammad was the last prophet, this one Bahá'í belief made the faith unholy, blasphemous—not a true religion. As a result, anyone who believed in or practiced the faith was not seen as human. We were deemed to be unworthy of basic human rights.

It became illegal for Bahá'ís to assemble for any reason, and acts of worship were expressly forbidden. Bahá'ís quickly found ways to work around this unjust rule. My friends and I worshipped at a place that will forever hold a special place in my heart: the soccer field. Every Friday morning, my good friends Siamak, Tofigh, and I, along with other members of our local Bahá'í youth group, showed up to score some goals and engage in a Bahá'í learning process known as "deepening." During deepening classes, one or two people share their expertise on a particular topic with a group. In team huddles, we didn't strategize about how to beat our opponent. That wasn't the point of the match. Instead, we enriched our understanding of our faith by discussing scriptures, histories, and texts from Bahá'í laws and books. To passersby, we looked like a bunch of guys playing soccer. In reality, we were attending church.

One of the biggest blows to Bahá'ís was the government's directive to ban followers from higher education. Javad had completed two years of medical school with excellent grades. Before he could start his third year, he was faced with an unfair choice: Recant his faith or be expelled. He left school. After four years working as a teacher, Mahin was fired. The authorities didn't want a Bahá'í instructor sullying the minds of impressionable Muslim children.

My high-school teachers encouraged me to lie on the university application. "Keep your faith in your heart," they said. "Write down 'Muslim.' No one will know. You have too much promise to throw away your future." Yet *I* would know, and I wouldn't betray my faith. As a point of pride, I studied hard and finished at the top of my graduating class. I also decided to take the university entrance exam. For religion, I proudly wrote "Bahá'í." When the scores came back, I was both elated and saddened to see that I had scored high enough to get into the architecture program at the University of Tabriz. It didn't matter.

It took several years to cobble together, but determined Bahá'ís who were removed from their university faculty positions, as well as doctors, lawyers, engineers, and other professionals banned from working in their fields founded an underground higher-education system in 1987. The Bahá'í Institute for Higher Education (BIHE) is rooted in the faith's strongly held belief that everyone has a right to an education—even if you might never get a chance to apply that knowledge due to unjust government restrictions.

Hundreds of Bahá'ís applied for admission when the school opened. I was one of the lucky ones accepted into the school's science program. Still, I knew I could never have a career in Iran as an architect. I would be learning for the sake of learning, which was both gratifying and frustrating. Even with the BIHE degree, I would be stuck doing menial jobs that paid meagerly and offered zero chance for advancement or intellectual stimulation. I feared I would be selling plastic bags and grinding eyeglass lenses forever.

Before the Internet existed, BIHE classes took place through mail correspondence or surreptitiously at people's homes. Teachers and students risked their lives for the sake of an education. Despite repeated efforts by authorities to shut it down, the Bahá'í Institute has thrived. Today, students can choose from more than thirty-five associate, bachelor, and master's degree programs. Professors from prestigious universities around the world, including Harvard, Columbia, and Yale, volunteer their time to teach online courses to Bahá'í students in Iran. Now that the Iranian government is issuing passports to Bahá'ís again, BIHE students are able to pursue graduate and doctorate degrees at universities in the United States, England, Canada, Australia, India, Germany, and many other countries.

I was set to start BIHE classes in the fall of 1988. Since I wasn't enrolled in an official university, the law dictated that I join the military as soon as I finished high school. But a lot of fresh graduates took their chances and didn't enlist. The punishment for not signing up was being forcibly enlisted *if* you got caught. I decided to take my chances. Violence went against my peaceful Bahá'í beliefs, but my reasons for not signing up went beyond that: I didn't see a compelling reason to put my life on the line for a government that viewed me as subhuman. In the eyes of my countrymen, I had no rights.

If I couldn't fight for the rights of every Iranian citizen, I chose not to fight at all.

My decision to dodge the military requirement was a gamble. One thing I had going in my favor was that the government was in disarray and didn't have a formal system for keeping tabs on citizens who didn't report to duty. I was safe unless someone turned me in, or a *basiji* or police officer stopped me and discovered I didn't have a military ID card that proved I had fulfilled my duties.

ID cards were important. High-school and university students carried cards to show they were temporarily exempt from service. Some people had cards showing they couldn't serve due to medical reasons. I didn't qualify for an exemption. But corruption and bribery were rampant in the Tabriz black market. With the right connections and some extra coin, it was easy to "oil the mustache," as it was called, and get whatever you needed.

I obtained a fake ID that identified me as my brother Javad, a student at Tabriz University. Javad was also supposed to enlist after he was expelled from the university. Like me, he had no desire to serve a country that treated him worse than a dog. Despite no longer being enrolled in school, he still had his student ID. These cards had no "Star of David," so to speak—nothing that identified us as Bahá'ís. The downside of having the same card as Javad was that he and I could never go anywhere together. If we were stopped, the *basiji* would certainly be suspicious of two people sharing the same identity.

I dodged military service for nearly two years this way. The few times an officer asked for identification, I gave my name as Javad, handed over my card, and was dismissed without incident. When I started to grow concerned about my luck running out, I subtracted a few years from my age and got a new card assuming the identity of my younger brother Iraj. It was good that I looked young for my age. According to my new ID, I was in high school again.

In reality, I was pushing twenty and trying to figure out my next move. My unwed siblings and I were still living at home. We either worked at *Agha's* appliance store or made shopping bags. The government restrictions made it difficult for any Bahá'í to find a high-paying job. Marriage and moving out didn't seem to be in anyone's future. Until my older siblings wed, there was no reason for me to put much thought into dating.

Fortunately, the shopping-bag business was going well. I was able to save money and purchase a car—a used, three-year-old burgundy Khodro Paykan, the first Iranian-made automobile. I didn't know many people my age who owned a car, and I was proud that I could afford one despite not having a university education. Next, I purchased a glass cutter and a grinder so I could start an optical surfacing lab and sell lenses to area optical stores. I ran both businesses out of the basement of my parents' home. When the optical lab took off, I sold the shopping-bag business to a friend and moved the optical lab into a rental home in a different neighborhood.

– – –

During the first four years that the Islamic regime was in power, militants executed more than 160 Bahá'ís. In June 1983, Islamic revolutionaries in Shiraz spent several days brutalizing ten Bahá'í mothers and daughters (the youngest was seventeen years old) before hanging them. Their crime:

teaching Bahá'í-faith classes to children. The men in their families—husbands, fathers, and sons—were killed a few days earlier. When the women were given a chance to save themselves by recanting their faith, twenty-eight-year-old Zarrin Muqimi-Abyanih replied, "Whether you accept it or not, I am a Bahá'í. You cannot take it away from me. I am a Bahá'í with my whole being and my whole heart." Thirty years later, despite pleas from the United Nations, authorities built a massive sports and cultural center complete with restaurants, a movie theater, and a mosque, at the site of the historic Bahá'í cemetery where the families' remains were interred. Of the 950 Bahá'ís buried there (many of them historic or prominent community figures), the remains of 50 were moved and dumped into a mass grave dug nearby. When Bahá'í community leaders asked that the center be built elsewhere or, at the very least, to leave the cemetery as a green space (the grave markers had already been destroyed), the guard commander overseeing the project replied that Bahá'ís had no rightful place in Iranian society. The Islamic regime, he said, wouldn't tolerate a "foul, unclean, and rootless sect."

The war between Iran and Iraq showed no signs of letting up. In February 1984, Iraq launched the first of a series of air raids and missile attacks on Iran's major cities. In what became known as the War of the Cities, Iran retaliated by bombing Baghdad, Kirkuk, and Basra.

These back-and-forth bombings went on for four years. The Iraqi Air Force had been rebuilt with help from the United States. It was bigger and more powerful than Iran's Air Force, which had been greatly handicapped by U.S. sanctions that limited the military's access to planes and even spare parts.

The first Iraqi aerial assault lasted for fifteen days and claimed the lives of more than 1,000 Iranians. Tabriz was pummeled. My family raced to the basement as loud sirens warned of impending airstrikes, and shelling struck the city. Every day I wondered, *Is this the day that I, or someone I love, dies?*

When the air raids showed no signs of stopping, residents of Tabriz packed up their valuables and fled the city to live with relatives in less targeted, rural areas. My family went to Tehran to stay with my Aunt Faridehe and her family. The capital city's eastern location near the Caspian Sea put it just slightly out of reach of Iraqi air bombers. Four years later, though, as the War of the Cities dragged on, Iraqi missile strikes would tear through the capital.

The picture was taken taken from the window of
the Optical Surfacing Lab, showing the next-door
house demolished as a result of bombshells.

In Tehran, my family's future was, once again, uncertain. There was no way to know whether our home, *Agha's* store, or the building that housed my optical lab would still be standing when we returned to Tabriz. It was possible that we would lose everything for a second time.

When it was safe to return to Tabriz, my heart soared when I saw that our neighborhood and home were unscathed. *Agha's* store was also intact. The area where my optical lab was located wasn't as fortunate. I didn't know what to expect as I made my way there. I choked back tears and bile as I saw massive piles of bricks, glass, and rubble, the shattered remnants of the building next door. By the grace of God, the building that housed the optical lab still stood.

It was surreal to go about everyday life while the country was at war. Many of my peers had gone off to fight. I was devastated to learn that the Muslim classmate who had stood up for me in high school was among the thousands killed. Every day, families received word that their sons were never coming home. Nevertheless, I didn't feel guilty for not taking up arms. My family and I had to fight every day to carve out an existence in a place where people despised us almost as much as they hated Iraqis.

– – –

In 1987, I rented retail space to open a store selling eyeglasses. I still hadn't fulfilled the country's military obligation, so my eldest brother Behrouz served as the store's front man. The business was in his name, but I was the person running it. I made frequent business trips to Tehran—now in the comfort of my car, not the bus. Soon, the store was doing so well that it became my family's main source of income. All of my siblings helped, just as they had with the shopping bags. With so few work opportunities open to Bahá'ís, most people were forced to find work in family-run businesses. For many, it was the only way to make a living. While this wasn't the life I had envisioned, I was doing okay. Many of my peers weren't so fortunate.

———

Chapter Eleven
1988

Mihrdad Maqsudi was a stranger to me, yet his existence forever changed my life. Mr. Maqsudi and I both stood up to high-school teachers who made false accusations about Bahá'ís. While I had the good fortune of having a classmate stick up for me, Mr. Maqsudi, then seventeen, spent more than a year in prison.

He was twenty-four when he was arrested for a second time. The trumped-up charge was probably spying, but nobody seems to know for sure. Mr. Maqsudi was held at the Central Prison of Urmia, located on the western side of the lake. There, he was repeatedly abused by officers and inmates. One month after his incarceration, inmates cornered a terrified Mr. Maqsudi in the shower while guards turned a blind eye. Someone had cranked up the water temperature to above boiling. They forced Mr. Maqsudi under the scalding water. There was no escape. He suffered agonizing third-degree burns from his scalp to the soles of his feet. He died a few days later after literally being boiled to death.

His parents brought their son's body back home to Tabriz for burial. Over the years, I had attended many funerals of Bahá'ís who had passed away either from natural causes or inhumane ones. I was one of several Bahá'ís who discreetly snapped photos to document our people's tortures and sufferings. Sadly, I was accustomed to seeing skin bruised, beaten, and mottled, eyelids swollen shut, fingers jutting at unnatural angles, and bloody toes minus their yanked-out nails. I had seen my share of gaping bullet holes and purplish-black rope marks around necks. But Mr. Maqsudi's death was exceptionally brutal.

On the day of the funeral, I arrived with my camera tucked into a small bag that contained a cotton cloth and a ring that were needed for the burial ritual. Because the body was so horribly disfigured, relatives were kept from attending the cleansing ritual. I was there with Uncle Shoá Allah, who oversaw Bahá'í burials, and a few others who had been photographing these atrocities for years. None of us were prepared for what we saw that day. The corpse was a leathery patchwork of black, white, and yellowed skin. Strips of flesh had been burned away exposing muscle, tendon, and what looked like bone. Mr. Maqsudi's hands were clenched into skeletal fists, and I swear his face—what was left of it—still held a look of absolute terror.

It was customary for the morgue door to be left open during cleansings to allow in fresh air and light. Today, the door was closed. The workers didn't want outsiders to catch a glimpse of the body. As I watched the workers prepare for the bathing, I choked down bile and reached a shaking hand into the bag to retrieve the camera. I knew I had a major problem: With the door closed, the room was too dark to get a good photo. If I used a flash, the bright light would alert the workers and the *basiji* who were patrolling the area to ensure the Maqsudi family didn't cause a scene. I didn't have much time to decide what to do. The morgue workers were as revolted by the state of the body as we were and were moving briskly to finish the task at hand. I felt I owed it to Mr. Maqsudi to document his monstrous death so that others would know his suffering. I glanced quickly at my uncle, who gave a terse nod. Before I could lose my courage, I pulled out the camera, turned on the flash, held it up to my eyes, and pushed the shutter button. The light temporarily blinded the workers. In an instant, my uncle snatched the camera from my hand and ordered me and the others to run. I hesitated for a second as I processed what was happening—my uncle was going to take the fall—and then a friend grabbed my arm, and we were sprinting through the cemetery toward an opening in the fence.

As I raced home, I kept expecting a bullet to pierce my back. *Maman's* face went ashen as I relayed what happened. She quickly called Aunt Nahid to let her know that Uncle Shoá Allah was in custody. It wouldn't take long for the *basiji* to collect the names of those attending the funeral. I didn't think my uncle would give me up. Nonetheless, torture has a way of spilling secrets. It was too risky for me to stay in Tabriz, and too risky to drive through checkpoints with my fake ID card, so I took the bus to Tehran to stay with my Aunt Faridehe until things calmed down.

No one would ever tell me how badly the guards treated my uncle during his weeklong interrogation. He stuck to his story that, while he was in possession of a camera, he hadn't used it in the morgue. The *basiji* thought they could catch him in this lie by having the film developed. A photo of Mr. Maqsudi's scalded body would mean certain death for my uncle. Fortunately, the *basiji* didn't realize that the largest camera shop in the city was owned by Bahá'ís who had connections at the city's film processing lab. When the photos came back, every picture was black—the lab technicians had ruined the film by exposing it to light. It meant we no longer had visual proof of the torture inflicted on Mr. Maqsudi, which was disappointing. But it was the only failsafe way to protect my uncle's life. Without any evidence of wrongdoing—and given my uncle's high military ranking—the *basiji* let him go. But they hadn't given up completely. They questioned every Bahá'í who was at the funeral. When they came to the house to question me, my parents told them that I was in Tehran on the day of the funeral. If my name was on the list of attendees, there must be some mistake, they said. The *basiji* didn't buy it.

In Tehran, I nervously jumped at every sound expecting the *basiji* to whisk me away at any moment and subject me to all kinds of unthinkable tortures. At Mr. Maqsudi's funeral, I had seen firsthand the horrors that people were capable of inflicting. As the days passed and nobody came for me, I started to consider my options. I knew I didn't want to go on living this way. I was a rebellious young adult raging against the establishment in the only relatively safe ways I knew how. So far, I had been lucky. If I continued down this path—taking photos and smuggling out information about the untimely deaths of innocent Bahá'ís—I would eventually get caught. The consequences would be severe. My friend's earlier warning resonated loudly in my mind, "They will peel the skin from your body." I now had a vivid image of exactly what that looked like. Visions of Mr. Maqsudi's scalded body haunted my days and nights.

Mr. Maqsudi was persecuted for his faith until his last breath. At age twenty-five, my own prospects looked bleak. I would never be allowed to get a degree or pursue my dream of becoming an architect. There was a time when I pictured myself as a husband and father. Now, I thought it was selfish to bring children into a world where Bahá'ís would never be accepted as equals or allowed to contribute to society. Many people my age harbored similar thoughts. At the start of the Islamic Revolution, thousands of Bahá'ís got visas and fled Iran. Then, the government changed the visa-application process, making it mandatory to declare your religion. If you wrote down Bahá'í, your request was automatically rejected. It was a head-scratcher: The people in power didn't want Bahá'ís in the country, yet they wouldn't let us leave. They wanted us to embrace Islam. The only way a Bahá'í could get out of Iran was through illegal means.

My friends and I were buoyed by stories we heard about people who had escaped the country and successfully forged better futures elsewhere. Persecuted Iranian Bahá'ís were being welcomed in America, Australia, Canada, England, and other places across the globe. My siblings, Bahá'í friends, and I quietly discussed the possibilities inside the safety of our homes: What might we accomplish if we were free to pursue our passions and be our true selves?

Years earlier, Siamak, Tofigh, and I had made a pact. We agreed that when one of us made the decision to leave, all three of us would go. I called my friends to give them the news. It was time. If either of my friends had second thoughts about leaving, I was prepared to go on the journey alone. But Siamak and Tofigh wanted out, too.

In fact, Siamak was already plotting when I called. His girlfriend, Jaklin, had fled to Turkey with her family earlier in the year out of fear for Jaklin's life. Four years prior, seventeen-year-old Jaklin had spent three months in the women's section of the same Urmia prison where Mihrdad

Maqsudi lost his life. Her crime: teaching children about the Bahá'í Faith.

The family's escape, Siamak said, had gone smoothly. They made it to the United Nations refugee center in two days. He was itching to be with her again and make her his wife. The three of us began reaching out to people within the Bahá'í community who had the connections to make our escape possible. In a week, we had a plan.

— — —

Siamak, Tofigh, and I would each pay the equivalent of $15,000 USD to the leader of a human smuggling ring. We paid half of the fee upfront to secure the services of three Kurdish men who would meet us in Urmia and lead us out of Iran. A trusted acquaintance would send the remainder of the payment after we arrived at our destination. Crossing the border into Turkey wasn't enough to secure our freedom. We needed to reach the capital city of Ankara, more than 750 miles west of the Iranian border. Ankara was the site of the United Nations headquarters. There, we hoped to be granted asylum based on Iran's long history of persecuting Bahá'ís.

We knew little about the actual plan or escape route. It was safer for everyone involved to know few details, in the event that one of us was captured. Based on Jaklin's experience, as well as stories of escape that were legend throughout the Bahá'í community, we expected to cross the mountainous range into Turkey in trucks and on horses. If all went well, I would call my parents from the safety of Ankara two days after my departure.

We planned to leave on *Nowruz*, March 20. It was my favorite holiday as a child, filled with fond memories of family and merriment. I took this as a good sign. It was a strategic move on the smugglers' part to leave during this busy national holiday. The roads would be packed with families traveling to usher in the new year with loved ones. Road checkpoints were sure to be overwhelmed with a high volume of cars. We were counting on guards to skip interrogations and wave cars through in order to keep traffic moving. The police would also be busy dealing with the antics of holiday revelers.

My parents were pained by the idea of me going away, but they, too, were in fear for my life. They also wanted more for their children than what the current political climate offered. At this point, the Islamic Republic had held a tyrannical reign over the country for almost a decade. There was no indication that life for non-Muslims would ever get better. If anything, the situation appeared to be worsening. Although heartbroken, my family understood and supported my need to go.

I longed to take all of my family with me, especially Javad, who deserved the chance to fulfill his dream of becoming a doctor. But I knew my parents wouldn't leave their homeland. The transition from the simple village life of Harvan to the busyness of Tabriz had been hard for them. Relocating to a new country, where they didn't know even the language would seem like an impossible feat. Besides, my family didn't have enough money to secure everyone's safe passage, and selling off the home and businesses would raise suspicions. At that moment, my life was the most in jeopardy, and at just twenty-four, I still had much living to do. I would be the only member of my family to go.

A few weeks had passed since the incident at the morgue, yet I still wasn't confident that it was safe to return home. When the departure date was set, I asked Javad to pick up supplies for me in Tabriz. Winters are brutally cold in Iran, and I would be at high elevation—above 12,000 feet—exposed to the elements for a period of time. Javad filled two backpacks with an extra pair of boots, a military-style canvas jacket, and wool hats, gloves, socks, and scarves lovingly knitted by *Maman* and Mahin. He also put in some cash and a few smaller-sized Persian silk rugs that I could sell or barter for cash when needed. It was important that I look respectable when I met with officials at the United Nations, so Javad also packed a suit.

The *basiji* would come down hard on my family if I were captured, so I took no photos, mementoes, or anything that might connect me to them. I had to pray that I would be strong enough to not give up names if the plan went awry. I didn't like to dwell on this possibility. The only personal item I took was a Farsi-English dictionary. I didn't know where I would spend the rest of my days, but I knew that English was the most widely spoken language in the world, and I intended to teach myself how to speak it.

Uncle Shoá Allah assured me that it was safe to return to Tabriz (without any photographic proof of the morgue incident, the guards finally gave up). I returned to Tabriz one week before my departure date to say a final goodbye to the people I loved. I made certain my brothers had all the information they needed to keep the eyeglass store and optical lab running successfully. To this day, the store continues to be my family's primary source of income.

Nowruz dawned crisp, cold, and bright. I had stayed up much too late the night before sharing stories of earlier, happier days with my family. Nobody wanted to turn in for the night. It was just as well; I was too excited and nervous to sleep. We had decided that *Maman* and Mahin would make the drive to Urmia with me. Their presence made my cover story—we're just one family among thousands traveling to celebrate the New Year—more believable than if I traveled alone. The decision to travel as the only male with two females was also strategic. If guards stopped our car for any reason, they would be less inclined to arrest me. They would never leave two women stranded without a man to accompany them to their destination.

Saying goodbye to my father and brothers tore at my heart. I flashed back to my family's separation in Harvan when *Maman*, Mahin, and Javad left for Tabriz. Back then, there was a chance that we would never see each other again, but we had faith that things would work out. I was going much farther this time, and I could be captured or killed. I knew this could be the last time I might ever lay eyes on my family. Even if I made it to Turkey and moved to another country, I could never return to Iran. I feared that I would be marked as a defector and traitor, which are crimes punishable by death.

In Persian culture, it's considered unseemly to be emotional. You learn to curtail feelings of love, sadness, fear, and hope. And, so, I bid a stoic farewell to my father and chided my brothers not to run the businesses into the ground. Then I climbed behind the wheel of my beloved Paykan to make one last drive through my homeland.

I took the longer, less-direct route south from Tabriz to Urmia because there were fewer checkpoints. As I drove past Ajabshir, I thought about the times my brothers and

I had walked there to go to school or to buy items at the market. I felt a strong urge to pull off the main road and point the car toward Harvan. I hadn't seen the village or the residents who drove away my family in almost a decade. It was my last chance to see what had become of my old home, to see Wolf and my other Muslim relatives who saved my life. Aside from nostalgia, I wanted the villagers to see me now: a successful businessman driving his own car. But I knew it was too risky. I was still a Bahá'í who had no rights or protections, and I was traveling with two Bahá'í women. On this holiday, Harvan would be filled with Muslims from other villages visiting their families. This wasn't the time for a trip down memory lane.

I stopped to get gas in Bonab and thought fondly of the many times I'd traveled to the city with *Agha* to sell fruit from our orchard. The people in Bonab had always shown my family the most kindness, not caring about our religious beliefs.

I drove a bit too fast around Miandoab, the city where Mr. Afnani and his son died under the sharp blade of a scythe. It was their horrific deaths that precipitated my family's flight from Harvan. At least my family had the chance to flee. To live.

During the five-hour car ride, *Maman* and Mahin sat quietly. Our attempts at small talk fell flat. Each of us was immersed in our own memories, regrets, and fears. No one could speak of the days to come or the possibility of not seeing one another again. The car quickly filled with the weight of worry.

— — —

I met Siamak and Tofigh, as well as my brother Behrouz, at a designated location in Urmia. Behrouz had taken a bus there. He would drive *Maman* and Mahin back to Tabriz—just another family driving to see family to celebrate *Nowruz*. Later, he would sell the car and pay back some of the money I borrowed from other Bahá'ís to pay for my escape.

Once again, it was time to say goodbye to my family. Mahin started sobbing. Until this point, she hadn't allowed herself to believe that I was truly leaving. With shaking hands, she unclasped a gold necklace from around her neck and placed it around mine. The necklace was engraved with a Bahá'í phrase "Alláh-u-Abhá," which means "God is most glorious."

"To remember me by," she said, as if I could ever forget my only sister, the one who had repeatedly forsaken her own future happiness to financially support our family. It would be another four years before Mahin felt our family was financially stable enough to say "Yes" to marriage. After a brief hug, a soft pat on the cheek, and a lingering look at my face as if trying to memorize every line, *Maman* shepherded an inconsolable Mahin into the car. I gave an awkward bear hug to Behrouz, promised to call in twenty-four hours, when I was safely in Ankara, waved goodbye, and watched my family drive away.

———

PART THREE

Escaping IRAN

Chapter Twelve

Day One: March 20, 1988

As the sun dipped behind the mountains, a pickup pulled up to the place where Siamak, Tofigh, and I waited. The truck was a patchwork of rusted steel with tires so worn I didn't see how they would get any traction on the snowy mountain passes we needed to cross. My friends and I wedged our bodies into the cab with the driver, a stout man in his thirties who smelled of wood dust and sweat. It was a tight fit. The driver grunted what I took to be "Hello" and steered the truck toward the mountains, carrying us away from the New Year celebrations.

Jaklin's family had traveled by truck and then bus, arriving in Ankara in two days. I found it reassuring that we might be traveling in the same truck her family rode in. Of course, her family had also traveled during more favorable weather, but I wasn't thinking about that at the time. My thoughts were positive: Her family made it out, and so would I.

The truck bounced over dirt and rocks. I couldn't make out a road, yet the driver seemed certain of where he was headed. Today would be the first of many days that required putting blind trust in strangers. I snuck a sideways glance at my friends and saw the same glimmers of hope and apprehension on their faces. I suspected we were each thinking the same thought: "We are really doing this! We are getting out!"

Less than an hour after I'd wedged myself into the truck cab, the driver stopped on an incline at the bottom of a steep, rocky mountain face. Had he seen something? A *basiji*? A checkpoint? A wayward villager trying to make his way home? I looked over at Tofigh, who was pressed against the passenger door. He was peering out the window at three men who had emerged from a cluster of trees. The men were dressed in traditional Kurdish garb: sand-colored, wide-legged trousers that tapered at the ankles; wool coats encircled with thick cummerbunds; and tattered-looking turbans perched on top of their heads. Their turbans were pulled low to protect their ears from the stinging cold.

The driver climbed out of the truck and began talking to one of the men, who, I assumed, must be in charge. He looked to be in his fifties, with black caterpillar-like brows obscuring dark eyes sunk far back in his head. His sunbaked face was a road map of deeply etched lines. He was surprisingly short, even for a Persian. I would never know the true identities of the three men tasked with getting my friends and me out of Iran. We used nicknames and dubbed this man "Shorty." His two partners were taller, trimmer, and looked about a decade younger. One sported a beard, so he was known to us as "Hairy." I questioned the judgment of the third smuggler, "Red." His bright-red head covering stood out starkly against the backdrop of dirt, rocks, and snow. It was as if he were wearing a target on his head. I didn't see any weapons, but I assumed all three men were armed.

Shorty and the driver exchanged words, and my heart sank as I realized that communication would be a challenge. The smugglers spoke Kurdish, a language that has very little in common with Farsi. My life was in the hands of three countrymen whom I did not understand and who could barely understand me. Through most of the journey, our conversations would consist of indecipherable words, a rudimentary version of charades, and a lot of gesturing and head nodding.

Hairy and Red pulled our backpacks out of the truck bed. Siamak, Tofigh, and I climbed out of the cab. "Maybe we're switching to another truck," Siamak said, hopefully. That would make sense, I thought, given the questionable condition of the vehicle we had just ridden in and the rugged terrain that lay ahead. Still, a quick scan into the darkening night showed no sign of another vehicle or even so much as a couple of horses or mules.

In the waning light, I made out massive boulders, vast scree fields, and nothing that suggested a path or road. The place looked ominous. My heart raced as a thought zipped through my mind: The smugglers weren't going to save us. They intended to rob us, shoot us, and keep their portion of the money. I frantically began to think of how I might reason with these would-be captors whose language I didn't speak. To my shock, the smugglers threw our backpacks at us, shouldered their own bags, and turned upward, toward the mountain. We were to follow.

– – –

My friends and I knew nothing about the escape plan. Were we walking to a rendezvous point, where another vehicle would be waiting for us? Were we headed to a village that had horses or mules to carry us and our loads? All of the escape stories I'd heard involved the use of vehicles to smuggle people out. I didn't understand. Why were we on foot, exposed to harsh weather conditions, and clearly visible to border patrols?

Winters in Iran's high mountains are notoriously brutal. Without the right clothes and shelter, a person can quickly lose fingers or toes, or die from hypothermia. My friends and I were dressed similarly in jeans, leather boots, canvas jackets layered over thick wool sweaters, and wool hats and gloves knitted by our dear *mamans*. Our backpacks held nearly identical sets of clean clothes to change into when we reached Turkey.

At a span of nearly 1,000 miles, the Zagros Mountains serve as a natural barrier between Iran, Turkey, and Iraq. Many of the peaks soar above 12,000 feet. The highest point, Mount Dena, reaches above 14,000 feet. The higher a person goes up these mountains, the thinner the air. I don't know how far up we were when we started to walk—perhaps 6,000 feet.

From the start, the trek was awkward and slow. I layered my two overstuffed packs on top of one another. With each step, the top pack shifted, throwing off my balance and causing me to pause mid-step to shrug both packs back into place. I could feel the straps carving grooves into my shoulders. In the dusky light, I could just make out Tofigh and the smugglers ahead of me. Siamak trailed behind. The Kurds had taken their first breaths in this thin air, their first steps on this rocky terrain. And it showed. Despite having no lantern to light their way, they moved at a sure-footed clip, their breaths calm and steady.

Within the first hour, I knew we had a problem. Siamak was falling farther and farther behind. Before we began hiking, Red had done his best machine-gun imitation to drive home the need for each of us to move quickly and stealthily up the mountain, or risk getting shot. Any noise could alert border-patrol guards or *basiji* to our presence. Still, I had to let the others know that Siamak was in trouble. I hollered to Tofigh to stop.

Growing up, Siamak, Tofigh, and I had played pickup games of soccer whenever we had the chance. We were part of the Bahá'í youth group that met at the soccer field to hold covert faith-deepening classes. All three of us were respectable players on the field. But since finishing high school, we had spent more time sitting than moving. Siamak now carried an extra thirty pounds on his midsized frame.

"I wasn't expecting to walk," Siamak said as he caught up to us and shrugged off his packs. His eyes scanned the snow-covered rocks around him as if searching for a comfortable spot to take a load off his feet. As he went to sit down, Shorty and Hairy hastily grabbed him underneath his armpits and pulled him upright. They were frantically gesturing up the mountain and shaking their heads back and forth. We understood. There was no time to rest.

"You have to keep going," I told my friend. If Siamak slowed us down too much, would the smugglers leave him behind? Shoot him? Before we started this adventure, my friends and I made a pact: The three of us would make it out together or not at all. I intended to honor that promise.

"It's my feet," he said, apologetically. "It feels like a thousand needles are jabbing me every time I take a step." Siamak was born with flat feet. With each upward step, the soles of his feet pressed painfully against the inner soles of his boots. When he switched up his gait to ease the impact, his calves cramped. Years ago, the condition worked to his advantage, exempting him from military service. Now those feet were a serious problem.

There was no way to tell how much farther we had to go—or for that matter, where we were going. Darkness limited my vision, but I was sure we had a lot more ground to cover before we could safely rest. At the moment, we were standing vulnerable and exposed on the side of a mountain. We had to keep moving. Pointing at Siamak's boots, I indicated to the smugglers that my friend's feet hurt. The three men exchanged a look and some words in Kurdish—undoubtedly all in disgust—and then Hairy and Red grabbed Siamak's packs off the ground and hoisted them onto their backs along with their packs. The only weight Siamak now had to carry was his own.

— — —

I rejoiced when we started heading down the back side of the mountain. I naively thought the descent would be easier. It wasn't. To keep from careening down the icy mountain face and smashing into sharp rocks, I edged my way down sideways, kicking to get a firm foothold in the hardpacked ice. It was painstakingly slow work, and Siamak struggled mightily. He motioned for us to keep going, waving us on with the promise that he would catch up. "Go on! Go on!" he shouted. Tofigh and I shook our heads and waited. We clapped our numb, gloved hands together when Siamak finally made it to the bottom.

We were on flatter ground but still moved cautiously around jutting boulders and icy patches. When we came to a slow-running river, I was crestfallen. There didn't appear to be a safe way to get across the fifteen-foot expanse. To my shock, the smugglers sat on the frozen ground and began taking off their boots, socks, and pants. They gestured and pointed at us to do the same.

"Off!" Shorty shouted at us.

"They're trying to kill us," Siamak said, half joking, half serious.

I watched as the three men shoved their clothes into their packs, tied their boots together, and flung them over their shoulders. Their gesturing became more urgent. As we gawked, they stood half naked in freezing temperatures. After Siamak, Tofigh, and I partially stripped, I was alarmed to see Red, weighted down with his pack and Siamak's pack, pad barefoot across the frozen tundra toward the river. Shorty motioned for us to follow. When Red entered the river, he reached behind and grabbed Tofigh. Hand-in-hand, the six of us waded across the waist-deep icy water. I had never experienced such painful, penetrating cold. Being swept away by the current wasn't a threat—the river had been slowed by the ice and snow—still, I didn't want to slip and take a polar plunge.

When we reached the other side of the river, Shorty, Hairy, and Red scooped up handfuls of river water to drink. Even though it was freezing outside, we were still at risk for dehydration. My friends and I drank, too, and then quickly grabbed our dry clothes and got dressed. I slipped on every pair of socks I had with me, but I still couldn't feel my feet. I prayed that this river was the only one we would have to cross. I prayed not to lose my toes to hypothermia. And I prayed for a truck to take us the rest of the way to Turkey.

— — —

We walked for several more hours before I heard the bleating of goats. We were nearing a village. Shorty motioned for everyone to stop. As he went on ahead, I sat on the frozen ground and rested with the others. I still didn't understand the plan, but I hoped that food and a bed in the near future were part of it. I had been up for twenty-four hours, and had eaten only dates and handfuls of river water.

Shorty returned about an hour later and motioned for the rest of us to follow. It was easier to pick my way over the rocks without stumbling now that the sun had started to rise, making obstacles more visible. The village sat precipitously on a steep incline within a narrow valley. As we drew closer, I heard the sounds of the sleepy village waking up: the tinkle of pails being filled with fresh goat milk and, inside earthen houses, the soft murmurings from mother to child. I smelled wood burning in preparation for the morning's meal, and my stomach growled.

We entered a home near the outskirts of the village. After we took off our boots, a woman who looked to be close to *Maman's* age gestured for us to sit on rugs spread on the home's dirt floor. She handed each of us a bowl containing a stew thick with goat's meat. It was time for the family's morning meal, but, for us, this was dinner. When the bowls were emptied, Siamak, Tofigh, and I were directed to a darkened corner of the room where the family's bedrolls were still laid out. I peeled off my layers of socks and hung them over one of my packs to dry them out. My feet rejoiced in being set free! The smugglers joined us, a fact that reassured me that they felt safe in this home. I used one of my packs as a pillow, my right hand looped through the other pack to thwart anyone who might try to steal it while I slept.

Sleeping when villagers are going through the motions of their day is not easy. Fortunately, I was exhausted. Siamak, Tofigh, and I barely spoke throughout the meal or as we lay down to rest. When we awoke hours later, we contemplated our fates while eating more stew.

"Do you think we're taking a truck from here?" I asked my friends hopefully. I hadn't seen anything resembling a vehicle as we walked through the village earlier in the day. But it had been dark, and I walked with my head down to avoid drawing attention to myself.

"Doubtful," answered Tofigh, as he sopped up the last of his stew with a piece of naan. He turned toward the smugglers and steered the imaginary wheel of a vehicle, while asking in Farsi, "Truck?" How desperately I wanted them to nod their heads "Yes." Instead, Shorty exchanged a quick look at his counterparts, chuckled, and shook his head back and forth. No truck. From the corner of my eye, I saw Siamak's shoulders slump. Without even a map for reference, the three of us knew there were hundreds of miles of hard mountainous terrain to cover before we reached Turkey. Surely, we weren't going to walk the entire way. We would never make it!

We stayed at the village until the sun began to set. We needed the night's darkness to shield us from the *basiji*. My heart sank as I realized that we would be traversing the mountainside again when temperatures had plummeted to their coldest. The villages were located so far apart that it took a day on foot to reach the next one. This spacing kept outsiders out—you had to really want to get to a certain village to make the difficult journey there—but it also meant that, if the next village didn't have a truck, we would remain on foot perhaps all the way to Turkey. The trip would certainly take longer than the two days I had anticipated. And the journey was going to be more perilous and physically demanding than my friends and I had ever imagined.

Chapter Thirteen

Day Two: March 21, 1988

I made it a point this time to stay closer to Siamak, so as to not lose sight of him in the night's inky blackness. The going was slower this evening—maybe because we knew we had hours and miles to go with no hope of rest.

The farther up the mountain we went, the icier the conditions, and the harder it became to find firm footing. Bowling-ball sized rocks littered the ground. My feet and shins constantly collided with boulders that were invisible in the darkness. With each uncertain step, I struggled to keep from tripping and being thrown flat on my face or spiraling backwards down the mountain. Lack of oxygen added to my fatigue. In the thin air, it felt a bit like walking through freshly poured cement. Each step was a slog. My head developed a dull ache that lingered for much of the trek.

Siamak fared even worse. The altitude, his flat feet, and a lack of food and water were taking a toll on him, physically and mentally. He could barely pick up his feet. The shuffling gait caused him to stumble often. He implored Tofigh and me to go on without him.

"I'll be okay. I just need to rest, and then I'll catch up," he said as he plopped down hard onto the frozen ground. Tofigh and I exchanged glances. The three of us would make it out together—or not at all. That was the pact.

"We're going to Turkey," I reminded Siamak. "The three of us. Together."

"I hear there is a pretty girl there," Tofigh teased. We dangled the prospect of Siamak's reunion with Jaklin like a carrot in front of a starving mule in an attempt to keep him motivated and moving.

The smugglers had no choice but to slow their pace to match ours, but they were growing increasingly impatient. Siamak was taking too many breaks, and it was costing valuable night cover. We needed to be sheltered by sunrise, or our exposure would make us easy pickings for the *basiji*. Unfortunately, I couldn't hear any sounds that might indicate a village was nearby. I feared there was still a long way to go.

"They are thinking about leaving us," Tofigh said to me as he glanced over at the smugglers.

Besides my brother Javad, Tofigh was the smartest guy I knew. He was the only one of my close friends who had served in the military. There, he discovered he had a knack for picking up languages. He didn't know Kurdish, but he was able to pick out and piece together certain words. He also paid close attention to people's body language. If he said we were in danger of being left behind, I believed him.

I looked up at Shorty, Hairy, and Red, who appeared to be engaged in a rather heated discussion. Dark clouds hung heavy in the night sky. The wind had gotten stronger. A storm looked to be brewing, and we didn't seem to be close to a village or anything that could offer protection. I saw the smugglers' eyes sweep over the barren landscape. Were they debating whether they could make it to the next village without the three of us as deadweights? The men had received half of their money before we started the trip. They would see the other half only if they succeeded in getting us out of Iran. I hoped that their need for cash was enough motivation to stick with us until the end.

Mercifully, Siamak recognized the danger and rallied. We pushed on for several more hours until the sky began to brighten. Hushed talks among the smugglers became increasingly more frantic and animated. With great urgency, they implored us to move silently.

"No talk!" Shorty whisper-shouted to us.

Tofigh thought we might be nearing a border-patrol station. If this were true, we would be sitting ducks when the sun resumed its place in the sky. Shorty pointed to a massive boulder up ahead. The stony formation ran the length of a train car and was several feet taller than any of us. It appeared that we weren't going to make it to the safety of the next village before sunrise. The new plan now involved sheltering behind the boulder until it was safe to move again at nightfall. We would be holed up for at least twelve hours and exposed to both Mother Nature and man.

As we huddled on one side of the boulder, Red passed around dates. I hadn't packed food or brought a canteen for water. There really wasn't room in my pack. Besides, I expected to reach my destination within forty-eight hours. I could survive that long without food or drink. I now saw the folly in this plan. I was eating snow and drinking river water to stay hydrated, but if the smugglers abandoned my friends and me, or we got separated, none of us had food. I took little solace in knowing that hypothermia would likely kill me before I starved to death.

Now that I was no longer moving, violent shivers racked my body. The temperatures hovered near freezing, and the wind howled. The sun continued to hide behind threatening steel-colored clouds. My watch suggested that the day had just begun, but the sky had an eerie evening feel to it. We stayed crouched behind that icy stone for five hours. As the minutes slowly ticked by, my fingers and toes went from being painfully pinpricked to unnervingly numb. I knew it wasn't wise to stay stationary for too long in such frigid conditions, but any movement was a chore. I sat on the frozen ground, my back against the rock, with my arms wrapped around my legs, which I pulled tight against my chest. Every twenty minutes, I stood up, stomped my deadened feet, and shook my arms and hands in a feeble attempt to get blood to move through my frozen veins. Each time, my friends got up and moved with me. None of us wanted to endure the painful act of freezing to death.

The wind worsened, and icy pellets stung my face. I began to fear that the boulder would be my grave marker. I thought longingly of my family back in Tabriz. Right now, they would be going through the motions of celebrating *Nowruz*, pretending to be happy and joyous, while not letting their concerns about me show. They would be gathered with family and friends, perhaps playing cards or trying to work up an appetite for the delicious cakes and sweets laid out before them. If people asked about my whereabouts, they planned to say that I was in Tehran ringing in the New Year with Aunt Faridehe's family. I knew if I froze on this mountain, my family would never know what happened to me. As I contemplated what a horrible son and brother I was to leave them in a state of perpetual uncertainty, the smugglers began talking animatedly among themselves.

Tofigh strained to pick up pieces of the conversation over the whipping wind. "They want to leave," he said.

"Leave?" I was shocked. It was not quite noon, and the sun wouldn't set for several more hours. When we took cover, we had left behind a forbidding landscape of snow and rock. "Where would we go?" I asked.

"Well, we're probably going to freeze to death before nightfall if we stay here," Tofigh stated. I was shocked at how matter-of-factly he described our imminent deaths. He and I looked skyward at the ice and snow falling fast from heavy, dark clouds. He was right. We couldn't stay here. "My guess is they think it's better to take our chances and see if we can make it to a village where there's shelter."

There was no question we were at serious risk of freezing to death. Yet, I didn't see how the six of us would make our way across the open tundra without being noticed. I was about to find out, though. In an instant, the smugglers grabbed our packs and thrust them out to Tofigh and me. I took it as a positive sign that Hairy and Red still shouldered Siamak's packs. I hoped it meant that they felt he was strong enough to make it to the next destination. Then a terrible thought struck me: Maybe they wanted his extra clothes to warm themselves. If this venture went really bad, they would likely take out all three of us and divvy up our belongings. I couldn't blame them for wanting to survive. I wanted to live, too. I wanted all of us to live.

Shorty pointed northwest of the boulder: We were to head that way.

We made it just a few hundred feet before we heard the sound of dogs barking. The dogs could have belonged to villagers who used them to protect livestock from predators and thieves. Or they could have been military-trained attack dogs. If we were close enough to hear their barks, then the dogs were close enough to smell our scents. There was nothing to do but move as quickly as possible in the opposite direction. We picked up the pace just as the storm that had taunted us all day showed up in full force. Fierce winds and swirling snow rolled in with a fog so dense I could barely make out the silhouette of Red in front of me. Quickly, I grabbed onto his backpack and yelled at Siamak and Tofigh to latch on to each other. I felt the weight of Siamak's hand as he grasped my pack. I could only hope that Tofigh had done the same. Loud whispers of "Hold on!" filled the air. It could have been this noise that alerted the guards or perhaps it was the barking dogs hot on our scent. Soon, I heard the unmistakable rat-a-tat-tat of machine guns.

Red froze in place for a second, and then took off running blindly through the foggy blizzard away from the sound of the gunshots. I held onto his pack as if my life—and the lives of my friends—depended on it, because that was the reality of the situation.

Running with two packs on your back in blinding snow over slippery rocks, with your hand looped onto a moving object in front of you is as challenging as it sounds. Red slipped and fell several times, taking me and my friends jarringly down with him each time. Still, we held tightly to one another. My lungs burned; my hands throbbed; my feet had long ago lost all feeling. I willed my body to keep moving.

There was no way that Red could gauge where he was going. I hoped he was able to see Shorty and Hairy. At this point, all I could do was try to maintain my grip—my lifeline—on his pack. Red slowed his pace as it became apparent that the dogs and guards had either smartly turned back or been swallowed by the storm. The blizzard raged through the afternoon and into the evening. Our snow-blind human chain never stopped moving. Looking back, it was foolish to continue walking in the whiteout. We could easily have stepped into a ravine or lost our footing and spiraled off the mountain face. Still, I knew if we stopped, we would never move again. Finally, the wind and snow started to peter out, and silvery stars peeked through the clouds. With relief and disbelief, I saw all six of us were still alive and together.

While my faith is strong, I am not one to believe in miracles. Still, I've never been able to explain the fateful timing of that snowstorm. The whiteout conditions kept the guards and their dogs from tracking us. Without the cover of that terrible weather, we surely would have been captured and killed. And despite the fact that none of us could see our own hands in front of us, we made it through the blizzard together.

Although we were alive, we were not safe. The smugglers exchanged fast and frantic words. Hairy set off alone, zinging angry words back at his comrades, who fired words right back at him. After a short distance, Hairy stopped and pointed west. Shorty and Red conferred and then pointed in the opposite direction. Our mad dash through the snowstorm had gotten us completely off track. We were lost.

Eventually, Hairy won out. We went west. After walking for an hour on frozen feet, Hairy seemed to reconsider his course of action. We backtracked and headed the opposite direction. But even that didn't seem right. There was much back-and-forth discussion among the three men. All seemed frustrated; none seemed to know precisely which way to go. Since we had already lost time backtracking, we continued in the direction we were now headed. We trudged on like this for several more hours, our boots slipping and sliding over deepening crusty layers of ice.

The frigid air, combined with the high altitude, made each breath feel like fire in my lungs. I couldn't recall the last time I had actually felt my fingers and toes. I hadn't eaten anything except dates in almost twenty-four hours. When we stopped for breaks, I forced myself to chisel out pieces of hardpacked snow with the heel of my boots, scooped the ice up with my gloved hands, and sucked out the moisture.

I now know that eating snow actually makes you more dehydrated, not less. The body works harder to melt the snow back to liquid, and the ice causes your core temperature to drop, hastening hypothermia. Plus, snow that's been on the ground for a long period of time—as this snow certainly had—can teem with bacteria that cause diarrhea, another problem that depletes your body of water. Even if I'd had this knowledge at the time, it wouldn't have mattered. A body can go longer without food than it can without water. I still would have done what I could to stay hydrated.

We had been on the move for almost twenty hours. All of us were struggling, but Siamak was by far the worst. The lack of food, oxygen, and rest made him delirious. Tofigh had agreed to walk behind Siamak to make sure he didn't unknowingly quit on us while I tried to keep the smugglers from leaving us far behind.

"Man, I sure hope this girl is worth it," Tofigh joked to Siamak. "You're looking pretty ragged there, friend. Better hope she doesn't decide to find another guy."

Tofigh bantered on and on. I was amazed that he had the energy to crack jokes. He was a good friend, reminding Siamak to keep his eyes on the prize: He would be free to worship as he liked, and to marry whomever he liked. He could attend university and have an actual career.

"I want a Pepsi," I heard Siamak say. I turned around in time to see my friend collapse to the ground. As I raced back, I could see that his breathing was raspy. "I want a Pepsi," he repeated.

I looked at Tofigh. "Is he joking?"

"More likely hallucinating," Tofigh replied. "And we don't have time for this." I followed Tofigh's concerned gaze up the mountain, where the smugglers were staring down at us. Even from this distance, I could tell they were not in the mood for any of this nonsense.

"Siamak, you have to get up. We are almost there," I lied. "Get up!"

"Pepsi?"

I could see the smugglers talking, and I sensed that they weren't going to wait around for long. Siamak's slow pace was the reason we hadn't made it to the second village before the blizzard struck. He was the reason we were lost. If the smugglers thought Siamak's pokey pace meant another exposed night on the mountain, there was a good chance they would leave him—or all three of us.

"Pepsi?" Siamak asked again, his outstretched hand shaped to welcome the sleek curve of a soda bottle.

"You want a Pepsi?" Tofigh asked as he kicked Siamak in the legs and rear, first gently and then more forcibly. "Here's your Pepsi."

Kick! Kick! Kick!

It was shocking to see Tofigh beat on Siamak when our friend was clearly out of his mind. But I got it. All of us wanted to rest. All of us wanted a Pepsi. None of us were getting these things anytime soon. If we were lucky, we'd find a village within the next couple of hours that would take us in, feed us, and give us a safe place to rest our weary bodies. Until then, we had to keep moving.

It didn't take long for Tofigh to expend what little energy he had and give up. With a sheepish shrug, he grabbed Siamak's left hand while I grabbed his right, and, together, we pulled our exhausted friend off the ground.

"You guys should go on without me," Siamak said as he held both of our hands. "You're good friends. But I'm no good. You can make it without me."

Tofigh and I shook our heads wildly. "No way," we said. No way were we leaving him behind. Siamak became angry. He shook off our grips on him, took a few bumbling steps backwards, and almost fell. "Go, just go. Please," he said, his eyes moist with tears.

Leaving our friend wasn't an option. Tofigh and I devised a plan. Tofigh would walk backwards in front of Siamak, holding onto Siamak's hands to pull him up the mountain. I got behind Siamak and pushed on his shoulders, his back, his rear—wherever I could get traction.

Push and pull.

Pull and push.

Slowly, the three of us made our way up the mountain.

———

Chapter Fourteen

Day Three: March 22, 1988

I was so delirious that I thought the village was a mirage. I had been on the move for more than twenty-four hours with only an occasional date to snack on. I was certain that the mountain would be my tomb.

Yet before me sat a small village.

About a dozen clay homes with slanted, snow-shedding metal roofs were perched a few miles below the ridgeline where the six of us stood. As we looked at our hopeful salvation, the smugglers talked, and then motioned for Siamak, Tofigh, and me to sit. Shorty and Red set off, presumably to see if a villager was willing to take the huge risk of sheltering and feeding three fugitives and their rough-looking smugglers for the night.

From what I had figured out, the smugglers originally had planned to move us on foot and horseback, traveling at night, sleeping during the day, moving unseen from one village to another until we reached the border. I surmised that the smugglers had ongoing agreements with certain villagers: The villagers provided food and shelter in exchange for money, livestock, protection, or some other payment. The smugglers knew and trusted these villagers, and the feeling must have been mutual for the villagers to take such risks to shelter us. Unfortunately, we were totally off course now and desperate for help. This village we had stumbled upon was unknown to the smugglers. A villager might agree to take us in, only to rob and kill us, or turn us in to the *basiji* for a reward.

These thoughts darkened my mind as I fought to stay hopeful. The villages that dotted this area were inhabited by Kurds, an ethnic group largely marginalized by the Iranian government. If nothing else, the Kurds and Bahá'ís were people united in ostracization. Perhaps that would be a sufficient reason for someone to take pity on us.

For two long, frigid hours, my friends and I sat and waited. I rummaged through my bags and found an extra pair of wool socks. I felt a pang as I pictured *Maman* knitting the socks for me. As much as I wanted to wrap my frozen toes in their wooly softness, I was afraid I might never get my boots back on if I took them off. Instead, I slipped the socks over my gloved hands in the hopes that some warmth might find its way to my numbed fingers. I desperately wanted to lie down someplace warm and sleep.

Many times, I feared that something had happened to Shorty and Red. Perhaps the villagers had threatened them. They could be on their way now to take us hostage and collect a reward for turning in three defectors and their traitorous smugglers. Or perhaps the delay meant that the villagers had turned us away. Had Shorty and Red decided to cut their losses and go on without the rest of us? Did they find refuge just for themselves?

Finally, we saw a red dot walking toward us. With relief, I saw that there was no mob with Red. He waved for us to follow him.

– – –

Red uttered a few words as we got closer to the homes and then forced the top of my head downward until my chin slammed into my chest. I understood: Keep my head down and don't look. I stared at the water stains on my leather boots and wondered if this posture was meant to keep the villagers from seeing our faces or us from seeing theirs. The less the villagers saw of us, the less information they could share with anyone who inquired about our passage. My stomach gnawed at my insides, and I hoped that food, water, and a bed—in that order—were nearby.

With my head bowed, I followed the smugglers into a home. An elderly woman pointed toward a crude firepit dug into the floor. My body hadn't been warm for two days. I wanted to pry off my boots and warm my toes, but my frozen fingers couldn't grasp anything. I sat there for at least thirty minutes while the wool socks I had pulled over my gloves dripped melting ice onto the floor. As my veins began to thaw, a fiery ache more intense than anything I had ever felt radiated out of my fingers and toes, sending shooting pain throughout my body. At one point, the painful burn of thawing out became so unbearable that I had to check to make sure that I hadn't actually thrust my hands directly into the fire. As this fiery feeling engulfed my body, my thoughts turned to Mr. Maqsudi. I only felt as though I was being burned alive. Mr. Maqsudi had actually endured it. *How excruciating his death must have been,* I thought sadly.

When I was finally able to use my teeth to pull off the layered socks and gloves, I was shocked at how stark white my fingers looked. They were as pale as the snow outside. Moving each digit was painful, yet I clumsily accepted a steaming cup of tea. I drank it too eagerly, scorching my tongue on the first sip. When I finished the cup, the old woman filled it back up. I was still so cold, and I knew I must be dehydrated, so I swallowed it down. Almost as quickly as I finished, the woman filled the cup again. I didn't want to offend her, so I continued to drink the tea. By the sixth cup, Shorty started to laugh. He leaned over and turned the cup on its side. With his hands he gestured "no more." I looked at the host. She smiled, gave a quick nod, and set down the tea kettle. I surmised that she had been waiting for me to signal that I was finished.

After we were partially thawed out, we followed an older man, who I presumed to be the woman's husband, outside to a livestock stable. Immediately, my nose was assaulted with the pungent smell of manure, hay, and dirt. The smell transported me back to my childhood home in Harvan, and a pang of homesickness washed over me. If I hadn't been so physically depleted, I would have laughed at the notion that the smell of sheep dung brought on a longing for home.

The smugglers threw their bags onto a pile of straw, plopped onto the ground, and began pulling off their boots and socks. They didn't utter a word, yet the message was clear: We would rest here for the night alongside the sheep and goats.

"At least the hay will provide some warmth," Tofigh said, as he yanked off his boots and searched his pack for a pair of dry socks. His toes were wrinkled like an old man's and as blanched as the snow outside. My feet looked equally alien.

"Maybe they'll let us take a horse," Siamak said, his voice tinged with desperation. I looked around at the sheep and goats in the stable. I didn't have the heart to point out that the family didn't own a horse.

We were still settling in, rummaging through our packs, and switching out wet clothes for dry ones, when a young boy of about ten arrived, carrying bowls of stew that still held a hint of heat from the family's earlier evening meal. I was famished and greedily used my fingers to shovel morsels of goat meat into my mouth. It may not have been mannerly, but the warmth of the stew helped thaw out my fingers more. With my belly full, I lay back onto the prickly straw. Adrenaline still pulsed through my body, and I worried I wouldn't be able to sleep, but I immediately drifted off, listening to the sounds of the livestock, the sounds of home.

– – –

I was awakened early the next morning by the smugglers' voices. Although I couldn't understand what they were saying, I knew we were in trouble. It was daylight, which meant it wasn't safe to travel. We were in a village that was foreign to the smugglers, and the villagers probably feared retribution from the *basiji* if we were found. Worse, one of them could have already set off to alert border patrol about our planned defections. Because we were now off course, if and when we could finally leave, the smugglers would have to risk their lives going into villages unknown to them in the hopes of convincing strangers to take in three armed men and three desperate fugitives. It was a dangerous situation for each of us. I hadn't expected the passage out of Iran to be without peril. Still, I never imagined that I would be trekking over desolate mountain ranges in the peak of winter. I had never heard of an escape going this awry. I berated myself for not considering such a scenario. *I should have packed warmer clothes*, I thought, *and food*.

The boy who had brought last night's meal arrived with more of the same stew. As he left, he led the sheep and goats outside so that he could muck out the stable. An older man, perhaps the boy's father, came in to talk to the smugglers. Tofigh tried to catch pieces of the conversation, but he couldn't make out what they were saying. Eventually, our smugglers and this villager must have reached a deal. After the man left, Shorty turned to my friends and me. "Stay," Tofigh understood him to say. I wondered if he meant for right now, for the day, for the week. "Shh!" he held his finger up to his mouth.

We were to stay. And be quiet.

"I think we're here until nightfall," Tofigh murmured to Siamak and me. Shorty shot him an angry look. Quiet meant no talking. Period. My body was still sore and exhausted. I welcomed the chance to give my feet a longer rest. I knew Siamak needed the break, too. Still, it was risky to be holed up in the village during the day. And the delay meant we'd reach Turkey even later. There was nothing to do except wait, rest, and recharge until the smugglers decided it was safe to head out again.

———

Chapter Fifteen

Day Four: March 23, 1988

Nothing could have prepared me for the trek that lay ahead. As soon as the skies turned a bruised, dusky color, Shorty gave the okay to go. I double-slung my backpacks and started off with my friends again. Ice soon crystallized on my eyelashes, and I burrowed my nose, mouth, and chin farther into my coat. The smugglers were taking us higher in elevation. If we lost our way now, we would need another miracle to survive.

The snow deepened the farther we went up the mountain. It looked as if no one had ever traversed this stark landscape, but I knew villagers must travel this way during the warmer months to trade and sell goods. Of course, nobody but we were foolish enough to venture up a snowy mountain range in the winter.

With each step, my foot sank deep into the crusty snowpack until the snow hit above my knees. I struggled to pull my back foot out of the snow and move it forward to take another step.

Step—punch through—sink—pull.

Step—punch through—sink—pull.

I tried to follow in the footsteps of the person in front of me. Still, it was exhausting work, and we were moving at a crawl. It seemed as if we were making little, if any, headway. I forced myself to think of a distraction, a happier time. Thoughts of my family made me homesick, so I latched onto the Tehran Derby that Siamak, Tofigh, and I attended five years earlier. The derby is like a superbowl matchup between two of Tehran's professional soccer teams: my beloved Esteghlal football club and Siamak's Persepolis team. Tofigh and I had traveled with several friends to Tehran, where we met up with Siamak. My last visit to Tehran—to hand over evidence of the execution of Mr. Tahqiqi and other martyrs of the Tabriz Local Spiritual Assembly—had been terrifying. This visit was all about pleasure. We hammed it up for photos in front of the capitol building and took in all of the sights.

My friends and I paid scalpers way too much money for tickets, but the game wasn't televised, and Azadi Stadium, which, at the time, seated about 100,000 fans, had oversold an additional 28,000 tickets. Fans climbed onto the stadium floodlights and hung onto metal fences. The game started an hour late, as people continued to pour into the stadium and jostle for seats. To this day, it is the highest attended soccer match in Tehran.

I smiled through chapped lips as I remembered the energy and hum in the stadium. It was electrifying. I had never experienced anything like it. When Esteghlal scored the one and only goal of the game, I screamed and thrust my fists in the air along with thousands of Esteghlal fans. Siamak was a good sport about the loss. "We'll get you guys next time," he'd said, neither of us knowing that it would be the last professional soccer match we'd see in Iran.

I looked ahead to my friend now, encrusted in ice crystals, slowly plodding, a dejected, "I-give-up" feel emanating from him. Tofigh and I had placed Siamak in between us so we could make sure he didn't fall far behind or get left altogether. Red trailed behind me, bringing up the rear. Siamak had regained some stamina during the longer stay at the village, but now the walk through the deep snowpack, coupled with the thinning air, conspired against him. We were a little more than an hour into our hike, and he was already floundering.

I watched from behind as he tried to place his feet into the gaping holes in the snow made by Tofigh and the others ahead of him. He carried just one pack, but the weight of it threatened to pull him off balance every time he aimed his boot for one of the existing footprints. When he finally fell (as I knew he would), I wanted to hurry and lift him off of the frozen ground. But it was impossible to move fast in knee-deep snow. I got to him as quickly as I could, while hollering to alert Tofigh, up ahead, that the group needed to wait. When I caught up to Siamak, his left leg was still stuck in a hole in the crusty snow. His other leg was twisted and caught up underneath him.

Please don't be broken, I thought in silent prayer as I tried to maneuver around my friend to see how bad the situation was. I didn't know what we would do if Siamak had fractured his leg. Perhaps we could build a makeshift sled to take him downhill to the last village. Then I remembered our circumstances: building a sled required tools and trees, resources we didn't have.

"Are you in pain?" I frantically asked Siamak. "Is your leg broken?"

Siamak was sprawled on his back, arms spread wide, feet still firmly encased in the snow in front of him. Responding to my alarm, Siamak hoisted up his upper body so that his butt sat firmly upon the hardpacked snow. He awkwardly reached behind him, grabbed the bent leg, and straightened it. Siamak had tied a shirt around his face to protect his nose and mouth from frostbite. The shirt had slipped down, and my heart skipped as I saw him grimace.

"Hurts a bit," he admitted. "Not broken, I don't think." I exhaled a breath that I didn't know I was holding.

"All right," I said. "Let's get you up."

"A bit of a rest would be good."

Was he mad? It was freezing. We were on a wide expanse of snow and nothingness. And we were certainly nowhere close to another village.

By this point, Red had caught up to us. "Up!" he shouted, as he kicked at Siamak's backside. This was clearly an order, not a suggestion. Red looked at me, pointed at Siamak's arms, and directed, "Pull!" I took hold of Siamak's forearms while Red grabbed Siamak from behind under his armpits, and together we pulled Siamak into a standing position. The back leg that had been twisted found its footing, crunched through the snowpack, and sank deep. Siamak teetered, threatening to fall down again and take Red and me with him. I held tightly to his arms to steady him.

"Give," Red said as he started yanking Siamak's pack off of his back. Siamak looked a bit chastened when Red added the backpack to his own, already-hefty load. Hairy was already carrying Siamak's other pack. I hoped that a less-encumbered Siamak would move faster and more steadily.

"We have to go," I pleaded with Siamak. "We can't stop here."

"You can leave me," Siamak said, again, half-joking, half-serious. I looked sternly at my friend. Siamak nodded, let out a hefty sigh, and punched his foot through the snow.

— — —

We had been on the move for close to an hour when a sound stopped me in my tracks. It was the unmistakable howl of a wolf. The howl was soon joined by others. Scanning the landscape, I counted four dark figures moving to the west of Shorty and Hairy, who were ahead of the rest of us.

As is their nature, the wolves were hunting in a pack. I expected they were hungry: Easy prey was hard to come by this time of year. I flashed back to the day in Harvan when wolves had killed two of our family's lambs. I knew firsthand the destruction wolves could do to animals. I didn't want to find out what those fangs could do to human flesh.

Everyone in the group stopped moving. From twenty feet in front of me, Siamak slowly turned and asked, "What do we do?" I could hear the fear in his voice. Siamak was a city boy, born and raised in Tabriz. He had never dealt with wild animals. Still, everyone knew that wolves were cunning and fast. Even in the best conditions, a person couldn't outrun one. And we were far from being in any position to run.

The wolves were still a fair distance away, but I knew how quickly they could cover ground. In the night cover, I could make out the silhouettes of Shorty and Hairy. I still had never seen a gun, but I was certain that each man had at least one weapon. Unfortunately, since taking our unexpected detour, the smugglers were no longer certain where the border patrols were located. Shooting at the wolves to kill them or frighten them off could alert anyone who was nearby to our presence.

We stood still as statues for what felt like an eternity. My legs started to cramp, and I worried that I might lose my balance and fall. Would the wolves see me as an injured animal and charge?

"Go. Slow," Red ordered from behind. Up ahead, I saw Shorty, Hairy, and Tofigh moving cautiously up the mountain.

"Time to go," I said to Siamak as I pried my back leg out of the snowpack and planted it firmly into the hole created by the others before me.

In the dim light, my eyes played tricks on me. At one point, I swore the wolves were racing our way. But when I looked, they seemed to be in the same spot as when we first stopped. Perhaps they were confused by our foreign human scent, or maybe they sensed there were too many of us to take on. For whatever reason, the wolves let us put more and more distance between them until my eyes could no longer make out their silhouettes in the inky darkness.

———

Chapter Sixteen
Day Five: March 24, 1988

For seven hours, we walked an agonizingly slow trudge through knee-deep snow.

Step—punch through—sink—pull.

There was a lot of time to think about the past, what lay ahead for the future, and what was happening in the present. I had so many questions I wanted to ask the Kurds. Why were they risking their lives for us? Where were their families? Why didn't they leave Iran, too?

An estimated thirty-five million Kurds lived in the mountainous region straddling the borders of Iran, Iraq, Syria, Turkey, and Armenia. They were the most oppressed ethnic group in the region, unwanted and persecuted by each country they tried to make their home. Like Bahá'ís, a disproportionate number of Kurds were imprisoned and executed without cause. They weren't allowed to hold government jobs, positions of authority, or to have high-paying careers. Unlike Bahá'ís, Kurds turned to violence to push back against their oppressors. At the time of my escape, the Kurds had been fighting to create a permanent nation state they called Kurdistan for ten years. Today, more than three decades later, this fight for Kurdish autonomy continues.

The mountains that the Kurds call home are rocky and forbidding—not suitable for growing crops or raising livestock. With income prospects bleak, many Kurds turn to smuggling to feed their families. No doubt Shorty, Hairy, and Red were helping us not because they wanted to, but because they had to in order to support their families.

– – –

When another village came into sight, Shorty went ahead to secure a place for us to stay. For someone with stubby legs, he was as surefooted as a mountain goat, and was often twenty feet ahead of the rest of us. While Shorty scouted out the village, we plodded along, trying to cover as much ground as possible before daybreak. The gray and gloomy sky frowned down, but I knew that morning was near. If we didn't find shelter at this village, we would have no choice but to continue the trek during the day.

Eventually, we caught up with Shorty as he walked back from the village. He had good news: A young newlywed couple had agreed to take us in. The couple shared their clay hut with an older woman, who, I assumed, was the bride's mother. The family was desperate for money to help them start their new life together. With our heads down to hide our faces, we quietly entered their small home and sat on the earthen floor.

I clumsily took a warm bowl of stew from the mother. Once again, I warmed my fingers and stomach by scooping up the meaty morsels and shoveling them into my mouth. With our bellies full, we made our way to a stable behind the house. The young man led a pair of goats out of the stable and then closed the stable door behind him.

Siamak, Tofigh, and I packed hay around us for extra insulation and warmth. We were just settling in when we heard loud voices and footsteps approaching the stable. We sprang to our feet and tried to brush the straw from our clothes and hair. An older gentleman—perhaps the younger man's father—entered the stable with the younger man fast on his heels. His eyes swept over us. Shorty approached him, and the two men exchanged words. From the tone of the older man's voice, I deduced that he wasn't on-board with his son's decision to take in guests. The man said a few clipped words to Shorty and his son, gestured at the six of us, and then left. I didn't know if the man wanted a cut of the money we had paid the young couple or if he planned to out us to authorities.

After Shorty finished talking with the young man, he walked over to his pack and shouldered it. The rest of us did the same. It seemed our stay had come to a premature end. There would be no rest today.

The six of us left the stable, walking past the older man and away from the village. We had been walking for about thirty minutes when Shorty made a U-turn. Instead of heading directly toward the village, we angled south. I didn't understand what was happening. Soon, I could make out the figure of the younger man who had welcomed us into his home earlier. We followed him up the hillside, clambering over rocks, and struggling for footholds in the snow. When we reached the top of the bank, we were on the back side of the stable. With the young man serving as lookout, the six of us scampered back inside.

The earlier incident with the older man had scared us all. Because we weren't sure if he would come back (perhaps with reinforcements), Hairy stood watch, while the rest of us tried to get some much-needed sleep.

———

Chapter Seventeen

Day Six: March 25, 1988

My spirits were low as I prepared to set out for another night of what felt like a never-ending nightmare. I had spent the night shivering, my body curled around my backpacks both to prevent theft and for extra cushioning and warmth. My bones felt as if they had been chiseled from ice. I was dismayed to feel a damp chill against my body when I slipped on what should have been my spare dry clothes. Snow had soaked through my pack, wetting everything inside. Little electrical currents of pain pulsed through my toes and fingers as I struggled to find the dexterity to pull on my boots and lace them up. My friends looked equally deflated. We were facing another night of wading through deep snow in search of another village to take us in. At the rate we were going, we might not reach Turkey for a month—if we made it at all.

Not for the first time, I found my thoughts wandering to my parents. They would have been expecting my phone call three days ago. The call wasn't terribly overdue. They would be worried, certainly, but not yet frantic. That feeling of panic probably wouldn't set in for another week. I knew they would envision the worst—my capture and torturous death. They couldn't know that the torture I was currently enduring was at the hands of Mother Nature, or that a snowy tomb constantly threatened my life. I prayed that the journey would move quickly once we crossed into Turkey. Surely, we wouldn't be walking all the way to Ankara. I would call my parents as soon as it was safe. Until then, I needed to press on with my friends.

After the prior night's long climb, we were now facing a steep descent. Eventually, we would need to go back up again to cross the Turkish border. The slippery mountain slope was even more difficult to go down than up. A firm foothold was a must, but securing one took a lot of effort.

Red and Hairy continued to shoulder the burden of Siamak's two backpacks, yet Siamak still struggled. I understood how he felt as my feet were now also in constant pain. A permanent frostiness had settled into my toes, and the damp socks created friction. I tried to ignore the watery blisters that pulsed on my heels and toes. Siamak had all of this discomfort along with the agony of flat feet. As I came down the mountain behind him, I held my breath each time I saw him stumble.

Then an idea came to me.

After high school, Siamak lived in Tehran with his sister while he learned how to repair broken appliances, televisions, and other electronics. During one of my visits to see him, Siamak and I went to the Eram Park Zoo. It was my first time at a zoo—my family could never afford to go. I was excited to see bears, alligators, and other animals that I had only ever seen in books. But I found the zoo overall to be dirty, smelly, and truthfully, a little barbaric with animals confined to small cages with very little room to move. I remembered the two of us laughing at a monkey that scooted around its cage on its butt.

"Siamak, wait up!" I hollered down to him. Farther ahead, Tofigh heard my cry and stopped.

I carefully made my way down to my friend.

Step—punch through—wedge—pull.

Step—punch through—wedge—pull.

My idea was this: Siamak would sled on his behind down the slope toward Tofigh, who would catch him. His buttocks would be frozen, and perhaps a bit bruised, but his feet and legs would be spared much of the arduous walk. Siamak laughed and shook his head. It was a crazy idea, but he agreed to give it a go. He sat on his bottom and lifted his feet and lower legs off of the ground. With my feet firmly planted in snow, I bent down and gave Siamak's backside a hard push. Off he went, skidding down to Tofigh, using his feet to control the direction and speed of his body. Shorty and Hairy, the leaders of the pack, appeared both appalled and amused. After Siamak reached Tofigh, Tofigh gave him a push and sent him on his way down the mountain again, toward Hairy, who sent him skittering downwards, butt bouncing off the ice, to Shorty. And so Siamak butt-sledded his way down the mountain. It may not have been the safest method, but it worked.

———

Chapter Eighteen

Day Seven: March 26, 1988

It took Shorty longer to arrange our stay at the next village. We waited with Red and Hairy for close to two hours, stomping our feet and clapping our hands to keep the blood moving and generate heat. I prepared myself for the worst—another six to eight hours of fighting through the bitter cold while hoping nobody saw us walking in daylight.

Fortunately, Shorty came through for us.

Tofigh made out the word for "money" in the quick exchange between the smugglers as we headed to the village. Getting so wildly off-course hadn't been part of the plan. Every interaction Shorty now had with a villager required a bribe to buy their cooperation and silence. He was forced to oil a lot more mustaches than originally intended, and funds were running low. Siamak, Tofigh, and I were carrying some cash, but we needed the money for our time in Turkey. We still had the Persian rugs, but no one in these small villages had the money or desire to buy them. The rugs were worthless while we were in Iran.

The family who took us in gave us a wide berth. I'm sure we looked bad and smelled even worse. It was clear they were not happy to be serving as our hosts. Perhaps they thought we had done something horrific to send us on the run. Maybe they feared we might do the same to them. I chuckled silently at the thought. None of us had enough energy to do any harm to another human being. My body was constantly hungry and thirsty. I was burning more calories than I was taking in, and my pants hung looser around my bony hips every day. There were many moments during the long nighttime walks when I dreamt of a soft bed to rest my tired bones. I may have even harbored thoughts about "killing" for a warm house and *Maman's Koofteh Tabrizi*, a super-sized lamb meatball stuffed with lentils, nuts, rice, or chicken. But I was truly too exhausted to fight anyone for anything. I hoped Shorty had paid them enough to guarantee our safety while we rested for the day.

After finishing my stew, I went to the stables, bedded down in the hay, and drifted to sleep. Hairy was on lookout. When it was time to go, I washed my face and hands in a communal bowl of frigid water brought by an adolescent boy who I assumed was a member of the host family. As I dressed, I noticed Tofigh frantically searching his belongings.

"Have you seen my belt?" he asked Siamak and me with a look of panic in his eyes. "I left it looped through my pants right here." Tofigh pointed to a wood post where his jeans—now beltless—still hung. "It's gone."

Siamak and I joined the search, rifling through Tofigh's packs and combing through the hay in case the belt had somehow fallen and gotten buried in the straw. The smugglers watched us search, and I wondered how the belt could vanish when one of them was supposed to have stood sentry while we slept. *Either one of the smugglers took it*, I thought, *or had nodded off on the job, giving someone the opportunity to swipe it*. A ball of dread formed in my stomach. What else had been taken? My heart raced as I snatched up my own packs to see if the rugs or cash were gone. Siamak and Tofigh did the same. We were relieved to find that Tofigh's belt was the only thing missing. Like the rest of us, Tofigh had lost weight and his pants were now much too loose. He needed that belt.

The teen boy who had brought in the wash water watched us closely. He seemed frightened by our manic actions.

"Do you have my belt?" Tofigh turned and asked him.

The boy, of course, didn't understand Farsi, so Tofigh grabbed his jeans and waved them in front of the boy's face. Pointing at the pants, he asked again, "Belt?"

Tofigh's raised, angry voice threatened to call attention to our presence in the stable. While Siamak tried to keep the situation from escalating, Shorty walked over to the boy and said something to him. The boy left and quickly returned with a chastened look on his face, Tofigh's belt in his hand. As Tofigh threaded the belt through his jeans, I realized we were lucky that the boy or another villager hadn't taken more of our belongings—or our lives. It was clear that my friends and I couldn't rely on the smugglers for protection while we slept. My friends and I needed to take turns standing guard, as well.

‐   ‐   ‐

The smugglers must have known that we were getting closer to the border when we started out that night. But as far as I knew, we were still days, perhaps weeks, away from freedom.

The six of us had traversed this snowy mountain range for seven days without encountering another person except those we saw at the villages. On this night, we had plodded along for three hours, slowly making our way up a precipitous rock face, when we crossed paths with two Kurds heading down the mountain. Their mule carried bulging sacks.

People weren't the only commodity smuggled out of Iran. I was certain that Shorty, Hairy, and Red each were carrying goods in their bags, such as cigarettes and small electronic radios, that they intended to trade with their Turkish counterparts. The men passing us had recently made a trade and were on their way to hawk their contraband.

My heart skipped a beat when I saw them. It meant we were getting closer to the border—but also closer to danger. Getting out of Iran was still just one step. I wouldn't feel safe until we were officially in the safekeeping of the United Nations.

Soon after we passed the men, we noticed that the cloudless night sky was lit up like daylight. A full moon hung low, while a searchlight swept over the terrain. This security measure surprised me. I sensed from the way the smugglers were looking at it that they hadn't expected so much brightness, either. It was challenging enough to slip past border patrol guards under the cover of night. How would we evade detection now?

Shorty led us away from the trail to a small rock outcropping below the mountain summit.

"Wait," he instructed us. "Here," he emphasized again pointing to the snow-covered ground. Red and Hairy handed Siamak his packs, and the three men set off up the mountain. It was the first time my friends and I had been alone in a week. And not just alone, but completely unprotected and at the mercy of anyone who found us. We shrunk back against the rocks into the shade of night to make ourselves less visible. We were high up on the mountain summit, and the wind was whipping mercilessly.

Thirty minutes ticked by, and then another thirty. Except for the time that we were lost in the blizzard, the smugglers seemed to have an excellent sense of direction. To me, the entire mountain looked the same, but they seemed to know when we were getting close to a village, as well as the safest routes to reach the next one. Still, I wondered if it was possible that they couldn't find their way back to where they left us. If they didn't return, there wasn't much my friends and I could do. We would either be forced to give ourselves up at the border and face our punishments or beg a passerby to risk his own life to save the lives of strangers.

By the time the second hour passed, I was convinced that the smugglers had deserted us, been arrested, or lost their way. We had never spent this much time so high up the mountain. Every inch of my body felt petrified by cold and fear. My hands and feet were in agony. As I contemplated my fate, I made a pact with God: If I made it out of Iran, I would dedicate my life to helping others. I would give up my aspirations of being an architect in order to honor my brother, Javad, who would never have the chance to fulfill his dream of becoming a doctor. Instead, I would be the doctor in the family. I would make my family proud, and bring help and healing to the world.

But first, I had to make it out of Iran.

Siamak, Tofigh, and I discussed our options. It was folly to remain sedentary in the brutal wind and cold for much longer. We could try to dodge the searchlight in the hopes of making it into Turkey undetected, but the odds of finding shelter or anyone who would help us once we crossed the border were slim. We had just agreed to head back to the path and beg a passerby for help when Shorty appeared. In his broken Farsi, Shorty explained that the situation was "not good."

"Guards everywhere," he said. "Need more money."

I knew Shorty was running low on cash after spending the week paying off villagers. Still, I was shocked at how much he wanted: the equivalent of 5,000 American dollars, a third of what each of us had already paid.

"No way!" Siamak shouted, outraged at the request.

He spoke for all of us, but we had little choice. We were not going to make it past border patrol without the smugglers' help. We had no idea how to get into Turkey unaided, and even if we made it across the border, we still had several hundred miles to cover to reach the United Nations headquarters in Ankara.

Siamak, Tofigh, and I walked away from Shorty to search our packs for money. The requested amount would leave us nearly broke. It would be critical to get the highest price possible when we sold the Persian rugs. Siamak begrudgingly handed over the wad of collected cash, which Shorty shoved into his coat pocket without counting. He motioned for us to follow him in the opposite direction from which he had just come, away from the probing light. We were no longer walking on anything that resembled a path. I had long since lost all feeling in my feet. I set my boots down hard on the icy terrain to get some sort of traction that would keep me from sliding down the slope. This exhausting work was made even harder by the thin air and freezing temperatures.

Shorty led us to an area with skinny trees and brush. Once again, he instructed us to wait. It would be more difficult for border patrol to make out our shapes among the trees, but the temperature also felt ten degrees colder in this part of the land, where the sun's rays never reached.

I was on the precipice of freedom—so close I could literally see Turkey. My mind raced with the possibilities of what my future could hold once I was free of my homeland's stifling restraints. Yet, there I sat, still stuck in Iran and at the mercy of Kurdish smugglers who kept delaying my freedom. I was fuming by the time Shorty returned with the smuggler who would lead us through Turkey. This journey had already taken nearly three times as long as anticipated. My family surely thought I was dead. I could almost touch the land of freedom, but my feet were still on Iranian soil. I wanted to be done with Iran for good.

So much time had passed that ice crystals dripped from our eyebrows, eyelashes, and mustaches. Siamak pointed at Tofigh's face and laughed, "You should see how ridiculous you look."

"I don't have to see," Tofigh replied, laughing and pointing back at Siamak. "You look just as funny."

The Turkish smuggler was not amused. He shot a look at Shorty, who shrugged, and said to all of us, "Good luck," before turning and walking away.

We didn't know it yet, but there were events unfolding in Turkey that made our escape even riskier. Crossing into Turkey required all of our waning strength. Fortunately, the smuggler knew precisely where to turn and when to stop to avoid the searchlight and border patrol. We crossed the border shortly before midnight, and my heart soared. I had made it! For the first time in my life, I was no longer on Iranian soil.

I would never return.

———

PART FOUR

TURKEY

Chapter Nineteen

Day 8: March 27, 1988

My native Azeri language is similar to Turkish, so I was able to talk to the new smugglers, who called themselves Osman and Demir. Both men had a rough, world-weary look about them, as if they hadn't gotten a full night's rest in the thirty-some years they had been on the planet. Osman had knotty black hair streaked with early strands of white. An inch-long scar curved to the side of his right eye, suggesting he had once come dangerously close to being partially blinded. Demir could have passed as Osman's brother (minus the scar and the silver streaks). The two shared so many similarities that I assumed they were related.

Unfortunately, the news that Osman and Demir shared as we walked to our new destination was not good. Two days before Siamak, Tofigh, and I crossed the border into Turkey, twenty-nine inmates had escaped from the Metris Military Prison in Istanbul. The prisoners had spent six months using spoons to dig a 200-foot underground tunnel. I was in awe of their determination to escape! All of the prisoners were members of illegal communist organizations. Most belonged to the war-hungry PKK, the Marxist-Leninist Communist Party of Turkey. The men were considered extremely dangerous: Eleven were awaiting execution, while eight escapees had been sentenced to a lifetime behind bars.

I also learned that we had crossed the border farther south than I had expected. We were just outside of Yüksekova, a city constantly ensnared in political unrest due to its close proximity to Iran and Iraq. The PKK was at war against the Turkish government for the right to form Kurdistan, an independent Kurdish state. Yüksekova was their main base and battleground. The escapees were likely headed this way. Iran, Iraq, and Turkey, along with the PKK, had active militaries here. The region was a war zone. The sounds of gunfire filled the air.

We still had to travel more than 700 miles to reach safety in Ankara, Turkey's capital. Getting there meant heading west directly toward the Istanbul prison. We now faced even more security than usual. The military and police had ratcheted up all patrols. They were manning more road checkpoints, stopping and searching trains and buses, and sending guards and dogs into villages. The entire country was on high alert. Our odds of reaching Ankara without being caught were greatly diminished. We couldn't have entered Turkey at a worse time.

– – –

We arrived at a small village outside of Yüksekova soon after the sun started to show itself, near six in the morning. It was a relief to be led into a home this time and not a stable. Siamak, Tofigh, and I huddled around the *korsi*, painfully thawing out and bringing feeling back into our fingers and toes. It was so cold that a thin layer of frost coated the home's interior walls and windows.

After we ate, Siamak volunteered to be the first lookout while Tofigh and I slept. We weren't certain that we could trust Osman and Demir. They could have arranged with the host family to rob us and leave us stranded. Given the earlier incident with the stolen belt, and our dwindling cash, we couldn't take a chance on anything else going missing. Tofigh and I tried to stay warm underneath the one blanket the family offered.

During the previous nights, I had drifted to sleep without much trouble, despite the sounds and smells of the stables, the uncertainty of our plight, and the freezing temperatures. But tonight, sleep was elusive. I was excited about finally making it out of Iran—the first time I had stepped foot out of my birth country. I was worried about how we would make it to Ankara with a full-scale search underway for the prison escapees. I was anxious about my family and the heartache they must have been feeling, not knowing where I was. And I was still so very, very cold.

I huddled closer to the *korsi* as my mind drifted back to Harvan. The *korsi* was the heart of my childhood home: My family gathered around it to eat, sleep, and take the chill from our bones. But listening to *Baba's* stories was my favorite *korsi* pastime. After my siblings and I finished our homework and chores, *Baba* treated us to stories about different Azerbaijani legends. One of my favorites was about a Turkish warrior named Hosayn. With his superhuman strength, Hosayn saved the residents of Tabriz and Isfahan from Mongol warriors who were terrorizing the cities, robbing and killing innocent civilians. It was reminiscent of the way Bahá'í families were still being treated.

Each night, *Baba* built the story up to an exciting climax—and then left us hanging in anticipation and clamoring for just ten more minutes of story time. Too often, we had to wait until the next night to find out what happened to our hero. As a child, I longed to possess Hosayn's superpowers. I envisioned fighting back against those who'd wronged my family and earning the respect of my countrymen. I was crushed when I learned that Hosayn was more myth than man. That night, I was longing for just a dash of Hosayn's strength to get me and my friends safely to Ankara.

It felt as though I had just drifted into a dream where Hosayn helps me rescue my loved ones from an angry village mob when Siamak nudged me to take over as lookout. Osman and Demir slept soundly. The smugglers didn't seem to be a threat to us, nor were they concerned about our safety with the host family. I envied their slumber.

When it was Tofigh's time to take over, I decided to let him sleep. We didn't appear to be in any danger, and I was still too restless to sleep. For the remainder of the day, I listened to the sounds of the village outside and watched the host family go about their daily tasks. The rest that I did get was fitful. Just as I felt a little relaxed, I jerked myself awake. For the remainder of our trip, I slept in fits and starts, drifting into a light slumber only to startle myself awake seconds later.

———

Chapter Twenty

Day Nine: March 28, 1988

The Zagros Mountains are a stunning backdrop to the plains of Yüksekova, where farmers raise wheat, barley, and cotton. At sundown, my friends and I followed Osman and Demir through these farmlands. Now fallow, these vast open fields offered poor protection for five men on the move. The trek was a little easier since we were moving on flat land, but we still had to punch our boots through crusty snow to keep from sliding and falling on the icy surface.

Siamak seemed to have newfound energy now that he was getting closer to seeing Jaklin. Although his flat feet were an ongoing problem, he moved more steadily now that he was no longer slipping and sliding his way up and over steep mountain slopes. We walked for almost eight hours that night, with an occasional stop to rest and snack on dates and nuts. Because of the extreme cold, I was rarely thirsty. Still, I knew the importance of staying hydrated, so I forced myself to chew on ice chunks when we stopped. Chewing on ice wasn't ideal: My body temperature dropped even lower. I feared I might never stop shivering. We skirted around villages and farmhouses, stopping in our tracks anytime we heard the distant barking of dogs, which could have belonged to villagers or search patrols.

When we reached the second village a little after six in the morning, we were surprised to find the home already occupied by seven other Iranian fugitives. The men had fought for the Iraqis during the war, taking up arms against their own countrymen. I didn't ask about their political views or religion—it was safer to not know (the same held true for the men knowing anything about my situation). But groups of Shi'a and Sunni Muslims, as well as communists, had organized throughout Iran in opposition to the new government. I assumed these men fell into one of those categories. "I don't agree with the Ayatollah's treatment of our people," one of the men said. "He is not a holy man helping his country. He thinks only of himself."

Indeed, Ayatollah Khomeini had a chance to end the war less than two years after it started when Saddam Hussein made a ceasefire offering. Instead, the Ayatollah continued to send thousands of young Iranian men into combat and to their certain deaths. After eight years, the war appeared to be coming to a resolution. It would, in fact, officially end four months later, on July 20, when the two leaders agreed to a United Nations-moderated ceasefire. Sadly, more than half a million soldiers and civilians had lost their lives in a war that had no true victor or purpose.

If the fugitive soldiers returned to Iran, they would be charged with treason and executed. In Iraq, they were still viewed as the enemy, regardless of their military actions against Iran. Political asylum in Turkey was their only salvation.

The men listened intently to the story of our escape but shared little about what they had been through. Although they were Muslims, they didn't condone the way that the Islamic Republic treated Bahá'ís or other marginalized populations. This abuse of power was one of the reasons the men had fought against their homeland. They seemed to respect and support our need to forge better lives elsewhere.

As elated as we were to meet these other Iranians, their presence was also problematic. Osman and Demir were now tasked with working with the soldiers' two smugglers to get all of us to Ankara. It would be more difficult to move and hide the ten of us through a country already on heightened alert. Food at the safe houses was already scarce. Now, there would be less of everything to go around. There wasn't anything my friends and I could do about the situation. We were at other people's mercy. We ate our small bowls of stew and then took turns standing guard while the others slept.

– – –

Around four on a gloomy, overcast afternoon, a van pulled up to the house. Osman got behind the wheel and instructed all of us to cram inside. With so many people, there wasn't enough room for everyone's belongings. The clothes and shoes I had worn for the past week were threadbare and smelly. I tossed aside my most worn-out boots, layered on extra clothes, and moved the rugs, cash, business suit, and dictionary into one backpack. Siamak and Tofigh did the same. I left behind anything that couldn't fit into my single pack.

About thirty minutes into the drive, Osman pulled the van onto the side of the road.

"Police!" he shouted, gesturing ahead to a string of cars coming in our direction. "You must go! Hide!" Demir threw open the van door and rushed all of us out—"*Çabuk! Çabuk!*" As soon as our boots hit the ground, Osman turned the van around and drove off.

Frantic, we scrambled up the hillside and tried to camouflage ourselves behind big rocks and sparse bushes. Ten pairs of boots had clambered up the snow-covered hill, disturbing the earth and scattering rocks, dirt, and debris. I feared that the police would see us barely concealed on the hillside or notice our hastily made boot tracks. I held my breath as three patrol cars sped by.

The smugglers hadn't given any instructions as to what to do next. It was too dangerous to walk on the road, so we huddled in place, waiting for the shade of night to come so we could safely move again. We didn't wait long. Osman returned twenty minutes after the police passed our hiding spot. We wedged our bodies back inside the van and returned to the village we had just left. A little more than an hour had ticked by, and we were right back where we started.

Around seven in the evening, Osman indicated it was time to try heading out again. I held my breath as we approached the hillside where we had previously taken cover, but there were no police in sight. Osman drove on.

When the van had first arrived at the house, earlier in the day, my spirits had soared. I was certain that my nights of walking through snow and ice in arctic weather were over. About two hours into the drive, Osman pulled onto a side road and put the van into park. He explained that the police had set up several checkpoints along the road leading to our next destination. In order to reach the house undetected, we needed to take a longer, more treacherous route away from the heavily patrolled road. And we needed to go on foot.

Once again, I fought to get toeholds on the slippery ice as I made my way uphill. When I reached the top, I was dismayed to see a river down below. We had crossed frozen streams and rivers during our trek out of Iran, but this body of water was wider—about thirty feet from riverbank to riverbank. The water would soon run swift and heavy as spring warmth brought a thaw. For now, the river, while wide, appeared shallow and solidly frozen.

Siamak, Tofigh, and I waited with Osman and Demir on the riverbank while the seven other men crossed first with their smugglers. I held my breath as each man gingerly took slow steps on the ice. A fall could mean a broken leg or an unexpected plunge into frigid water. As the lead smuggler got closer to the other side of the river, the ice cracked. Water hit midway up his calf. It was late March, and the river had already started to thaw. Soon the crack splintered, submerging the other men's feet in the icy river. Having done this before, the smugglers were better prepared than the rest of us. They hadn't stripped off their pants and boots like their Kurdish counterparts in Iran. They wore rubber wading boots that reached their knees and kept their feet dry. The rest of us wore ankle-high, lace-up, leather combat-style boots.

Tofigh contemplated taking off his boots to keep them dry, but Siamak pointed out that socks offered zero traction on ice and no protection from the cold. Instead, Siamak offered to carry Tofigh piggyback style across the river. It was a generous offer: Siamak's way of saying "Thank you" to Tofigh for not giving up on him and helping him get this far. But it was a risky move. Even though the river was shallow, if Siamak fell with Tofigh on his back, both men would be completely submerged in the icy river. Siamak insisted, and I offered to carry his backpack. At least his spare clothes would be dry if he went for an unexpected swim.

Knowing that the ice was already fragile where the other men had traversed, Siamak and I decided to cross farther upstream, where we hoped the ice would hold. Siamak was almost to the other side of the river when his left foot punched through the ice and into the water. I watched him wobble and then regain his balance. By some miracle, he didn't fall. He and Tofigh made it across.

Except for Tofigh, who had been carried and kept dry, and the smugglers, who wore rubber waders, the rest of us were at tremendous risk for losing toes and feet to frostbite. I thought longingly of the boots I'd left behind at the last home. I had busted through the seams of the right shoe, so it wouldn't have offered much protection from the snow and rocks. Still, the boots would have been dry.

Our excursion took on a new urgency. We needed to get to the next home quickly in order to warm our feet and save them. We followed Osman as he walked upstream hugging the river on one side. We were still trying to avoid getting too close to the village, where the police were staked out.

I forced myself to ignore the currents of pain shooting from my toes and up through my legs and spine. In time, I lost all feeling from the knees down, and the pain mercifully stopped. It was as if I were walking on dead stumps. It's a testament to the human body and the will to survive that I kept going. Each of us was enveloped in our own personal misery. It did no good to complain. My suffering was no different than the others'. What I, and everyone else, needed was shelter. And fast.

It is impossible for more than a dozen men to step quietly through the woods on deadened feet. As much as we tried to move stealthily, I had grown accustomed to the sounds of labored breathing, crunching ice and twigs, and the occasional muted cry of someone stumbling over an impossible-to-see tree root or rock. So, when foreign sounds joined in—snarls and very fast scampering—I immediately noticed.

I don't know who broke the silence and shouted "Run!" but all of us took off as fast as our frozen feet could carry us. We were being hunted not by humans, but by a pack of stray dogs. Feral dogs are common in the Middle East. They prowl city streets and villages on the hunt for food. Villagers train dogs to be vicious and keep them outside of stables and courtyards to protect livestock, property, and families from predators. Sometimes, these attack dogs escaped from their owners and joined their feral friends on the prowl. Hungry packs were known to attack and kill humans. They were ruthless. Some people survived a dog attack only to succumb to rabies later.

I willed my legs to carry me faster as the sounds of dozens of growling, hungry canines flooded my ears. To my surprise, I saw Siamak fifteen feet ahead of me, running swiftly, his flat feet no longer a problem. Demir and the other two smugglers had been in the rear, but they quickly caught up to the rest of us.

Running only triggered the dogs' instinct to chase. As with most pack animals, their goal was to separate the weakest prey from the rest of the herd and go in for the kill. All of us were weak and exhausted, though. None of us had much strength to run far or fast. We stopped running and picked up rocks, fistfuls of dirt, snow, twigs, and branches, and hurled them at the pack. I heard dogs whimper when they were hit. In our panic, we forgot the importance of being quiet and shouted at the dogs. The fight between the pack and us seemed to go on forever. Eventually, the dogs backed off.

The terrifying incident provided one benefit: adrenaline had sent blood coursing through my extremities, and I was actually sweating from the physical exertion. Plus, instead of fixating on how cold I was, I was now focused on listening for sounds that I was still being stalked. Thankfully, the dogs didn't return.

———

Chapter Twenty-One
Day Ten: March 29, 1988

Dawn was breaking when we reached the next house on the outskirts of Van, a city situated on the eastern shore of Lake Van, the second-largest saltwater lake in the Middle East and the largest body of water in Turkey. We had been on the move for nearly ten hours, yet the Iranian border was still only sixty miles behind us.

I was frozen, bone tired, and mentally wrung out. I felt as if I had just survived a war. Each of us collapsed onto rugs spread on the dirt floor of the home and yanked off our boots. It was only then that one of the Iranian soldiers, who went by the name Ardeshir, discovered that he had lost his left boot while running from the dogs. He was so flushed with adrenaline that he hadn't noticed that he had been walking for several hours in nothing more than a sock. Everyone's toes were a frightening gray-white color—no blood had reached those digits for far too long—and we were all experiencing some degree of frostbite. But Ardeshir's foot had a hard, grayish-yellow, waxy appearance. It looked plastic, swollen, and bruised. I had discarded my holey socks at the last house and layered on all of the remaining ones before starting out for the night, so I had no dry socks to put on. I pulled my wool hat off of my head and stuffed my frozen feet into it.

Fourteen of us crowded into the host family's small earthen hut. The family was clearly poor, yet they generously passed around a plate of figs, bread, and goat's milk cheese. While we nibbled on the offerings, Siamak, Tofigh, and I quietly discussed who would take first watch. It was clear from my friends' haggard faces and half-drooped eyes that none of us were up to the task. We were exhausted. I suggested that we take our chances and rest instead of acting as lookouts. My friends readily agreed.

− − −

When I woke in the middle of the afternoon, the house had cleared out. The seven Iranian fugitives and their smugglers were nowhere in sight. Their belongings were gone. I never saw them again. I knew not to ask about their whereabouts. If I were detained, I would have virtually no information to share about these men, and that was safest for all of us.

Siamak, Tofigh, and I were in for another shock: Osman and Demir said they wouldn't escort us any farther. They claimed that we hadn't paid enough to take us all the way to Ankara. I suspected that they were growing increasingly concerned about our low odds of making it to the capital without getting caught. When they originally agreed to smuggle us out, they had no way of foreseeing that a countrywide manhunt would be underway. Because of the prison outbreak, there were more checkpoints than ever. Getting into Ankara undetected would be difficult and dangerous, and the smugglers must have decided it wasn't worth risking their lives to save ours. We argued with the men, emphasizing that the deal had been for them to get us to Ankara. If they bailed now, they wouldn't receive their full payment. They weren't convinced the little extra money was worth it. Siamak switched his strategy. He begged them to take us to Sivas, where we could meet up with Jaklin's family.

"Her family can help us if you just get us there," Siamak pleaded. Osman and Demir exchanged a look. "Wait here, and do not leave this place," Demir said. With that warning, both men headed out the door. I didn't know if they were coming back, what their new plan might be, or if there was a plan at all. All I knew was that Siamak, Tofigh, and I were in a precarious situation in a hostile part of an unfamiliar country, and still very much at the mercy of strangers. I could only hope that Osman and Demir would change their minds and come through for us.

I spent the remainder of the day attempting to dry out my wet socks, boots, and clothes. It was an impossible task. When Osman and Demir hadn't returned by nightfall, I was certain they had deserted us. My friends and I discussed what to do. We had little money to pay the host family for another night's stay. Besides, we needed to save our funds in case we needed to take a bus or train later. We had no map, no idea of where we were, or which direction to go. We also had no clue about checkpoint locations. We were trapped.

My friends and I were still debating our next steps when Osman and Demir returned. They had arranged for a taxi to pick us up a short distance outside of the village at the break of dawn. The taxi driver would take us farther west, to Erzurum. The city was a major transportation hub for people traveling between Iran and Anatolia, the Turkish peninsula where Asia and Europe meet. Once there, we would hopefully blend in with other travelers as we caught a train from Erzurum. If we were lucky, we could take the train all the way to Ankara.

———

Chapter Twenty-Two
Day Eleven: March 30, 1988

Demir handed me a map of Turkey as we walked through the woods to meet the taxi around four in the morning. A permanent cold seeped through my still-damp jeans, socks, and boots. I was concerned that the taxi plan was a ruse. Maybe the smugglers had turned us in when they left, and we were walking toward a trap. My legs felt like lead. I was so tired of walking in the cold. If Osman and Demir had betrayed us, I wasn't sure that I had the energy to run or fight. Yet, I also wasn't ready to give up on my dream of freedom. I was so close, yet still so far, from asylum and safety. Suddenly, we were startled by the sound of tires crunching over snow and gravel. The taxi—with headlights off to evade detection—pulled up. Relief washed over us, and we profusely thanked Osman and Demir for their help. After exchanging hearty back-slaps and good lucks with the smugglers, my friends and I climbed into the taxi.

When the sun offered enough light, I looked at the map and tried to get my bearings. The driver was going around the northeastern rim of Lake Van to reach Erzurum. I calculated that it would take up to six hours to cover the more than 230 miles—longer if the driver needed to take side roads to avoid checkpoints. If we were stopped, there was little we could do except offer up the last of our cash and possessions, and hope the bribe was enough.

– – –

For the first three hours, our journey was uneventful. The driver seemed to know precisely when to take side roads to get around checkpoints. As we entered the Agri Province, I strained to catch sight of Mount Ararat, the country's highest volcano. This mountain rises nearly 17,000 feet and separates Turkey from Iran and Armenia. Christians believe Noah's ark came to rest in these mountains after the great flood. Today, volcanic deposits make the soil fertile for growing grains and grazing livestock.

We were about thirty miles west of the city of Agri when a police car came up behind the taxi and switched on its lights. Siamak, Tofigh, and I exchanged nervous glances as the taxi driver pulled over. My heart pounded, yet our driver didn't seem concerned. "You take care of police," he said to us, implying that the officer would let us go—for the right price.

The officer peered inside the car and took a long look at Siamak, Tofigh, and me. We looked like bums. Or perhaps like men who had just dug their way out of the earth's belly to escape prison. We hadn't bathed in more than a week. Every day despite the cold, we had sweated through all of our clothes, which were now soiled and tattered. I had grown used to the stench emanating from my body, but the officer sniffed, wrinkled his nose, and grimaced.

The officer motioned for the taxi driver to step out of the car, and the two men walked several feet away. We saw both men look our way once or twice. The taxi driver gestured and nodded his head. The officer walked back to the car, opened the back door, grabbed Tofigh by his upper arm, and pulled him out of the car. *This is it*, I thought. I felt the blood drain from my face, and I prayed for the officer not to notice how ashen white I had become. I was thankful I was still seated in the taxi. I feared my knees might have buckled if the officer had taken me out of the car instead of Tofigh. I braced myself for what was certain to come next: interrogation, prison, torture, death. After ten exhausting days on the run—just two of them outside of Iran—I couldn't believe this was how my story would end.

To my surprise, the officer motioned for Siamak and me to remain inside of the car. He shut the door. He and Tofigh walked behind the car and out of sight. After a few minutes, Tofigh opened the taxi door and instructed me to hand over all of the remaining money. At the start of the journey, I had been unofficially proclaimed the keeper of the funds (although each of us kept a small stash of bills in case we became separated). I was so relieved to not be going to jail that I eagerly rummaged through my pack and handed over the cash. I hoped that the officer wouldn't search my backpack where a few bills and coins remained hidden at the bottom. The officer looked displeased as he counted the money. If he demanded more, we would have no money left. But if we balked, we could be taken into custody and sent back to Iran to face unthinkable consequences. I was willing to hand over everything.

The taxi driver rolled down his window and shouted urgently to the officer, his fingers pointing toward the road ahead. Another police car was coming our direction. That officer would most likely pull over to make sure everything was okay. Once he saw what was going on, he would want a cut of what little money the officer had extorted from us. The officer knew this and motioned for Tofigh to get back into the taxi. He didn't want to share his spoils. We were free to go.

We sat in silence for the next thirty minutes while the taxi driver drove on to the city of Horasan. "You get out here," the driver told us as he pulled into the train station. I was confused. We were officially in the province of Erzurum, but we were still fifty miles east of the actual city, where we planned to catch the train to Ankara.

"No, we paid to go to Erzurum," I firmly reminded the driver.

"Not enough money," the driver insisted. "You get out here."

I suspected that the police encounter had shaken the driver. He knew we were low on money, and we wouldn't be able to bribe our way out of another sticky situation. We also didn't have the ability to bribe him to take us farther. I was certain that Demir had sufficiently paid for the entire passage to Erzurum, but there was nothing to do now that the driver had refused. We would have to catch a train from Horasan instead.

Unfortunately, we soon discovered that the westbound train wasn't running because a bridge was out. The train was the fastest, most direct way to reach Ankara. Taking a bus was riskier due to the many stops and increased road checkpoints, but we had no choice. Horasan was a relatively small town of about 15,000 people. I knew that three ragged-looking outsiders walking down the road would draw people's attention, so I pleaded with the taxi driver to take us to the bus station. To my surprise, he agreed. There, we boarded a *dolmus* bound for Erzurum. *Dolmus* is the Turkish word for filled, stuffed, or full—all appropriate descriptions for these mini-buses that are jampacked with people. Taking a *dolmus* proved advantageous. The little bus was so crowded, noisy, and smelly that the checkpoint guard who came on-board did a cursory scan from the front. He didn't attempt to muscle his way toward the back, where I was sitting with my friends, head lowered, heart in my throat, fervent prayers going up to the heavens.

We arrived at the Erzurum train station around ten in the morning. We had planned to buy tickets for passage all the way to Ankara, but we quickly learned that we were too short on funds after paying the police officer to let us go. We had enough money for only one of us to reach Ankara. To add to our woe, we had already missed the westbound train, and another one didn't leave until the next day. We couldn't risk hanging out that long, but we had nowhere safe to go. The militia were everywhere, randomly accosting people and asking for identification. I watched as guards, guns at the ready and ominously dressed in combat-style black boots, pants, and vests, boarded outgoing trains and scrutinized the faces of incoming passengers. My heart sank as I realized that the trains were no longer a safe option: They were too heavily patrolled.

Short on cash and having no other choice, Siamak found a payphone and called Jaklin's father, Mr. Habibi. It was the first time any of our loved ones knew that we had made it out of Iran. The Habibi family was living about midway between Erzurum and Ankara in a city called Sivas, while waiting to gain entry to what they hoped would be their new homeland, Australia. Siamak planned to petition the United

Nations to let him join the family in Sivas, and eventually Australia. But first, he had to make it to the United Nations office in Ankara.

Mr. Habibi suggested that we take another *dolmus* to Sivas. We would stay with the Habibi family for a short time while figuring out our next steps. By the time we walked to the bus station, we had already missed the morning bus to Sivas. The next bus departed at six in the evening, leaving us with seven hours to fill. At this point, we had been on the go for more than twenty hours. We were physically and mentally exhausted, and our stomachs churned with hunger.

The bus depot had a teahouse where passengers could stop in for a light meal and drinks as they waited to catch their next ride. Siamak, Tofigh, and I sat at a table in the far back of the restaurant. From my vantage point, I watched as grim-faced soldiers patrolled the area, getting on and off buses at random, shiny black machine guns in hand. My stomach clenched. I didn't know how we were going to make it past security.

Since the three of us were occupying seats in a restaurant, we were expected to buy something. Loitering wasn't tolerated. Fortunately, at twenty cents a cup, tea was very affordable. Plus, the warm liquid tricked my stomach into thinking I was full. I had been told to bring Turkish lira with me. This bit of advice proved invaluable. Handing over Iranian rials to the cop or the tea-shop proprietor would have clearly marked us as outsiders. I was grateful for the lira.

Cups do not sit empty for long in Turkish teahouses. Servers quickly refill them—for an additional charge. Even though twenty cents was a small sum for a cup of tea, I had to slowly sip my drink to make each cup last as long as possible. In addition to paying for refills, I also had to pay to use the restroom. I waited until my bladder felt ready to burst before paying to relieve myself. By the time I boarded the bus for Sivas that evening, my stomach sloshed and my bladder ached.

I kept my head down as I boarded the bus, avoiding eye contact with any soldiers patrolling nearby. I noticed nearly all of the other passengers taking the same approach. Even if a person hadn't done anything wrong, you could still be taken into custody. I followed my friends to the back of the bus, where we sat on deeply cracked and torn leather seats, the flattened, yellowed stuffing popping through. I hoped once again to blend in with the crowd.

Throughout the ride, I was jumpy and nervous, worried about the checkpoints. Still, I surprised myself by dozing off a few times—and then jolting myself awake—during the eight-hour trip. I knew it wasn't wise to nod off when I was at risk for theft or a security search, but my body was simply that tired. I was in disbelief when the bus stopped only at its designated locations to let passengers on or off. We didn't hit a single checkpoint! Our luck was improving.

———

Chapter Twenty-Three

Day Twelve: March 31, 1988

When we arrived in Sivas at two in the morning, Mr. Habibi and another Iranian Bahá'í named Mr. Sahriyari were there to greet us. I wanted to wrap both men in an enormous embrace, but I was highly conscious of my stench and filth. Besides, it was unseemly for Persian males to show emotions. Mr. Habibi didn't care about odors or decorum. He sobbed as he tightly hugged each one of us, and soon we were all crying and hugging and crying some more. We were quite a spectacle, and my eyes worriedly swept the station to see who might be watching. Thankfully, there wasn't a soldier in sight at this early hour. The passengers who got off the bus with us kept their eyes down and scurried away to their destinations like frightened mice. They probably knew that there was something unusual about this highly emotional reunion of five grown men, but they wanted no part in it. Everyone was focused on acting invisible to protect themselves.

As we drove to the Habibi residence, we quickly shared the highlights of our escape. Mr. Habibi was shocked to learn how very different our journey had been from his family's. It had taken Siamak, Tofigh, and I almost two weeks to cover the same ground that his family covered in just two days. The Habibis had traveled almost entirely by vehicles. We had moved almost exclusively on foot, traversing snowy mountain peaks and frozen rivers, and sleeping in unheated stables. The Habibis never had to bribe corrupt smugglers or police, never had to flee a pack of wild dogs, never had to find their way through a blinding snowstorm, and never worried about being mistaken for escaped convicts.

During the car ride, Siamak was unusually quiet. "What? Are you worried Jaklin will not want you when she sees how ugly you look, and . . ." Tofigh inhaled deeply through his nose. "Phew! And how bad you smell!" Tofigh was joking. Still, there was truth to what he said. Siamak was ashamed of his appearance. We all were. The closest any of us had come to a bath during the past eleven days was a shared bowl of cold water to wash our faces and hands.

Like most Persian couples at the time, Siamak and Jaklin kept their feelings for each other secret. This wasn't unusual. Emotions like love simply weren't openly expressed. The concept of boyfriend and girlfriend wasn't part of Persian culture. Mr. and Mrs. Habibi probably had their suspicions about the two, but they never said anything. A couple was expected to be modest when showing affection even after announcing their intention to marry, and Siamak hadn't yet spoken to Mr. Habibi about making Jaklin his bride. But as Siamak's best friend, I knew how he felt about her. I was happy that the couple would be able to start a new life together someplace safe as husband and wife.

Siamak and Jaklin hadn't seen each other for almost a year, so it really was unfortunate that he looked and smelled like a vagrant when he walked through the door of the Habibi family's apartment. The couple awkwardly nodded at each other. When Mrs. Habibi offered us a chance to clean up, Siamak was the first to head to the shower. Tofigh and I had no qualms with that. It was more important that Siamak look his best.

I didn't want to sully the furniture with my filth, so I sat on the floor until it was my turn to shower. For the first time in what felt like forever, I let my guard down. I felt safe. The aromas of home filled the small apartment as Mrs. Habibi and Jaklin prepared Persian dishes. My growling stomach reminded me that it had been too long since I had eaten.

When it was my turn to shower, I scrubbed ruthlessly at the layers of dried sweat and grime that had settled in my hair, ears, and every crevice of my body. Afterwards, I slipped on clean clothes borrowed from Mr. Habibi's son. Once my friends and I were presentable, we gathered at the small wooden kitchen table and tried not to gorge ourselves. It was almost morning, but Mrs. Habibi and Jaklin had prepared a *Nowruz*-type dinner feast. Mrs. Habibi cautioned us not to eat too much—our stomachs had shrunk and were no longer used to such rich foods. As Jaklin set platters of food on the table, she and Siamak exchanged sly glances and smiles. While we ate, Mr. Habibi told the women about our harrowing trip. Jaklin's eyes brimmed with tears as she heard about the blizzard and realized how close she had come to losing Siamak on the mountain. I wished that the couple could find solace in each other's arms.

Instead, Jaklin and her mother cleaned up the kitchen and then retreated into the apartment's one bedroom. The sun was up, yet none of us had slept. In fact, my friends and I had been on the move for almost forty-eight hours. Our bodies desperately needed rest. I smiled at my friends before bedding down on the floor in the apartment's main room.

No one had to stand guard. We slept safely and soundly for the first time in more than two weeks.

− − −

I awoke to the smells of more delicious cooking and was surprised that my stomach—so full when I went to sleep—was once again growling in anticipation. I desperately wanted to call my family and let them know that I was okay, but it wasn't safe to do so from the Habibis' home. I couldn't be sure who might be listening in on my parents' phone conversations, and I didn't want to put a target on the Habibi family, who had been so kind to me. Besides, I reasoned, it would be best to call from Ankara when I could share the good news that I had been granted asylum.

Mrs. Habibi insisted on washing my filthy clothes. I was embarrassed to hand her such foul-smelling rags, but I also couldn't bear the idea of putting them back onto my now clean body. I wore Mr. Habibi's son's clothes while mine were in the wash. Even after they were laundered, I found that my old clothes still held a sense of despair.

Having recently been through the process of obtaining refugee status, Mr. Habibi walked us through what to do and what to say at the United Nations office in Ankara. "Tell them you are Bahá'ís who were persecuted for your faith," Mr. Habibi instructed. He assured us that this information alone was enough to receive asylum.

Mr. Habibi's face fell when he learned that we had crossed the border in the southern part of Turkey near Yüksekova. The United Nations' main office was in Ankara because it was the country's capital. All refugees had to go there first to be processed, but there wasn't an actual refugee camp in the city. Instead, refugees were sent from Ankara to Van, Hakkari, or Agri, the city where we had the run-in with the police officer. Mr. Habibi explained that refugees were sent to a location based on where they first entered Turkey. Our crossing meant that we would be placed at the camp in Hakkari in the southern part of Turkey near the Iraqi border. This location was not good, Mr. Habibi gravely informed us. The camps in Hakkari and Agri were tent cities that lacked basic sanitation. There was much overcrowding, filth, sewage, and disease. The Hakkari camp's proximity to Iraq also made it more dangerous for Iranians.

"No, you say you crossed farther north, closer to Mount Ararat," Mr. Habibi said. Had we not wandered so off course during the second day of our escape, this likely would have been where we crossed. This little lie would ensure our placement into the refugee system in Van. Here, we would pay a nominal fee to stay in hostels reserved for refugees. We would be safer and more comfortable. "Van is the best place to be," Mr. Habibi assured us. The irony that we had nearly died while wading through a frozen river and fleeing rabid dogs in order to reach Van the first time wasn't lost on me. Eventually, we could request to live anywhere in Turkey while waiting for a permanent placement in another country. Siamak, of course, wanted to move to Sivas to be closer to Jaklin. Tofigh and I had nowhere else to go, so we planned to tag along.

———

Chapter Twenty-Four

Day Thirteen: April 1, 1988

We left Sivas shortly after midnight. Siamak nodded his head in Jaklin's direction in a bashful goodbye. Because we were short on cash, Mr. Habibi paid the taxi driver to take us the remaining 270 miles to Ankara. Assuming we didn't encounter any problems, we would be the first people in line when the United Nations office opened. We took no extra clothes, supplies, or money from the Habibi family. They had already done so much to help us. Plus, we didn't want to have anything in our possession that might connect us to the family if our plans went awry.

For the first time in almost two weeks, I was clean and well fed. But I was still exhausted. I had too much nervous energy flowing through me to relax during the six-hour drive. Even Tofigh couldn't seem to concentrate enough to harass Siamak about his short time with Jaklin. We sat in silence for much of the trip, holding our collective breaths and praying that this long, grueling ordeal would soon come to a satisfying close.

Nothing about this journey had gone as I expected, and I couldn't stop thinking about two Bahá'í women from my community who had made it to Ankara only to be deported back to Iran, where they were imprisoned. I knew Hamila and Gila from our years serving together on the Bahá'í youth committee. Although I hadn't been bold enough to express my feelings, I was enchanted by Hamila. She had long, dark hair, slender fingers, and chestnut-brown eyes that exuded kindness. She was smart, funny, charitable, and, like me, she railed against the Islamic government's restrictions that stifled her potential. I may have been kidding myself, but I thought she had feelings for me, too.

Months before I began to plan my own escape, the Bahá'í community was buzzing with concern about Hamila and Gila's plight. The women had made it safely to Ankara— quickly, uneventfully, no trekking over mountains in the dead of winter. The United Nations had long ago recognized the Bahá'í persecutions taking place in Iran and swiftly granted their request for asylum. Still, something had gone terribly wrong. Hamila and Gila were now in an Iranian prison, their parents distraught, all contact cut off. The scenario was what all hopeful Bahá'í refugees and their families feared most.

I wouldn't learn the full story behind Hamila and Gila's deportation and imprisonment until decades later, when I reconnected with Gila in Canada, where she now lives. As Gila tells it, while in Ankara, the women were dismayed to find out that they weren't part of a group of refugees scheduled to take a bus to the Van refugee site. In fact, she and Hamila feared that they were deliberately singled out to stay behind because they were young, attractive, and traveling without male protection. Most of the refugees that they had befriended in Ankara were boarding the bus. With their friends gone, Gila and Hamila feared they would be easy prey for sexual assaults. Gila, the only one of the two who spoke a little Azeri and Turkish, marched over to one of the police officers and demanded that she and Hamila be put on the bus with their friends. The officer assured Gila that she and Hamila were scheduled to go on the next bus to Van. But Gila insisted: She wanted to be on this bus that was leaving today. The officer again suggested that she wait. When Gila persisted, he shrugged his shoulders, added Gila and Hamila's names to the roster, and ushered the ladies on-board.

There was much celebration—singing, chanting, and dancing in the aisles and on seats—as the bus headed east, toward Van. Everyone was elated. It was rare for a refugee to be deported after being placed into a United Nations site. Hamila and Gila, along with the others on-board, rejoiced at their good fortune. The bus sped east, past Sivas, and on toward Erzurum with two police cars trailing behind as escorts. But then instead of heading south toward Van, the driver kept going due east. Soon, they were in the Agri Province, with Mount Ararat in sight. A scant twenty-two miles stood between the refugees and the country they had just fought so hard to escape. Still, the bus rolled on. Gila recalls the somber hush that came over everyone when they realized the bus wasn't taking them to safety in Van. They were headed straight back into hell. When the bus came to a stop at the Iranian border, each passenger—Gila and Hamila included—was shackled and arrested. As Gila looked around at the shocked and shattered faces surrounding her, she realized that she and Hamila were the only Bahá'ís on the bus, the only refugees *entitled* to asylum due to religious persecution. The officer in Ankara couldn't warn Gila about the doomed fate of these passengers. Yet more than once, he had urged Gila—practically pleaded with her—to wait for the next bus. She wouldn't hear of it. And now, she and

Hamila were back in Iran. They were released from prison after six months of beatings and starvation.

Defeated, the women moved back home with their parents. Eventually, they married and had children. Although Hamila and Gila had grudgingly come to accept their fate and a life of oppression, they wanted more opportunities for their children. After the Iranian government started issuing passports to Bahá'ís again in the late 1990s, Gila and her family flew to Turkey, where the United Nations granted them legal asylum. In 2014, nearly thirty years after her failed attempt to escape Iran, Gila and her family set down roots in Canada. Hamila and her family also used their passports to legally settle in Australia.

— — —

We were anxious to get on our way to Ankara and had grown used to moving at night. As a result, we arrived two hours before the United Nations office opened. We passed the time at a teahouse, and when the office doors opened at eight, Siamak, Tofigh, and I were ready. A clerk took down information—name, age, citizenship, reason for seeking asylum, and border-crossing location. That was it. We were officially entered into the United Nations system. We wouldn't be fully protected until the United Nations confirmed our information and admitted us into one of the refugee camps. Until then, we could be sent back to Iran at any time without cause.

The next stop was the local police station. The police were very familiar with the treatment of Bahá'ís in Iran. I was issued temporary protection documents with a case number linked to my *kimlik*, a personal identification number required of everyone living in Turkey (similar to an

American's Social Security number). I was to carry this documentation with me at all times. The entire process took less than four hours.

Only after I had these documents in my hand—with signatures from United Nations representatives and police—did I finally allow myself to believe that I had made it. I could finally let my family know that I was alive and in Turkey—exactly as we had dreamed.

Siamak, Tofigh, and I headed to the post office, the closest place with payphones. Two weeks had passed since I last spoke with my family. My parents had been expecting my call within three days of my departure. With each passing day, they grew more convinced that something terrible had happened. They envisioned me captured. Beaten. Tortured. Injured. Left to go insane in an overcrowded, dangerous prison where no one would ever find me. Dead. They clung desperately to hope while fearing the worst.

I dialed my home number. *Maman* picked up on the second ring. "*Maman*," was the only word that I got out before she shouted, "Mansur! Mansur! Mansur!" She broke down in sobs, and then I was crying, too. In the background, I heard another woman whose voice I didn't recognize.

"Siamak? Siamak?" she shouted. *Maman* and Siamak's mother had become so consumed with worry that they had started spending alternating days at each other's homes, waiting for the phone to ring and propping one another up. I let Siamak say a few words to his mother, and he arranged to call her once she was at her home. I spoke briefly with Mahin, sharing just enough information so that everyone would know that I was unharmed. I also gave her the phone number for the hostel that would be my temporary home until I moved to a camp. Because it was the middle of the day, *Agha* and my brothers were at work. When they called me later that evening, more tears were shed. I didn't know whether the authorities were listening to my parents' phone calls, so I didn't share details of my plight. My family caught me up on the latest happenings, such as how the businesses were doing. I spent a lot of time trying to convince them that I really was okay. And for the first time in what seemed like forever, I felt like I was telling the truth.

Mansur with Tofigh and Siamak immediately after receiving refugee status in Ankara, Turkey.

Chapter Twenty-Five

Spring 1988

The United Nations held Turkish police accountable for the safety of Bahá'í refugees for as long as we stayed in the country. To help police keep tabs, I was required to check in at the police station every morning. If I failed to show up, the authorities would investigate my disappearance. I was taken aback by this commitment to my well-being. It stood in stark contrast to police in Iran, who celebrated, and oftentimes directly orchestrated, the disappearance of Bahá'ís.

After the Islamic Revolution and throughout the Iran-Iraq War, more than one million Iranians fled to Turkey. In 1984, the Bahá'í International Community established a Refugee Desk to coordinate relations with the Office of United Nations High Commissioner for Refugees (UNHCR) in order to aid Iranian Bahá'í refugees seeking asylum. In ten years, the program helped more than 10,000 Iranian Bahá'í refugees immigrate to other countries from refugee settlements in Turkey and Pakistan. I was one of them.

Today, Turkey is home to the world's largest refugee population, with more than four million refugees. The vast majority of today's refugees are Syrians who have fled their country's deadly civil war. But there are probably a few hundred Bahá'ís also seeking refugee status elsewhere.

– – –

My first meeting with a United Nations representative went well. I smoothed the wrinkles out of my suit and answered various questions about myself: my work experience, my reasons for seeking asylum, my future aspirations. My answers would help determine which country I might one day call home.

As long as I had my identification documents with me, I was free to explore Turkey's capital. I cautiously ventured out with Siamak and Tofigh. We bartered for a good price for our rugs and secured enough money to continue paying for our room at the hostel, as well as food. If Bahá'í refugees arrived penniless in Ankara, other Bahá'ís collected money to cover their expenses. To my knowledge, nobody was ever turned out onto the street. Money was always a concern, though. We were expected to pay for our transportation to wherever the United Nations sent us. There were other expenses to cover, too: lodging, food, and necessities like shoes, clothes, and blankets.

Because we were not citizens of Turkey—and were supposed to be in the country only temporarily—we weren't allowed to work. At the start of our trip, Siamak and Tofigh appointed me the group's accountant. With two successful businesses under my belt, I had a good head for money, and I knew how to budget. We ate a lot of bread, cheese, fruits, and vegetables that were readily available and affordable at open-air markets. For a small man, Tofigh had a bottomless stomach. In Tabriz, he was famous for putting away two restaurant meals in one sitting and finishing with dessert. He was endlessly hungry and especially didn't like to hear that he couldn't spend more money on food.

After sleeping for days on the frozen ground, the hostel's sparsely furnished room with three twin beds and a communal hall bathroom felt luxurious. Two weeks after we arrived in Ankara, my friends and I received notice that we were to be bussed with other refugees to the United Nations site in Van. Thanks to Mr. Habibi's good counsel, we were headed to the nicest, safest place.

Tofigh, Siamak, and I were the three most subdued refugees on board the bus to Van. You would have thought we were headed to a funeral. While fifty of our countrymen chanted, sang, and celebrated, my friends and I sat quietly, each of us haunted by Hamila and Gila's story. "Why so glum?" an older man asked as I sat rigid in my seat. "You are free now! Free!" I couldn't tell him or his boisterous clan what I knew: nothing was certain yet. The threat of deportation was a constant worry. I wouldn't trust that I was free of Iran until I was completely out of the Middle East.

I sat between Siamak, who stared out the window, and Tofigh, who kept trying to stretch his legs into the aisle, but there were too many people dancing and moving around. I watched out the window, too, as the hillsides, farmland, and cities blurred by in the opposite direction from where my friends and I had recently traversed. I held my breath as the bus passed signs for Sivas, and then Erzurum. At Horasan, the bus headed south, which was the right direction for Van, but also on the way to Iran. I started to panic when I saw signs for Agri, and the road where the police had stopped our taxi just a few weeks before came into sight. Agri was directly east and not on the way to Van. Siamak turned and looked at me, his eyes wide, his face pale. We looked over at Tofigh, who stared straight ahead, a death grip on the seat in front of us. He was watching the road as the driver angled the bus south. "Yes!" Tofigh shouted. He thrust his arms into the air in celebration and then wrapped Siamak and me in an embrace. For the first time on that long drive, I shouted out in triumph, my cries of joy finally mixing with the others on the bus. I couldn't believe it. We were really going to Van!

After we settled into our hostel, Siamak, Tofigh, and I spent our days exploring the city, which is known for its medieval settlements. We visited Van Castle and Fortress, home to seventh-century Urartian kings. We walked the stone halls of the seventeenth-century Hosap Castle. And we took a ferry across salty Lake Van to Akdamar Island to see the Church of the Holy Cross and other Armenian monastery ruins. We nibbled on bread and cheese while picnicking with other Iranian refugees. And we waited for word about where life would take us next.

———

Chapter Twenty-Six
Summer 1988

A month and a half passed before I was told to gather my things and buy a bus ticket to Kirsehir, a city almost 700 miles west of Van and 100 miles southeast of the capital. With stops, the bus ride would take close to sixteen hours. To my dismay, Siamak and Tofigh received notice that they were going to Nevsehir, about sixty miles south of my destination. I would be completely on my own.

We were given one day's notice to pack our belongings and prepare to leave. I sat down with Siamak and Tofigh to divvy up the remainder of our cash. As I handed the lira to Tofigh, I admonished him to spend it wisely. "You can live on bread and cheese a while longer," I told him. Tofigh clasped the money to his chest and smiled broadly. I could tell he was already calculating how much he could afford to spend on lambchops. "Perhaps Siamak should hold on to your money," I suggested with a laugh, but now that Tofigh had cash in hand, he wasn't giving it up.

Saying goodbye was hard. We took solace in the belief that our parting was certainly temporary. Each of us had already put in a request with the United Nations to be relocated to Sivas. With our ties to the Habibi family, we were confident that we would be reunited there.

When I arrived in Kirsehir, I went straight to the police station to check in and find out where I was supposed to stay. "You are Bahá'í?" the officer asked me. He didn't say it in a derogatory way; still, I was taken aback by the question. People didn't generally inquire about your faith in Turkey.

Was there a problem? I wondered.

"Yes," I replied, my heart in my throat. The officer ran his finger down a long list of names, stopped at one, hastily scribbled something on a torn piece of paper, and handed me the address of my new home.

I didn't know what to expect when I knocked on the door of the fourth-floor apartment. Putty-colored paint was peeling off the walls; water stains tattooed the ceilings; tumbleweeds of dust, dirt, and hair had made their homes in the hallway corners. The air was thick with the scent of saffron, onions, and sweat.

A man a few years younger than me with narrow shoulders and cinnamon-colored skin answered the door and welcomed me into the apartment. It turned out that the officer had inquired about my faith in order to place me in the same apartment with another Bahá'í man named Sabar. I also shared the two-bedroom apartment with a married couple (who occupied one of the bedrooms), a young single woman (who had the other bedroom), and another man named Baharan (we three single men slept on the floor in the main living room).

It was common for refugees to have as many as a dozen people sharing a place in order to make rent affordable. Because we couldn't get jobs, most of us relied on our families to send money to live on. In addition to having multiple roommates, we refugees took other cost-saving measures like skipping breakfast and eating only twice a day. I wondered how Tofigh, with his bottomless stomach, was faring.

I didn't mind the arrangement. I planned to be in Kirsehir only until I received the okay to move to Sivas, and I was grateful to have a warm, safe place to rest my head. But four weeks later, I found out that my relocation request had been denied. I called my friends, concerned that Siamak would be devastated after receiving the same news. To my surprise, both Siamak and Tofigh's requests had been approved. They were moving to Sivas together, while I would remain alone in Kirsehir. Instead of a two-hour bus ride, my friends would now be almost five hours away. Fortunately, I could travel freely around the country as long as I let the police in Kirsehir know where I was going, when I was returning, and who I was visiting. If I stayed overnight, I was required to check in with the local police. One requirement of travel was that you had to know someone in the area you planned to visit. Otherwise, you couldn't go. This wasn't as challenging as it might sound. With the Bahá'í network, you were almost certain to know the name of another Bahá'í refugee living in a different city. And now I would know lots of people in Sivas.

I was disappointed about the continual separation from my friends, but overall, I was mostly relieved to be anywhere that wasn't Iran. The Turkish people were graciously accepting of most Iranian refugees. They warmed to you more when you spoke their language. I witnessed many of my Farsi-speaking countrymen struggle to communicate in broken Turkish, and saw how some Turks looked at them in disgust. My familiarity with Azeri was a tremendous advantage: I was fluent in Turkish after one month in the country.

Still, there were instances that reminded me that I was merely a guest passing through. Unlike tourists, who at least contributed to the economy, I felt more like a parasite, taking and taking. I was used to being on the giving end of charity, not receiving it. I was used to working and paying my way. Doing nothing was hard.

When Sabar invited me to play a friendly soccer match—refugees versus Turks—I eagerly said yes. I had been a respectable player on the field back in my youth, able to kick a ball with either foot. I missed the sport. We met at a field at a nearby park, and our team quickly went up one to zero. The Turks had come back and tied the game when I took a shot with my left (nondominant) foot and scored. While my friends slapped me on the back, my stomach knotted. I saw the Turks exchange heated looks. They started getting more aggressive on the field after I scored, their actions suggesting that they didn't care if one or more of us refugees got hurt. We knew things could get really ugly if we embarrassed the Turks by winning the game. After a quick huddle, it was agreed: no more scoring. We threw the game, and then watched silently from the sidelines as the Turks celebrated their big win.

– – –

I have never been the type of person who sits back and waits for something to happen. I need my life to feel purposeful, with structure to my days and to-dos to fill my hours. Since I wasn't allowed to work, I helped clean the apartment and shopped at the market. I even learned to cook, a chore that *Maman* and Mahin had always done because it was considered women's work. I learned that cooking is much harder than it looks. Also, I'm not very good at it.

Because none of us had anything better to do, Sabar and Baharan often stayed up into the early-morning hours playing cards with others in the apartment building. They went to bed late, purposefully slept through breakfast, and woke up in the middle of the afternoon. I excused myself from card games at midnight and rose at seven every morning, hours before anyone else stirred. I gave myself a job: learning English. At my first meeting with the United Nations representative in Ankara, I expressed a desire to go to an English-speaking country. I didn't know if that would happen, but I wanted to be prepared just in case. In school, I had learned the English alphabet and some words like *hello, thank you*, and *goodbye*. I knew I needed to know more than this to make my way in a new country.

For five hours every day, I sat and copied words from the Farsi-English dictionary that I had carried with me like a life preserver over the mountains. Aside from the necklace from Mahin, the dictionary was my most valued possession. I filled sheets and sheets of paper with funny-looking scribbles and attempted to memorize the meanings of the words. I got through almost all of the words in the dictionary during the eighteen months I was in Turkey. I could recognize words by sight, but I had no idea how to pronounce them. I needed to hear the words spoken, which meant finding people who knew the language.

Nevsehir, the city where Siamak and Tofigh stayed before relocating to Sivas, was a popular place for tourists because of its proximity to Cappadocia, home to some of the world's largest underground cities. Tourists come to explore the sprawling network of rooms and tunnels carved from ancient stone eight levels underground. Historians believe that more than 20,000 people may have once lived here inside the earth's belly, hidden from invaders and predators.

Tourists also flocked to nearby Goreme National Park, where fourteenth-century Christian monks once lived and worshipped inside ancient cave dwellings.

It took about two hours by bus to reach these popular tourist destinations, making it an easy day trip. Once there, I eavesdropped on Turkish tour guides who spoke in English to groups of European tourists. I heard so many people speaking English that it confirmed to me that English truly was the universal language. I rarely understood what was being said—everyone talked so fast!—but occasionally I'd pick up a word or two and secretly congratulate myself for knowing it.

— — —

The refugee-relocation process could take a long time. I had heard discouraging stories from refugees who had been in Turkey for more than three years and were still waiting to go to their new home. Some refugees submitted their applications, endured lengthy interviews, and waited months for word only to have their hopes crushed. Often, no reason was given. Each host country accepted a limited number of refugees. Once that quota was met, you had to wait until the next year to apply again. Because a refugee could apply for admission to only one country at a time, you could spend a year or more in limbo, get denied entry, and then have to start the process all over again with a different country. Your life was forever on hold.

About a month after I settled in Kirsehir, I met with a woman who worked with the Bahá'í Refugee Desk. Mrs. Mozhgani had connections with other faith-based groups around the world and helped find homes for people fleeing religious persecution. It was her job to learn more about me—the languages I spoke, my goals for the future, any connections I had to Bahá'ís already living in host countries—to help make a good match.

I told Mrs. Mozhgani that I spoke Azeri, Farsi, and Turkish, and that I was learning English. My goal was to get a college degree. I wanted to become a doctor. My cousin Shahin had fled Iran several years ago and was living in Australia. I had been counting on him to sponsor my move to Australia. Sadly, less than three weeks after I made it to Turkey, my parents called with news that Shahin had died in a car accident. My heart hurt for my cousin, whose life was just getting started, and for my Aunt Nahid and Uncle Shoá Allah, who couldn't bury their son. With Shahin gone, I no longer had any family residing outside of Iran who could vouch for me.

Mrs. Mozhgani jotted down my answers, considered my responses, and thumbed through a stack of papers before stopping on a folder. She flipped through it. "What about Argentina?"

When I was twelve, I cheered on Iran's national soccer team, Team Melli, as they competed for the World Cup in Argentina. Like everyone else in Iran, I was glued to the games, listening to the matches on the radio with my father and brothers from our home in Harvan. I couldn't see the matches, so I had no idea what Argentina looked like. My knowledge of the country was limited to the team's experience there—and that experience, like many events in my life, was tainted by the Islamic Revolution.

The 1978 World Cup coincided with Ayatollah Khomeini's rise to power. The team was fractured—some pro-Shah, others pro-Khomeini. Despite winning the Asian Cup three consecutive times, Team Melli fared poorly in the World Cup, losing two matches and tying one. The poor showing was due largely to politics. The Shah's regime kept team captain and star player Parvis Ghleechkhani from playing at the games. He had been detained and arrested several times by secret police for opposing the regime. The players who did go to Argentina were in constant fear for the safety of their loved ones back in Iran. I associated Argentina with this bad time in Iran's history, but I knew Argentina wasn't to blame for any of it.

"Do they speak English?" I asked hopefully. Mrs. Mozhgani shook her head, "No, mostly Spanish." That was disappointing. I didn't know Spanish. Still, I told her that I was willing to go anywhere. Certainly, any country was better than the one I just left, I said. She smiled and agreed.

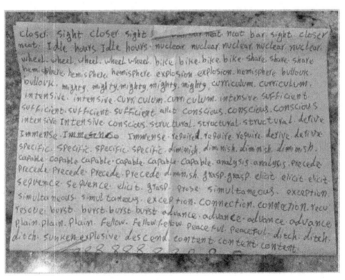

A sample sheet of terms copies multiple
times-used to learn spelling

Picture of the Dictionary used to
memorize English words.

After mulling it over, Mrs. Mozhgani scanned more
folders, and threw out another suggestion: Norway. "They
have a very good education system, and they speak English,"
she said. Yes, I told her, I would be happy to go to Norway.

Still seemingly not satisfied, Mrs. Mozhgani continued
to dig through the mound of papers on her desk. Suddenly,
she stopped, looked up at me with a broad smile, and said
confidently, "Alaska! You would do great in Alaska!" She
flipped open a folder and pointed to a map of North America.
A large swatch of land (just slightly bigger than Iran, I
would later learn) sat surrounded on three sides by ocean.
A short distance to the west was the Soviet Union, a country
struggling with its own political turmoil as its people fought

to break free from a communistic government. To the east sat Canada, a country whose friendly reputation mirrored that of its southern neighbor, America. Nobody ever had a bad word to say about Canada. On the map, Alaska looked more like America's unwanted stepchild—part of the United States, but only in concept.

The idea that I might become an American thrilled me. I knew my parents would be proud. Despite what Americans thought of Iranians (and they had reason not to like us given the embassy-hostage situation and ongoing squabbles over oil), most Iranians thought fondly of America. Before the Islamic Revolution, there was a brief period of time when Iranians were able to watch American shows dubbed in Farsi. As a teenager, I was enamored with *The Six Million Dollar Man*. I watched Muhammad Ali win several prizefights. And I was as hooked on Pepsi and Coca-Cola as any soda-crazed American. America was a place of freedom, of acceptance, of unlimited potential. It was definitely a place that I could call home. "Yes!" I said eagerly. "Alaska sounds perfect!" Even better, I remembered that a former classmate from Tabriz, whose name was also Siamak, now lived in Alaska. I would know someone! Mrs. Mozhgani smiled at this good news. Having a contact would help my case. Together, she and I filled out my application requesting entry to the United States.

———

Chapter Twenty-Seven

Fall 1988

During my time in Turkey, every few weeks I dialed a number at the United Nations to check my application status. Months went by with no news. I tried not to get discouraged. I knew the wheels turned slowly. I was fortunate that it wasn't a hardship for my family to support me while I bided my time in Turkey. My brothers were doing an excellent job running the optical businesses in Tabriz.

Phone calls were expensive, so my family and I communicated mostly by mail. It was common for Iranian authorities to intercept and read letters from refugees (in their eyes, we were defectors). I was concerned that they would censor or keep my letters. I decided to handwrite two copies of each letter so I would be able to find out from my family later if they had actually received all of the news I shared.

I was mostly untouchable now that the United Nations had granted asylum, but the Islamic Republic could potentially decide to go after my loved ones. Knowing this, I never wrote anything about what happened during my escape or my relocation status, nor did I mention Siamak, Tofigh, the Habibi family, or anyone else by name.

My parents confirmed that my letters frequently arrived already opened. Even though I wasn't sharing sensitive information, this invasion of privacy angered me. It was another way the government wielded power over my family and me. When I voiced my frustration to Sabar, he told me he sent letters to his family in Iran using the name of a business—not his real name—as the return address. His family sent letters addressed to the business, not him. Since making this change, he said, letters to and from his family arrived unopened. It seemed too simple. I couldn't believe the Iranian authorities hadn't figured it out. But I gave it a try, writing Ankara University in the return section of the next envelope I mailed. My parents caught on and replied with a letter to Ankara University addressed to my post office box. From that point on, we exchanged mail without any issues. Just in case, though, I still wrote two copies of every letter, keeping one for my personal records.

I craved information about what was happening in my country, especially since the war with Iraq had finally ended, but it was too risky for my parents to share such news. I was in contact with my loved ones, yet I still felt very cut off. I remember one particular letter from *Agha* that lifted my spirits. He wrote that he was proud of me for taking this brave step to pursue a better life. He was confident that I would study hard, succeed, and make the family proud. It was the best love letter I ever got.

In October, I received a frantic phone call from *Agha*. Javad and a cousin had been stopped on the street by a *basiji* who quickly discovered that their identification cards were fraudulent. After spending two days in jail, Javad and my cousin were sent away to fulfill their military duties. Our families never had a chance to say goodbye. This news was upsetting, but the outcome could have been worse. At least, Javad and my cousin had avoided serving during wartime. But in the two years that Javad was gone, I wasn't able to write to him. I couldn't risk getting him in trouble with his commanding officers if they discovered that his brother was a defector. Later, I would learn that the military knew, and Javad (and then Iraj) paid a price for it.

— — —

With little to do but wait for word from the United Nations, my days grew long and monotonous. I filled my time exploring nearby cities, hopping on buses, returning the same day or staying overnight, always checking in with the local police. I visited Siamak and Tofigh in Sivas, and met up with them in neighboring cities. Regardless of where I was, I always dedicated five hours of each day to my English studies.

There was a large, informal Bahá'í network within Turkey, which made it easy to connect with others. I taught classes to younger Bahá'ís in Kirsehir and surrounding cities, tapping into my knowledge of the history of the Báb and the sacred Bahá'í texts that I had memorized years ago. For the first time in my life, I was free to share this information and express my beliefs without fear of imprisonment, beatings, or death. It was an amazing feeling.

I also returned to Ankara quite often. There was much to see and do in the country's capital. I always stopped at the hostel to welcome new Bahá'í refugees. During one of these visits, I met a lovely family—husband, wife, and their four children—who had arrived penniless after being robbed. They didn't speak Turkish. The fear in the mother's eyes was heartbreaking. She was worried about getting enough food for herself to continue nursing her baby, as well as food for her husband and older children. I had enough money with me to cover frivolous expenses on my trip—food, shopping, and museums—nothing I really needed. I counted out enough fare to purchase a return bus ticket to Kirsehir and handed the remaining bills and coins to the father. I could see him struggling with this gesture. His pride wanted him to decline, but his family desperately needed help. It was only a handful of lira—perhaps the equivalent of forty dollars. After I left, the father told many people about a young Bahá'í man named Mansur who generously helped his family. When he received funds from his relatives in Iran, he paid me back. It wasn't necessary, but he spoke of how he had been at his lowest when he met me—questioning whether he'd made the wrong decision taking his young, vulnerable family out of Iran. After being robbed in Turkey, he had lost faith in mankind. My small act of kindness had restored it.

− − −

I tracked down my friend in Alaska (also named Siamak, who had been in the Tabriz Bahá'í youth group with me) and told him that I hoped to see him soon. Siamak sent a postcard from Juneau, the city where he lived (and the state's capital, I learned, from reading the back of the postcard), and the place that I hoped to call home, too. The postcard showed a city on the banks of a river with soaring, snow-covered mountain ranges in the background. My heart sank when I saw those white-tipped granite peaks. I wanted to be done with wintry weather and steep, rocky mountains. Still, the area looked beautiful. And very, very cold. I would need new boots, a parka, and other cold-weather gear. I wrote to *Maman* and Mahin asking them to knit more hats, gloves, sweaters, and scarves. "I may be going someplace very cold," was all I felt comfortable sharing in my letter.

In the meantime, Tofigh was growing impatient waiting for word about his request to immigrate to America. Siamak and Jaklin were planning a wedding. Besides consecrating their love for each other, marriage ensured that they would be sent to the same country. They had applied to go to Australia.

The wedding was set for the last day in November, and I looked forward to the celebration. Due to the circumstances—everyone's refugee status, limited finances—the wedding wouldn't be a lavish affair. Still, it was nice to have a happy occasion to look forward to. Right before I was to depart for Sivas, I got a phone call: My application was moving forward. I needed to meet with a United States immigration official in Istanbul immediately. It would take me at least eight hours by bus to reach Istanbul from Kirsehir. I didn't have enough time to attend the wedding in Sivas *and* make it to my interview. Sadly, I had no choice. I phoned the soon-to-be newlyweds and offered my heartfelt congratulations, and then I boarded the bus to Istanbul.

At the immigration office, I answered the same set of questions I had answered since arriving in Turkey: reason for seeking asylum, languages spoken, family or friends living outside of Iran, plans for the future. There was no way to gauge whether my answers fit with what they were looking for, or if I gave a response that would keep me out. At least I had made it to this critical second step, I reassured myself. I had answered every question truthfully. The only thing that I could do now was remain hopeful.

As I continued to wait, I tried to learn as much as I could about Alaska. My letters to Siamak were filled with questions: What was Juneau like? Where could I study? Where could I find a job? Were Americans friendly to Iranians? His responses were reassuring: The University of Alaska had its main campus in Juneau. There wasn't a medical school, but I could get my college start there. I could stay with him for as long as I needed, and he would help me find a job. He declared that there were many jobs available for immigrants who were willing to work hard. Americans, he assured me, were very welcoming. He bolstered my spirits by sharing that the Bahá'í community was strong and extremely supportive in Alaska. There was even a Bahá'í National Center in Anchorage, but it took a long time to get there, he warned.

Identical copies of letters written to my family about my escape. These letters would serve as a tremendous source of information for this story.

Letter written to Javad describing part of the escape.

Chapter Twenty-Eight
Leaving Turkey: Summer 1989

The waiting continued well past spring and into summer. I felt as if I had explored every square inch of Turkey, aside from the cities where I didn't feel safe because they were too close to the Iranian or Iraqi borders, and affluent cities like Izmir and Antalya, whose beautiful Mediterranean beaches attracted celebrities and the well-to-do. A visit to those ritzy cities was beyond my financial means.

Tofigh grew tired of waiting to hear back from the United States. He took matters into his own hands and scheduled a meeting with the Canadian Embassy in Istanbul. Tofigh had taken private English lessons in Iran. Like my brother Javad, Tofigh had been on the path to becoming a brilliant doctor before the Iranian government declared that Bahá'ís didn't deserve a proper education or professional careers. The Canadian immigration official was extremely impressed with Tofigh's mastery of English and his initiative to handle matters on his own. Two weeks later, Tofigh received word: He was going to New Brunswick, Canada.

When Siamak, Jaklin, and the Habibi family were notified that they were to leave within the week for Sydney, Australia, I went to Sivas to say goodbye. It was June. I had been in Turkey for more than a year. Six months had passed since my interview with the United States immigration officials. I still hadn't heard whether I was definitely going to Alaska. I promised Siamak that Australia would be next on my list of countries to try if things didn't work out with America. But the idea of starting the process all over again, and living for another year in uncertainty, was disheartening.

Even though Canada quickly approved Tofigh's immigration request, he was still waiting to leave. He and I received our relocation information around the same time in July: Tofigh would go to Canada in one week, while I was bound for America. I couldn't believe I was finally going to start my life in my new home!

A few days before my departure date, I arrived in Istanbul, where I was to catch an international flight. I had flown a few times within Iran, but never such a long distance as this. I was nervous about leaving behind everything familiar—the people, the languages, the food, the cultures. Because of the way I fled Iran, I feared that I would never be allowed back to see my family, my home, my friends. It was so permanent and real.

After I picked up my exit permit at the police station, the next stop was the United States Embassy and Consulate. There, a representative handed me a folder with my travel plans and airline tickets.

"You will fly to Athens, Greece, and then on to Kennedy International Airport in New York City," the representative told me. I nodded my head. "From there, you'll catch a flight to Chicago, and then on to your final destination, Milwaukee."

I looked at him in puzzlement. I did not understand. "What is Milwaukee?"

"Milwaukee?" He appeared as confused as me. "It's a city. That's where you're going. Milwaukee is your new home."

My new home? I thought. There clearly was a mistake.

"No, my new home is Juneau," I explained to the man. "I am going to Alaska."

The representative thumbed through my papers, closed the folder, and handed it to me. "Well, there must have been a change in plans," he told me. "You're going to Milwaukee."

I felt like I might throw up. "Where is Milwaukee?" I asked, trying to suppress my growing panic.

"It's in Wisconsin. Not far from Chicago. A big city in Illinois," the man talked to me in short, clipped sentences as if I were too slow to digest anything more. He was right. I didn't understand. "It gets cold there in the winter," he added.

Cold. Now that was something I understood. I was not going to Juneau, where it was cold. I was going to someplace called Milwaukee, where it was also cold.

"You leave tomorrow," the man reminded me as I walked away, stunned, still processing this unexpected turn of events. I was happy that I was still going to America, but I had spent months getting familiar with Juneau. Siamak was going to take me under his wing. I had never even heard of Milwaukee. The word felt strange on my tongue. I couldn't even find it on a map. Who would I stay with? Where would I study? How would I find a job when my English was still so poor?

My hand was shaking when I called Mrs. Mozhgani with the Bahá'í refugee desk to see if she could shed light on what was going on. She was equally shocked. "Let me look into it. But Mansur," her voice softened, "it is too late to change anything. I'm sorry, but you're going to have to go to Milwaukee."

I wiped away tears as I hastily sent off a letter to Siamak informing him that we wouldn't be seeing each other in

Juneau. I sent a letter to my family as well. Until I was out of Turkey and safely in America, I still didn't feel safe telling them where I was going. I explained that I would be traveling, and I would write as soon as I was settled into my new home. *Milwaukee*, I thought, swallowing the knot that had wedged in my throat.

When Mrs. Mozhgani called back, I learned that there had been a clerical error. An intern had sent my paperwork through the United States Bahá'í National Center, which is located north of Chicago. He wasn't aware that the Illinois location could place people only in the continental United States. My request should have gone through the Bahá'í National Center in Anchorage, which operates independently. (Hawaii also has its own separate Bahá'í National Center.) As a result, I would start my new life in Milwaukee, not Juneau.

"You won't be far from the Bahá'í Temple in Illinois," Mrs. Mozhgani said in a feeble attempt to boost my spirits. "It's the oldest Bahá'í house of worship in the world, and the only one in the United States. Won't that be wonderful?"

− − −

In the early morning of July 21, 1989, I boarded a plane in Istanbul, along with three Iranian Bahá'í families headed to various pockets of America. I was the only one traveling alone. The plane was heavy with nervous energy. On the flight from Greece to New York, the flight attendants learned that one of the children, a little girl named Roza, was celebrating her fifth birthday. "Happy birthday!" I said to Roza in English. She wrinkled her forehead and looked in confusion toward her parents. *"Tavalodat mobarak!"* I said again in Farsi so she would understand. I told Roza she was a lucky girl to be getting the gift of freedom on her birthday. She smiled brightly. Almost twenty years later, I would see hints of that same little girl's smile when I attended Roza's wedding.

An interpreter greeted us when we touched down in New York. As I waited for my paperwork to be processed, I thought about all of the immigrants who had come to the United States before me seeking a better life. I couldn't see the Statue of Liberty, but I knew her torch was out there, still welcoming people to the land of the free. I felt humbled to be one of them.

Different people escorted us to our respective gates. I was the only one from the group headed to Chicago. As I waited anxiously to board, I glanced around the vast concourse. I had never seen such a massive building. There seemed to be hundreds of people frantically rushing to get somewhere else. I could read certain words: exit, Coke, gate. I could confidently speak a few words in English: hello, thank you, water, bathroom. I was still learning how to say "Milwaukee" and "Wisconsin," the *wha*-sounds tripping up my tongue.

O'Hare airport was also sprawling and busy. I was grateful for the woman who greeted me when I got off the plane. I wasn't wearing any identification, but she must have known that the frightened-looking Persian man wearing the dark-blue handknit scarf was the person she sought. She took me directly to the departure gate for the Milwaukee flight.

She didn't speak Farsi, and I was too nervous to try English.

"Welcome to America!" she said as she left me at the gate.

"Thank you!" I said in response. It was my first English conversation in America.

Flight from Athens to New York—Celebrating
little Roza's birthday in 1989.

— — —

Almost a day had passed since I left Turkey. It was approaching midnight when my plane touched down in Milwaukee. The Bahá'í National Center had arranged for an Iranian couple, Mr. and Mrs. Rouhani, to meet me and take me in until I found a job and could afford to get my own place. I greeted Mr. Rouhani with the traditional Persian greeting, planting kisses on both of his cheeks. Mr. Rouhani had been living in the United States for more than thirty years, and my enthusiastic greeting caught him off guard and embarrassed him. I didn't realize that men didn't kiss on the cheeks in America. There was much I needed to learn about American customs.

Although I had eaten well throughout my travels, Mrs. Rouhani didn't believe that I wasn't hungry. "You must eat," she insisted. I politely declined, stating emphatically that I wasn't hungry.

In Iran, there is an etiquette game of sorts that people engage in, called *taarof*. The rules are simple: before saying "Yes" to something that you want, you must first give several convincing "No's." After two or three rounds of offers and refusals, a person can finally say "Yes" without appearing rude.

I truly wasn't hungry. My stomach was still in knots from the stress of the travel. But Mrs. Rouhani assumed I was *taarofing*. She insisted I eat; I politely declined. We did this exchange until, eventually, Mrs. Rouhani won (which is precisely how *taarofing* works). I gave in and had my first meal: a McDonald's Big Mac, fries, and a Coke. I was already on my way to becoming a true American.

———

PART FIVE

AMERICA

Chapter Twenty-Nine

1989

When my plane touched down in America, I had about $400 to my name and a well-worn, dog-eared dictionary. My English was choppy and rudimentary, at best. I had been sent to some foreign city I had never heard of. I knew no one, and I had no idea how I was going to get a job and support myself. I had survived many terrifying moments while in Iran and Turkey, but my family and friends were always there for support. Now, I was on my own.

I met my first American friend, Kia Saeian, through the Local Spiritual Assembly. Kia was still in diapers when his family fled Iran. Kia embodied everything I hoped to achieve one day: He was a medical student at a California university, and he could switch effortlessly between Farsi and English. With Kia's help, I navigated the stacks of paperwork needed to ensure I could legally stay and work in the country, and take the right steps toward obtaining citizenship.

Through a temporary staffing agency, I landed my first job. I made $4.25 an hour working as a night janitor at the Ambrosia Chocolate Factory, located on the outskirts of downtown Milwaukee. In Greek mythology, ambrosia is food for the gods. I quickly learned that Americans worshipped chocolate. The factory made just one candy bar—the Trixie Bar—which was a mix of milk and bittersweet chocolate, pecans, almonds, and cashews. Mostly, the factory made chocolate chips that were used in mass-produced Keebler and Nabisco cookies.

My primary job involved scrubbing and sanitizing the large vats that churned the chocolate mixture. After donning overalls, plastic shoe coverings, goggles, gloves, and a hairnet, I climbed a ladder down into the pit and brushed, scraped, and peeled the many layers of dried chocolate from the walls of the ten-foot steel drum. Then, I hosed the debris down a drain. The metal retained the high temperature needed to keep the chocolate in liquid form. The base of the drum felt like one hundred degrees. The work was hot, sticky, and unpleasant. The drum echoed every time a scraper handle struck the sides, which was often. The sickly sweet smell of cocoa permeated my clothes and seeped into my pores. Rivulets of sweat trailed down my back. My goggles fogged up. I worked in perpetual fear that someone would accidentally start up the vat's mixing mechanism, and my pummeled body would be found the next day covered in milk chocolate.

Being the only immigrant worker at Ambrosia forced me to practice my English. One early morning as I was leaving the grounds to catch my bus, I passed an employee named Virginia, as she was coming in for her day shift.

"What's up, Mansur?" she asked.

I stopped and looked up at the sky. I squinted, shielded my eyes from the sun, and swiveled my head left, and then right. What was she referring to? What was I looking for?

"I don't see anything," I said, quite seriously.

Virginia doubled over in laughter as I stood confused, glancing back and forth between her and the sun-drenched sky.

"What's up?" she explained, as she wiped tears from her eyes, "is an expression. It's like saying, *What's going on?*"

"Oh," I said, still trying to make the connection. "I'm leaving work. That is what's up."

Virginia slapped me on the shoulder and laughed all the way into the building.

Working night shifts could get lonely. Some nights, the enormity of my situation made me weep. I had left behind loved ones and friends, a successful business, and the only home I knew. I had risked everything only to find myself scrubbing toilets and chocolate vats. The first part of my journey—getting out of Iran—had been much more difficult than I had anticipated. I knew making my way in America was going to be hard. Still, I had underestimated how much I would miss my family and all that was familiar.

Mr. and Mrs. Rouhani were kind and gracious hosts. For the first week of my stay, I shared a room with the eldest of their four sons, a college student. I was shocked to learn that he was in the process of moving into his own place. Without a wife! In Persian culture, adult children live with their parents until they're married. My older siblings, who were in their thirties or close to it, were still single and living at home. I was older than any of the Rouhanis' children. The couple never said I needed to move out, but I felt it wasn't right for me to stay if this wasn't the American custom.

When I asked Kia to help me find a place, he balked. "You have a place with the Rouhanis," he said. "You should stay. Get familiar with Milwaukee. Save some money." But I insisted. One week after starting the job at Ambrosia, I moved into a ground-level studio apartment on the corner of Cambridge and Oakland in East Milwaukee. The apartment wasn't in the best part of town, but it was a straight shot on the bus to Ambrosia. I didn't have the funds to cover the deposit and the first month's rent ($275). Kia was right. I should have thought through my situation. I couldn't afford to move. But the Local Assembly came through for me once again. After a long shift, I would come home and collapse onto a twin bed donated from some Bahá'í family. That saggy mattress with its threadbare sheets and stained navy-and-white striped bedspread served as my bed, couch, desk, and kitchen table. I ate off of mismatched plates, scrubbed my clothes in the bathtub, and flung them over the shower rod to drip dry. The scenario took me back to Tabriz, when my family had to rely on charity to forge a new start. Here I was, almost exactly ten years later, repeating history in a different country.

A few weeks into my job, my supervisor called me to his office. I was nervous, wondering if I had done something wrong. I was still learning English, and I hoped that I would be able to follow what he said and participate in the conversation. I didn't know it yet, but my supervisor, Patrick McDonald, would become one of my biggest advocates. His support helped me get to where I am today. Mr. McDonald had no complaints about my work. Instead, he encouraged me to sign up for English as a Second Language classes at Milwaukee Area Technical College. He even helped me complete the application. I wasn't used to people who weren't Bahá'ís wanting to help. It occurred to me that he didn't know what religion I followed—more importantly, it didn't matter to him. It would take some time for me to stop questioning these kindnesses from Mr. McDonald and others like him.

ESL class started after Labor Day—just a couple of months after I arrived in Wisconsin. The teacher was impressed with my mastery of English. Every two weeks, I advanced to the next class level. I started in a beginner class in September and completed the entire program by December. I still wasn't as fluent as I would have liked, but I had gone as far as that particular program could take me. With the encouragement and aid of my teacher, who knew my dreams of becoming a doctor, I applied for a scholarship to attend an intensive ESL program with a special focus on science and technology at the University of Wisconsin-Milwaukee.

I was thrilled when I got a scholarship that covered tuition, but my heart sank when I learned that classes were held on weekday afternoons. I wouldn't be able to start my night shift on time. To my surprise, Mr. McDonald modified my work schedule, allowing me to work mornings from six to eleven. I had just enough time to get back to my apartment, shower off the cocoa stench, and get to school. After class, I went back to Ambrosia to complete another shift. When possible, I worked overtime on weekends, nights, holidays and school breaks—anything to help me earn money for medical school.

I spent what little free time I had with people from the Bahá'í community. I had never seen so much diversity! The only Bahá'ís I had ever known were Persians. In America, I met followers from Japan, China, England, Mexico, and other countries. I met Native Americans and African Americans who shared my faith. There were very few Persians in Milwaukee. I found I preferred that, because it allowed me to focus on improving my English while learning more about American customs. My initial year in America was filled with many life-changing firsts. I went to the Bahá'í House of Worship in Wilmette, Illinois, just north of Chicago, next to Lake Michigan. It was the first time that I had been to a Bahá'í Temple. I had read about the Temple and seen photographs, but the reality of its splendor outshone anything I had envisioned.

Architect Louis Bourgeois spent ten years designing and constructing the building, even seeking input from 'Abdu'l-Bahá, the son of the Bahá'í Faith founder. With its sweeping white dome, soaring pillars, and intricate designs, the building earned its moniker: The Temple of Light and Unity. In the Bahá'í Faith, the number nine symbolizes oneness and unity. Each of the Temple's nine exterior pillars are adorned with symbols from various world religions, including the Jewish Star of David, crucifixes, and the Islamic star and crescent. At the time, the Temple was one of seven Bahá'í houses of worship in existence worldwide. The Wilmette Temple, which opened in 1953, is the only one in North America. It's a National Historic Landmark and considered to be one of the Seven Wonders of Illinois. More than a quarter million people visit the site every year. In 1989, when I was one of the masses, I wept at the Temple's awe-inspiring architectural splendor and the beauty of its messages of unity. I prayed inside the House of Worship and meditated outside at one of the Temple's nine gardens. I had never felt more at peace.

A few months later, I traveled ninety miles northwest to Green Lake, where I attended my first Bahá'í conference. More than 2,000 Bahá'ís from across America, Canada, and other countries attended this weekend event. I had never seen so many Bahá'ís in one place. It made my heart happy to see people of varying ethnicities and races openly embracing the faith. It was a true reflection of the faith's focus on one God creating one human race. When I told my family in Iran about these experiences at the Temple and conference, we all marveled at the idea that such a large number of Bahá'ís could gather and worship without fear of persecution or threat of imprisonment or death.

I spoke with my family every few months. I needed to hear their voices, even though each treasured phone call cost about five dollars per minute. The time difference and my long work hours made it challenging to connect. I wrote letters home often, and sent letters to Siamak, who was living in Australia with Jaklin, and Tofigh, who was in Canada. I missed my friends dearly. Like me, they were struggling to adapt to the customs and ways of their new homelands.

I did well in the advanced ESL class. In May of 1990, just nine months after I came to America speaking barely passable English, I passed the Test of English as a Foreign Language (TOEFL) exam. Now that I was officially deemed fluent and proficient in English, I could start my college studies. Once again, Mr. McDonald helped me apply for scholarships to continue studying at the university. He promised to adjust my work schedule so I could attend classes.

Even with financial aid to offset college costs, I needed to work a lot of hours to cover rent, food, bus fare, and other expenses. The summer before my first year in college, I worked eight hours at Ambrosia from six in the morning until two in the afternoon. I went home, changed, and then started my shift as a grocery-store cashier, working six more hours, from four to ten at night. The fourteen-hour workdays were exhausting, but I was proud to be making it on my own in America. That fall, I enrolled in math and science courses at the University of Wisconsin-Milwaukee, avoiding any subject too heavy in English.

To my surprise, I was elected to serve on the Local Spiritual Assembly. I hadn't been in Milwaukee for long, but I had immersed myself into the Bahá'í community. Bahá'ís were the people I most identified with, regardless of nationality. One of my first tasks as an Assembly member was to meet with the mayor of Milwaukee. He had asked for our input on how to ease racial tensions between the northern, predominantly Black part of the city and the southern, mostly White section. This experience opened my eyes to the injustices that seemed to plague Black Americans; it was similar to how Bahá'ís were treated in Iran—as less than human. At Bahá'í conferences, I was inspired by an overall feeling of inclusivity. Now, I saw that prejudices and segregation were universal problems present in America, too.

As I had done in Iran and Turkey, I continued to teach and work with Bahá'í youth. Every other week, I drove students to volunteer at the Wilmette Temple. One December while school was on winter break, I offered to drive seven teenagers to a Bahá'í youth conference in Atlanta. I was still getting comfortable driving on America's busy interstates, which were much more chaotic than Iran's two-lane roads. It was snowing when we left Milwaukee in a rented 10-passenger van sporting questionable tread-worn tires. The snowfall intensified the farther south I drove. It brought back memories of the white-out blizzard that nearly claimed my life. This time, I was responsible for the lives of seven young people. By the time we hit Louisville, Kentucky, conditions were so bad that the highway department was shutting down the roads. I had never driven in weather like this. The time was close to midnight, and I had no idea where I was or where to go. I fishtailed the van into the parking lots of hotel after hotel. There were no vacancies. At the fourth and final hotel I tried, without luck, I wandered over to the lobby payphone and flipped through the chained-up phonebook. The Yellow Pages had a listing for a Bahá'í Information Center. I really didn't expect anyone to answer at such a late time, but I dialed the number anyway. I didn't know what else to do. To my surprise, a man answered the phone. From his groggy voice, I could tell he had been sleeping. I explained the situation. There was a long pause and then a muffled conversation.

"Do you have a pen and paper handy?" the man asked when he got back on the phone. I did. "Bring those kids to our house." And he gave me the address.

About forty-five minutes later, the students and I were sprawled out on the couch, chairs, and floor of this gracious family's home. In the morning, they made us a hearty pancake breakfast, checked the road conditions, and sent us on our way.

Compared to Milwaukee, Atlanta seemed to pulse with nonstop energy. Thousands of Bahá'í youths from across the country had come to the city to connect, celebrate, and worship. There were two Black young people in the group from Milwaukee with me. On Christmas Eve, they made plans for our group to attend a church service in the inner city. To this day, that service, at an all-Black church, remains the most joyful and jubilant worship service I have ever attended. Everyone was singing, dancing, clapping, and hugging.

Unfortunately, my euphoria quickly evaporated a few days later, when it was time to head back to Milwaukee. I had asked parents to send their children with enough money to cover the costs for a hotel on the return trip. I planned to stop midway through the 15-hour drive. But as the students piled into the van, I learned that most of them were broke. I hadn't thought to collect their cash up front, and they had blown everything on souvenirs and food. I didn't have enough money to cover hotel rooms for everyone. I could have reached out to the Louisville couple again, but I felt it was asking too much. I made the long drive back to Milwaukee in one shot.

———

Chapter Thirty

Early 1990s

I finished my first year at the University of Wisconsin-Milwaukee with high marks. As a result, I was one of two dozen students accepted into the university's fast-track medical school program. With this accelerated program, I could finish my undergraduate studies in three years, plus have guaranteed admission to the Medical College of Wisconsin, also in Milwaukee. My hard work in school had paid off. I continued to work hard outside of school, as well.

One day in late July 1991, I showed up for my shift at the Ambrosia Chocolate Factory to find the place swarming with cops. My heart raced. It would take years for me to think of police as civil servants who wanted to help and protect people—not harm or terrorize them. I headed toward the employee entrance, where an officer stood blocking the door.

"Stop," he said when I was about six feet away. "You can't go in."

"I work here," I told him. I pointed at the Ambrosia logo stitched on my shirt and fumbled for my employee identification card, which I held out to him with a shaking hand.

"No one's allowed in."

I didn't understand what was happening. I glanced at my watch and panicked. I needed to clock in. I was going to be late! I couldn't afford to lose a day's pay. Out of the corner of my eye, I saw a couple of co-workers waving at me from the employee parking lot.

"Mansur, come here!" they shouted.

"My shift's starting," I said as I got within earshot of the men. "I need to clock in."

"Dude, none of us are working today," one of the guys said. "There's some messed-up stuff going down in there."

"What's going on?" I asked.

"The cops are sweeping the place for body parts."

I was certain I had misunderstood. Maybe *body parts* was an American slang term for drugs or money. "What are body parts?" I asked, completely serious.

"Body parts?" My co-worker looked at me as if I were daft. "You know, a dead man's hand, his eyeballs, maybe his skull. You know? Body parts." He swept his hands down his body to make sure I understand what a body was.

Now, I was even more confused. Why would a corpse's eyeballs be in a chocolate factory?

Finally, another co-worker stepped in to explain things. "Mansur, they think one of the workers here is a serial killer. Do you know Jeffrey Dahmer?"

‒   ‒   ‒

Jeffrey Dahmer worked nights at Ambrosia for several years, but our paths never crossed. He was a chocolate mixer, so it's likely that I cleaned some of the vats at the end of his shifts. I later learned that police had found gruesome photographs along with the severed heads and remains of some of Dahmer's victims in his apartment, just blocks from the factory. Under questioning, Dahmer told police that he sometimes kept skulls from his victims in his employee locker at Ambrosia. It was my job to clean that locker room. I had likely wiped down the locker door that entombed the remains of some poor tortured soul. I shuddered to think that I had worked in the same place with anyone who was capable of such horrific acts. My co-workers who knew him said Dahmer kept to himself and never caused trouble. Unfortunately, the publicity surrounding Dahmer's employment, and the subsequent police search that turned up no skulls or body parts, blemished the Ambrosia name.

─ ─ ─

I was thrilled to be on my way to earning a medical degree and grateful to have a job and a boss who worked with my school schedule. Still, I came to realize that something was missing. I was lonely. Through the Bahá'í community, I met Jerry and Jenny Lerner. Jerry was a doctor; Jenny was involved with the university theater program. They lived within walking distance of the school. The couple often opened their home to Bahá'ís new to the city. When they offered me a chance to save some money by moving in with them in May of 1992, I readily said "Yes." I no longer cared if it wasn't customary in America for a man who was nearing his thirties to share living space with another household. I desperately missed being a part of a family.

I quickly became big brother to eleven-year-old Gabriel, five-year-old Ariel, and three-year-old Geneva. Gabe and I became fast friends. He taught me a lot about American pastimes like football. In turn, I taught him about the football game (soccer) that I loved. Like most boys who grew up in that area, Gabe was a huge Green Bay Packers fan. The two of us spent hours watching Packers games while Gabe explained the various positions, plays, and rules to me. I blame Gabe for turning me into a big cheesehead! Gabe didn't have as much luck teaching me about baseball. No matter how many Brewers games I watched, I just couldn't get excited about the sport. Baseball moved much too slowly for my liking.

When I was settled, I called Tofigh to give him my new phone number and address. Tofigh and I had grown closer over the years. We both stayed in touch with Siamak, but communication with him was more challenging, given the significant time difference and high phone-call fees, between North America and Australia. When Tofigh answered my call, I sensed immediately that something was wrong. By this point, Tofigh was in his third year of undergraduate studies at the University of Toronto. His admission to medical school was contingent on how well he finished the semester. His grades, Tofigh admitted, were not good. Tofigh had no other ambition in life except to become a doctor—and my friend was certainly one of the smartest men I knew—but a woman had broken his heart.

Tofigh had been certain she was "the one."

She wasn't.

After their breakup, he was too hurt to concentrate, too depressed to study. It was all that he could manage to shuffle his crestfallen body to class each day until the semester mercifully ended.

Badly.

It was late by the time I hung up the phone, but I dialed another phone number anyway. "I'm concerned about Tofigh, and I'd like to leave for Toronto tomorrow morning," I told my friend Ron Enyati. "Are you up for a road trip?" Ron, a Persian Bahá'í, pulled into the Lerners' driveway bright and early.

During the 11-hour drive to Toronto, I called Tofigh from a payphone to let him know Ron and I were on our way. An unshaven, slovenly man answered the door. Tofigh looked thin, pale, broken. I was so glad I'd made the trek to see him. Ron and I spent the next week with Tofigh, listening to him pour out his heart over this girl and helping him figure out next steps, since medical school was temporarily off the table. It was awkward, and I felt guilty that I would be going to medical school while Tofigh's plans were on hold. He was the one who'd always dreamed of becoming a doctor. I had wanted to be an architect. But, I had made a promise to God to become a doctor and help people if my friends and I survived that frightful snowstorm on the Zagros Mountains. I intended to make good on that promise.

To lift Tofigh's mood, we visited Niagara Falls. (In hindsight, this was probably a bad idea, since newlyweds often honeymooned there, and the town's slogan—"Niagara Is for Lovers"—was visible on billboards, T-shirts, and teddy bears.) We attended Bahá'í events. We watched funny movies and ate too much junk food. By the time Ron pointed his car west, toward Milwaukee, five days later, I could see a bit of the old spark back in my dear friend's eyes. I knew he would be okay.

— — —

In November, I traveled with about fifty Bahá'ís, including the Lerner family, to New York City, to attend the Bahá'í World Congress. It was only the second time that the international Bahá'í community had held an event of this magnitude. I was an infant when the first conference had taken place, in London in 1963. I had been looking forward to attending this world event ever since I found out that I would be living in America. More than 30,000 Bahá'ís from across the globe came together to mark the 100th anniversary of the passing of Bahá'í Faith founder Bahá'u'lláh. The four days of presentations, music, arts, and social gatherings did not disappoint. I met Bahá'ís from all corners of the world. Some, like me, had fled their homelands seeking refuge from religious persecution. Many were able to openly practice their faith the way I was now doing in America. Everyone seemed committed to ending religious persecution and ensuring that Bahá'ís everywhere could worship freely. These stories made me hopeful for my family and friends in Iran.

– – –

As I began my last year in the accelerated undergraduate program, I noticed that textbook pages looked blurry, and I was having frequent headaches. I was still wearing the eyeglasses made in my optical lab in Tabriz. The Lerners suggested I go to LensCrafters. That simple recommendation changed my life. At the vision center, an optometrist examined my eyes and diagnosed me with nearsightedness. Throughout the eye exam, I was fascinated by the optometrist's job. I had never heard of this profession. When I was growing up in Iran, only an ophthalmologist could diagnose eye problems or prescribe eyeglasses. You went to an optician to get your corrective lenses. Many people couldn't afford to see an ophthalmologist, so they went about life with blurred or double vision and chronic headaches.

I peppered the optometrist with questions about his training and profession. I was shocked to learn that I could become a Doctor of Optometry in slightly less time than earning a medical degree to become a physician. With my years of experience in the optical lab and my knowledge of corrective lenses, I was essentially already an optician. Optometry seemed like the perfect career for me!

Unfortunately, the University of Wisconsin-Milwaukee didn't have an optometry program. And despite being fast-tracked for medical school, I felt like optometry was my calling. I applied to three optometry schools in the Midwest, which I selected mostly because I could afford to drive to the campuses from Milwaukee. Out of the three, the University of Missouri offered the best financial-aid package. I was headed to St. Louis.

––––––

Chapter Thirty-One

Summer 1993

Before starting optometry school, I decided to fulfill a dream to visit the site of the first Bahá'í Temple in Ashgabat, the capital of Turkmenistan. Built in the early 1900s, the Ashgabat Bahá'í Temple had been badly damaged in an earthquake that shook the country in the 1940s. Its ruined remains were demolished some twenty years later. Still, many Bahá'ís continued to make pilgrimages to the sacred site. I also wanted to visit Turkmenistan because I was fascinated by Russian history. Turkmenistan had just become a sovereign country two years earlier in 1991, after nearly seventy years of Soviet rule. I first became enchanted with Russia after reading Leo Tolstoy's *Anna Karenina* and the works of Russian poet Aleksandr Pushkin. Even though Turkmenistan and Iran share a border, no one in my family had ever been able to go. For much of my time in Iran, Bahá'ís were forbidden to leave the country. None of us could get a passport. On this—my first trip back to the region since fleeing five years ago—I would be achingly close to my homeland and loved ones, yet I knew I couldn't see them without risking their safety or mine.

For me, this trip was very much a pilgrimage, a spiritual journey. While some college students backpacked through Europe, I was forging a different route through the Middle East and into Central Asia. My plan was to return to Istanbul and make my way through several countries, staying in hostels or with Bahá'í families along the way. I wanted to connect with as many Bahá'ís as possible and share my knowledge and experiences. I knew a lot about the faith's history from my earlier experience during my teenage years memorizing Bahá'í writings. Many followers in these countries didn't have access to Bahá'í texts. The only opportunities they had to deepen their understanding of their faith was through discussions with people like me. I also wanted others to know what I had learned about the faith's impact worldwide, based on my brief time in America attending conferences, the World Congress, and the Wilmette Temple.

From the Istanbul airport, I took a bus to the opposite side of Turkey and into Armenia, stopping to visit with Bahá'í communities along the way. Being back in Turkey felt surreal. I was essentially traveling the opposite direction I had traveled when I fled Iran. Thankfully, this time I didn't have to walk or evade authorities.

After Armenia, my next stop was Azerbaijan. Azerbaijan and Armenia, both former Soviet Republics, were ensnared in a decades-long war. Their borders were heavily militarized, making it impossible to cross from one country to the other by bus or car. I had to go back to Turkey to catch another bus into the Nakhchivan Autonomous Republic. This self-governed, 2,000-square-foot patch of land is a part of Azerbaijan, and borders Armenia, Iran, and Turkey. Being in Nakhchivan, even for a short period of time, carried its own risk. Much of the fighting between Azerbaijan and Armenia took place here. My plan was to fly from Nakhchivan to Baku, the capital of Azerbaijan.

I assumed flying was the safest way to go—until the bus pulled up to the airport. As I stepped off the bus and walked toward the entrance, it was evident that the war had taken its toll on the airport, which is also an Azerbaijani military airbase. Sections of the roof were sagging. The walls were pockmarked. Peeling strips of paint hung down. I dashed into the building, worried that the entrance overhang would collapse on top of me.

The airport was in bad shape, but the plane was even worse. I walked across the tarmac to a puddle jumper that reminded me of my Toyota Corolla after it was stolen, taken for a joyride, and wrecked in St. Louis—except my car had real seats, decent tires, and less rust. The plane had several metal benches bolted to the floor. I took a spot on one of the few seats with a backrest and searched frantically for a seatbelt. There wasn't one. As I looked around, I was shocked to see a dozen passengers sitting on the floor holding on to small cages with chickens or ropes attached to goats. One woman sat with a piglet in her lap. For almost ninety minutes, I breathed through my mouth as the pungent stench of manure and body odor filled the small cabin.

I had been speaking Turkish for much of my trip, but when I landed in Baku, I effortlessly slipped back into Azeri. Hearing so many people speaking my native tongue took me back to happier times in Harvan: playing soccer, climbing cherry trees, listening to *Baba* tell stories around the *korsi*. The Azeri words tasted sweet.

Because I wasn't yet a United States citizen, immigration services had issued me a refugee travel document, a piece of paper that unfortunately didn't carry the same weight as a U.S.-issued passport. Being fluent in Azeri came in handy when a border-control officer took off with my travel document. I had no idea where he was going or why. Without that document, it would be extremely difficult for me to return to Turkey, let alone America. I dabbed at the sweat forming on my brow and asked another worker if he knew where his colleague had gone. The guy shrugged, unconcerned about my situation. After about ten minutes, the officer came back with my travel document in hand. When he saw how sweaty and nervous I was, he laughed and slapped me on the back. "This is the first American travel document I've seen," he explained. "I wanted to show the guys." And with that, I was free to go.

– – –

Like Iran, Azerbaijan is a predominantly Shia Muslim country. After the Soviet Red Army invaded the country in 1920, Muslims, Bahá'ís, and other faiths were forced to take their religions underground. The Soviet Communist Party intended to replace all religious beliefs with what they called "scientific atheism." While organized religions were never banned, many mosques, temples, and churches were destroyed or seized for other purposes. Believers of any faith were forced to worship secretly in teahouses or private homes. Communist materials distributed to school-children and touted by the media ridiculed religion while endorsing atheism.

Nearly twenty years later, when dictator Joseph Stalin rose to power, the Soviets forced thousands of Bahá'ís to leave Azerbaijan. Bahá'ís from Iran were sent back to their homeland. Others went to Siberia. Some Bahá'ís pretended to be atheists so they could stay in Azerbaijan. Most of these secret followers settled in Baku.

When the Soviet Union collapsed in 1991, Azerbaijan declared its independence as a secular state. The new government revised the country's constitution, ensuring that all citizens are treated equally regardless of religious beliefs. The amended constitution gave citizens the right to worship any faith of their choosing (or not worship at all), and openly express religious views—an act that had been forbidden under Soviet rule.

I couldn't have timed my visit better. The Bahá'í community elected a new National Spiritual Assembly in 1992—the country's first in more than seven decades. The community had been oppressed for a long time, and they were hungry to learn more about their faith. There were few Bahá'ís left in the country who had the knowledge to teach Bahá'í history, practices, and learning processes. I was a source of information waiting to be tapped. It seemed as if God had directed me to Azerbaijan during a time when my presence could have a significant impact.

In Baku, I met and later shared a residence with Ghassam Yari, a retired Iranian army general. Now in his seventies, Mr. Yari had left Iran as a much younger man before the Islamic Revolution. He was now a citizen of Brazil. A native Azeri speaker like me, Mr. Yari was answering his own calling to introduce more Azerbaijanis to the Bahá'í Faith. He had been in the country for almost a year translating Bahá'í texts into Azeri. At the time we met, he was working on *The Hidden Words*, ethical teachings written by Bahá'í Faith founder Bahá'u'lláh during his 1858 exile in Baghdad. It seemed Mr. Yari and I had both been pulled to Azerbaijan for similar reasons.

Mr. Yari guided me through the ins-and-outs of life in Azerbaijan. The country was nothing like what I had expected. Like most Persians, I had grown up in awe, and even fear, of the superpower that was the Soviet Union. I assumed (incorrectly, I now saw) that all Soviet Republics were lands of plenty—much like America. Instead, what I saw in Azerbaijan was a country whose growth and fortunes had been stifled. The country's infrastructure was old and ill equipped to serve the needs of its growing population. Water service was available from 4:30 to 6:00 every morning. Those ninety minutes were the only time that you could take a shower, flush the toilet, and fill water jugs to get you through the rest of the day. Markets were cleaned out of breads, meat, and produce within an hour of opening, and only sparsely restocked until the next day. Electricity flickered sporadically and sometimes went out for hours. In sharp contrast, the city had one of the region's most modern subway systems. The metro stations, built in the late 1960s, reflected a Soviet architectural style. Spanning twenty-two miles, the Baku Metro was a point of pride for Azerbaijan, the first Islamic country to have a subway system.

The calling I felt to help Bahá'ís in Azerbaijan kept me there for six weeks. I never made it to Turkmenistan or the site of the first Bahá'í Temple. Still, I had gotten all that I wanted out of the journey—and more.

I hadn't told my parents that I would be traveling to the area. I didn't want to tip off Iranian authorities to my whereabouts. I was less than thirty miles from the northern Iranian border, and yet it was as if there were still an ocean between my family and me. I wasn't sure whether Iranian intelligence services were monitoring my parents' communications. Still, toward the end of my trip, I took the risk and called them from a payphone, taking care not to share details that might give away my exact location. It was always good to hear everyone's voices, and since the phone fees weren't as high, I was able to talk to my parents and siblings for longer. I could tell my family was proud of the work I was doing to educate others about the Bahá'í Faith and the continual oppression and persecution of followers. It was only through efforts like this that we could hope to bring about change in Iran.

About a month after I returned to the United States, a Muslim relative visited *Agha* at the appliance store. He came with a warning. "Tell Mansur not to call you when he is in the area," the relative said. Through his message, we knew that the Iranian Intelligence services had monitored our phone call. They were aware that I had been close by. I was mad at myself for being so reckless. Being in the area and speaking my native tongue had stirred such a homesickness in me. But my need to connect could have jeopardized my family. It was unbelievable that, five years after my escape, Iranian authorities still thought I posed a threat.

———

Chapter Thirty-Two

St. Louis, 1993–1997

Back in Milwaukee, I went through the painful act of saying goodbye to my second family, the Lerners. I would miss watching football with Gabe and his father, and being a part of American traditions in their home, like Thanksgiving. At the time, I didn't know that Jerry and Jenny's relationship was floundering. In two years, Jenny would call to tell me that the couple was getting divorced. The news shook me as if the split were happening to my own parents. I reconnected with Gabe, who was sixteen at the time and struggling through one of the most difficult times in his life.

I met Paul Olson through the St. Louis Bahá'í community. Paul was a doctoral student studying biology and biomedical science at neighboring Washington University, and he let me stay with him for a few weeks while I got my bearings and found a place of my own. My one-bedroom apartment on the outskirts of Ferguson was affordable but farther away from the university and the Bahá'í community than I would have liked.

The first two years of optometry school involved a lot of classroom instruction. I relied on scholarships, student loans, and a job I'd landed at an optical shop to help cover expenses. I needed a car to get to work, so I bought my second American automobile. The white, twelve-year-old Toyota Corolla sported lots of dents, dings, and rust spots. The cracked, tan vinyl seats gave off a slight odor of sour milk every time you sat down. The car was certainly a step down from the Iranian-made Khodro Paykan I had proudly driven around the streets of Tabriz.

One day after pulling into a parking spot at my apartment building, the car key wouldn't budge from the ignition. I twisted and pulled. It was stuck. Not seeing any other option, I left the key in the ignition and used my spare key to lock and unlock the car. My locked-and-loaded Corolla greatly amused my classmates and was often the butt of stories and jokes published in the student newsletter. I shrugged off the good-humored ribbings. The car got me from point A to point B, and that was all I needed.

Until one snowy day when the car vanished.

Small shards of broken glass glimmered in the parking lot's wintry slush. Someone had smashed out a window and used the stuck ignition key to drive off with my car. Three days later, the police called to say they'd found my car. In actuality, the police found my car the same day it was stolen—they just forgot to tell me. They also didn't tell me what sort of shape the car was in. A group of teenagers had gone on a joyride and backed the car into—and then got it stuck on top of—a fire hydrant. I paid $160 in impound fees to reclaim a car that was stolen from me and then so severely damaged that it was no longer drivable. It cost an additional $135 to have the car towed to a junkyard, where they offered me $75 for the scrap metal. The theft left me car-less, broke, and feeling a bit broken inside.

Looking back, I was most likely suffering from depression. The first year of optometry school was extremely challenging. While my ability to speak English had improved, it was still a struggle to keep up with fast-talking professors, especially those who were immigrants like me and spoke English with a foreign accent. I missed my family in Iran. I hadn't realized how much the Lerners' presence had kept me going. I had always turned to the local Bahá'í community for friendship and support, but I was the only Bahá'í in the area, and I no longer had a car to get to Bahá'í functions and events. For the next year, I relied on the generosity of friends and public transportation to get around. At one point, I drove a white Toyota Corolla (almost identical to my stolen car) that someone had donated to the Local Spiritual Assembly.

Eventually, I saved enough to purchase another Toyota for $700. I was thrilled to be able to enjoy the independence that comes with owning a car. This excitement lasted less than twenty-four hours. A taxi driver rear-ended the car the very same day that I bought it. Ironically, I was on my way to meet with an auto-insurance agent. The taxi driver didn't want to involve the taxi company or their insurance provider. He offered to pay cash for the damages, which totaled $650. I accepted, pocketed the money, and never fixed the car. In essence, that car had cost me only $50.

I was still feeling pretty low, though, and I didn't really know what would make me feel better. One Friday night, after finishing work at the optical lab, I came home and said a prayer, asking for guidance. That night I heard a voice in my dreams telling me to move to Saint Charles, a suburb fifteen miles northwest of Ferguson. A move to Saint

Charles didn't make sense. I would be even farther—thirty miles—from the university. Still, I got up the next morning and went to look at apartments.

On Sunday, I attended Race Unity Day at a park in downtown St. Louis. This annual worldwide Bahá'í-sponsored event typically takes place the second Sunday in June. Activities are open to everyone as a way to promote racial harmony and understanding. I sat down with my picnic lunch across from a Black man who introduced himself as Emmanuel Ankrah from Saint Charles. When I told him I was hoping to move to the city—and had, in fact, just been checking out apartments the day before—Emmanuel Ankrah got the biggest smile on his face.

"Would you be interested in serving on the Local Spiritual Assembly?" he asked. When I told him "Yes" and that I had been elected to the Milwaukee assembly, Emmanuel Ankrah started clapping and cheering.

"We have eight people elected to serve on the assembly in Saint Charles, but we need one more," he explained. "I think you are meant to be our number nine."

The entire meeting seemed fated. Moving to Saint Charles and getting involved again with the assembly and the youth group was exactly what my lonely soul needed.

— — —

From the moment I found out that I would be living in America, I focused on achieving two dreams: becoming a doctor and becoming a United States citizen. While I studied eye anatomy and vision problems, I also immersed myself in learning about the country I now called home: its history, founding fathers and leaders, the constitution and amendments. My apartment was littered with index cards with questions written in Sharpie: "What did Martin Luther King, Jr. do?" and "Name one of your state's senators and representatives."

I have taken many exams in my life. None made me as anxious as the one I took that day in February 1995 at the U.S. immigration center in St. Louis. The small room where the oral exam took place had just enough space for a small faux-wood table and two plastic chairs that looked like they had been salvaged from a condemned school. The unventilated room was unseasonably warm. I was thankful that I had worn my suit jacket not only to make a good impression, but to conceal the rings of sweat that pooled under my armpits. The immigration officer was a no-nonsense man. He didn't waste time with pleasantries or trying to help me relax. In quick succession, he asked personal questions about my arrival in the United States, places I had lived, worked, and studied, and my past life in Iran. When he asked if I had ever been part of a militia or military group, I could truthfully say "No."

When the officer fired off ten civics questions, not one of them stumped me. Finally, with a shaky voice, I read five different sentences out loud in English, not tripping over a single word. I was pretty confident that I had passed. Still, I didn't exhale until the immigration officer stuck out his hand and said, "Congratulations!" After the swearing-in ceremony, I would officially be a naturalized United States citizen. My parents wept at the news. My classmates surprised me with a party. I was both proud and oddly conflicted. Despite a lifetime of cruel and unjust treatments, it still pained me to renounce my Iranian citizenship. With that step, I knew I had no chance of ever returning to Iran again.

In addition to shedding my citizenship, I also slightly modified my identity. Americans, I had discovered, pronounced my Arabic name, Mansour, exactly as it was spelled—*mansour*—as if I were a bitter man. (The correct pronunciation sounds more like "man-soor.") To help guide people to the proper pronunciation, I changed the spelling of my name to Mansur, dropping the letter "o." My naturalization certificate was the first of many U.S.-issued documents issued to Mansur Nurdel.

— — —

After two years of lectures, labs, and tests, it was time to put my optometry knowledge to work. Besides the healthy financial-aid package, another reason I chose to attend school in St. Louis was for the opportunity to work in the university's eye clinic. The free or low-cost clinic provided services to people who couldn't otherwise afford vision care. Growing up in Harvan, nobody had access to routine medical, vision, or dental care. You saw a doctor only when something was seriously, often life-threateningly, wrong. It wasn't until my apprenticeship at the optical lab in Tabriz that I discovered I had a vision problem. By that point, I was almost an adult. I had spent my childhood viewing a fuzzy and out-of-focus world. I assumed the world was a blur for everyone. I didn't realize there was something wrong—and fixable—with my eyes. I was shocked the first time I held an optical lens up to my left eye and watched letters and objects come into crisp focus. Once I started wearing eyeglasses, I marveled that I had done so well in school while reading hazy words. It didn't seem right that anyone should go through life with poor eyesight. I felt everyone should be able to get vision care regardless of ability to pay.

For this reason, I chose to complete my first clinical internship at the Rosebud Sioux Tribe Reservation in South Dakota. At the end of May 1996, I loaded up my dented and damaged $50 Toyota Corolla with my few possessions and headed west. One of the many things I loved about America was its vastness. I enjoyed exploring different states and cities. During the drive, I checked out Iowa and Nebraska. I had never seen such flat topography. There were fields of corn, wheat, and soybeans as far as my eyes could see.

Shortly before I made the drive to South Dakota, I read *Bury My Heart at Wounded Knee*. The book helped me understand the persistent marginalization of Native Americans at the hands of White settlers throughout history. Anytime I read about a group of people who were run out of their homes and treated as less than human, I couldn't stop from comparing their plight to that of the Bahá'ís. But even the Bahá'ís and Turks in Iran fared better than Native American tribes.

At Rosebud, I witnessed a level of poverty I had never seen before—not in my small village in Iran that lacked running water and electricity, or in war-torn countries like Azerbaijan. The magnitude of the reservation's despair shocked me. It was heartbreaking to see Native Americans— those who walked this land first—living in such squalor in the heart of America. Deserted, boarded-up homes pockmarked the landscape. Multiple generations of families crowded into dilapidated trailers. Rusty cars and beat-up trucks sat in weeds outside of the homes.

Equally appalling were the health conditions of the homes' inhabitants. I hadn't seen so many people with rotted or missing teeth since leaving Harvan. Due largely to Western influences, Native Americans today have some of the nation's highest rates of obesity, diabetes, heart disease, and high blood pressure. Left untreated or poorly managed, diabetes and high blood pressure can cause lasting, irreversible eye damage.

I was one of three optometry interns providing care at an eye clinic at Rosebud Hospital, a decent, yet perpetually short-staffed facility. Indian Health Service managed the hospital, which served the tribes in the region. While examining the eyes of one twenty-something-year-old patient, I was shocked to see signs of advanced diabetic retinopathy. It usually takes ten years of poorly controlled blood sugar for this condition to develop. This early presentation suggested that this young man had been living with diabetes that was either undiagnosed or poorly managed since his early teen years. He was already at severe risk for blindness.

During my four months at Rosebud, I treated more people with diabetic retinopathy than I have at any other point in my thirty-year optometry career. The number of people experiencing premature vision loss and advanced eye disease was staggering. Even though the hospital provided free eye exams and eyeglasses to those living on the reservations, no-show appointments were extremely common. When I called to reschedule these missed appointments, I often heard the same story: I couldn't get there. The roads were horrific, poorly maintained, distances long and I imagine getting time off work was difficult or impossible. Sadly, this situation often affected the children, whose parents couldn't bring them in for much-needed eye exams.

I understood why the hospital struggled to attract and retain quality medical staff. Seeing such a high number of people living in poverty and poor health day in and day out was depressing. For stress relief, I often ventured out—sometimes solo, sometimes with other interns—to check out the surrounding area. I paid my respects at the site of the Wounded Knee Massacre at Pine Ridge. I drove east to see the "world's only" palace made of corn in Mitchell, South Dakota. I saw Mount Rushmore, the Badlands, and was a curious observer at the annual Sturgis motorcycle rally. About fourteen miles south of Rosebud, I learned to shoot pool in a bar in Valentine, Nebraska. I was the only one there sipping a Coke.

The Fourth of July fell on a Thursday that year, and I had four days off. I drove to Denver, Colorado, to find a place to stay during my next clinical rotation, which was set to start the next month. I was too broke to afford a hotel, so I slept in my car and showered at a highway truck stop. I had the good fortune of meeting Dwight and Marian Kimsey while visiting the Bahá'í Center in Denver. The couple was known for taking in Bahá'ís who were either passing through the area or looking to make Denver their home, and they opened their doors to me. This generous offer lifted a huge financial burden off of my shoulders. I would be in Colorado for only four months, which made renting an apartment difficult. Plus, as I plugged quarters into the truck-stop public shower, it was evident that I was running low on funds.

During my last week at Rosebud, I treated an eight-year-old girl who needed glasses to correct a vision problem. Hearing my accent, the girl's mother asked where I was from. "I'm from Iran," I told her. "I am a Bahá'í." I don't know what compelled me to share this last bit of personal information. She hadn't asked about my religion. The woman's eyes widened. "My grandmother is a Bahá'í! She would love to meet you!" I had wondered whether there were Bahá'ís on the reservation. On the few occasions that I asked around, many people weren't familiar with the faith.

Soon, I was seated on a sagging, faded rust-and-brown floral print couch inside Mrs. Littlemouse's mobile home. I wanted to hear about her life as a Native American Bahá'í (one of fewer than a dozen on the Rosebud and Pine Ridge Reservations, I learned). But Mrs. Littlemouse had never traveled beyond the South Dakota-Nebraska border. She was much more interested in hearing about Bahá'ís who worshipped in other parts of the world. I sat for hours, sipping warm Coca-Cola and sharing my experiences in the Middle East and in America. I feared that my descriptions of the Bahá'í Temple in Illinois were woefully insufficient. But Mrs. Littlemouse closed her cataract-clouded eyes and smiled, revealing multiple gaps of missing teeth. "So beautiful," she said.

– – –

In August, I moved into the Kimseys' home in Denver. Mr. and Mrs. Kimsey treated all of their Bahá'í tenants like extended family, and the feeling was mutual. I felt valued and supported throughout my stay. My internship at a surgical eye center focused on procedures like cataract surgery and radial keratotomy to correct nearsightedness (a precursor to today's more advanced corrective laser surgeries). My interactions with patients weren't as intimate as they had been in Rosebud. By the time I saw patients, another doctor had already diagnosed the problem and decided on a treatment. I enjoyed the intricacies of surgery, but I missed getting to know people through one-on-one interactions.

My co-workers also wanted to get to know me, I dis-covered. Most of them seemed to accept that I didn't drink alcohol because it was against my religious beliefs. But my lackluster dating life raised some eyebrows. My co-workers desperately wanted to set me up despite the fact that I was in Denver for only a short time. "So-and-so would be perfect for you," they'd say. I had learned early on that Americans have a much more relaxed view of dating than Persians. In Iran, young adults go out in groups, not as couples. A man expresses interest in a woman only if he thinks it might lead to marriage. Casual dating—and certainly casual premarital sex—simply aren't done. For the first time, I felt peer pressure to be "more American."

"Don't you want to meet someone nice? Have some fun?" my colleagues asked.

"The one girl for me is already taken," I told the recep-tionists when they asked every Monday if I had gone out with anyone special over the weekend. That "girl" was actually royalty: Princess Diana. In addition to finding her beautiful, I always sensed that she was a truly kindhearted person. The receptionists would laugh and shake their heads. "You need to lower your standards," they said. I disagreed: I saw no reason to settle for anything less than perfection.

In the seven years that I'd been in the States, I had gone on few dates. Those women were also Bahá'ís. It wasn't that I was opposed to dating outside of my faith—Bahá'í doctrines fully encourage and support interfaith marriages—but my teetotaler ways didn't appeal to a lot of women, especially Americans. And explaining my life story along with an abbre-viated version of my religious beliefs to those who'd never heard of the Bahá'í Faith (which is a lot of people) felt too intrusive. Besides, I saw how quickly a woman had derailed Tofigh's aspirations to become a doctor. I was determined to have my career first, a love life second.

I might not have fallen in love with a woman during my stint in Denver, however, I fell head-over-heels for the Rocky Mountain State. With its majestic mountain range and semi-arid climate, Colorado shared many similarities with Iran. I had visited close to half of the States. None of them felt more like home than Colorado. I decided that I would start my professional career in the Mile High City.

As I prepared to temporarily leave Denver, the receptionists at the eye center created a going-away present for me: a poster of Princess Diana with pictures of the two of us together. They had pasted photographs of my face on top of the men lucky enough to actually be by Diana's side in real life. Laughing, I pointed out that the princess and I were a striking couple. When Diana died in a car accident later that year, those pictures lifted me up.

— — —

I returned to the University of Missouri in January of 1997 to finish my last rotation at the university eye clinic in East St. Louis, Illinois. Two years earlier, when I'd received my naturalization certificate, I had modified my first name—from Mansour to Mansur—in the hopes that more people would pronounce it correctly. The change mostly worked. But now, I was facing a new problem.

"Dr. Noodle," the call would come over the intercom system, "your patient is ready."

"Dr. Noodle, there's a call for you on line two."

"Dr. Noodle, please come to the front desk."

I patiently explained to the receptionist that my last name was pronounced Nur (rhymes with fur) dell (like the farmer in the dell). Nur. Dell. Nur-dell. For whatever reason, she simply couldn't say it correctly. When patients and even colleagues started referring to me as Dr. Noodle, I asked everyone to simply call me Dr. Dell. Legally, my last name is Nurdel, but thirty years later, my patients and staff still know me as Dr. Dell.

One patient who had no problem saying my last name was a fellow Persian. During his examination, I noticed that the optic nerve in his right eye was enlarged, a problem that could indicate an earlier injury or trauma. "Have you been hit in the eye in the past?" I asked him. No, he said, not that he could remember. We chatted a bit about our past lives in Iran. As he was headed out of the exam room to pick out eyeglasses, the patient stopped, turned back, and looked at me, his eyes wide. "Wait! I was kicked in the face while in high school in Arkansas," he said. "It was during the U.S. Embassy hostage siege. A classmate went after me because he knew I was Iranian. I didn't see the attack coming. He punched me in the stomach, and while I was doubled over, his boot connected with my eye. I couldn't see for a week." Yes, I told the patient, that traumatic incident twenty years earlier could have damaged his eye.

———

Chapter Thirty-Three

Denver, 1997

Receiving my Doctor of Optometry degree should have been the highlight of my year. It is still one of my proudest moments. Eight years after arriving in America with a tattered Farsi-English dictionary, I was both a citizen and a doctor. But my elation was surpassed by news from Iran. My parents finally had passports!

In the mid-1990s, the government had started issuing passports to older Bahá'ís who were no longer considered to be threats. Still, being allowed to have a passport and actually receiving one are two different things.

In 1994, *Agha* and *Maman* made several trips to the passport office to submit their applications. At each visit, *Agha* was interrogated about his faith. "Your parents were Muslims," the passport official said while looking over *Agha's* application. "You shouldn't be a Bahá'í. Go back to being a Muslim, and I'll give you a passport." When *Agha* said no, he was laughed at, ridiculed, and called *najis*. No one would even acknowledge *Maman*, who sat silently in a chair tucked in a far corner, listening to people belittle her husband. "Go home, old man," they told my father. "And don't come back."

But *Agha* and *Maman* persisted. After his trips to the passport office, many interrogations, and humiliating moments, the officials gave *Agha* a passport. They still wouldn't acknowledge *Maman*. *Agha* refused to travel without her, so the passport was useless. It expired after two years.

Mansur with his parents in Istanbul, Turkey, in 1997.

I had hoped to finally see my parents after I finished optometry school, and we made plans to meet up in Turkey. But they still needed passports. During one of the visits to the passport office, *Maman* pled with the official, tears welling up in her eyes. "Please, I haven't seen my son in ten years. We are only going to Istanbul. Please, think of how your mother would feel being away from her son for so long." The official wasn't moved. "You can become a Muslim and get a passport," he sneered at my parents. Then, with a finger pointed at my mother, he told my father, "Don't bring her back here. She's not getting a passport." *Maman* let out a sob. Clutching *Agha's* hand, they left the office defeated. I was as heartbroken as they were when they shared the sad news with me. I couldn't muster the energy to be angry at my country. This is how it had always been for Bahá'ís.

About three months later, *Agha* received notice that the passports were ready. *Agha* and *Maman* were shocked and so happy. But when they got to the office, the worker handed one passport to *Agha*. Once again, there was no passport for *Maman*. "I want you go to Turkey and see Mansur without me," *Maman* told *Agha*. "You need to see our son." *Agha* didn't like the idea, but it seemed that *Maman* was never going to get a passport. At least one of them could visit with me. When they got home, *Agha* handed the passport to Iraj and explained that he would be going alone to Turkey because the office still wouldn't issue a passport to *Maman*.

Iraj was furious as he took the passport from Agha and looked it over. "*Maman*! *Maman*!" Iraj shouted excitedly, a big smile on his face. "You can see Mansur! You're on *Agha's* passport!"

My illiterate parents didn't understand the writings on the passport. Iraj pointed to *Maman's* name on the passport and explained that she was listed as *Agha's* companion. As long as she traveled with *Agha*, she could go wherever he went. I don't know if the passport office made this stipulation because of their faith. The government has never thought highly of women overall, so it's possible that even Muslim women weren't allowed at the time to travel out of the country without a male escort.

Agha later shared that *Maman* literally jumped for joy, shouting, and hugging everyone. While she had encouraged *Agha* to go without her, it was clear from her enthusiastic celebration that it would have broken her heart to stay behind. I jumped for joy, too, when they called with the news that they could both legally leave Iran. I would see my parents for the first time in almost a decade!

Immediately after my May graduation, I flew to Istanbul, where I was reunited with an older, frailer version of the parents I had left behind. When we embraced at the airport, none of us cared about Persian decorum or the reining in of emotions. We were blubbering messes. We hugged. We cried. We left wet kisses on each other's cheeks. In the years since I'd fled Iran, I had seen a lot of the Middle East, Central Asia, the United States, and the former Soviet Union. But this trip to Turkey marked the first time my parents had crossed the Iranian border.

For ten days, I showed them some of my favorite places in Turkey. Even though Iran bordered the Arabian and Caspian Seas, *Maman* had never seen the ocean. I watched her face light up with delight as her feet sank into the sand and the cold salt water encircled her ankles. *Maman* had never worn a hijab or burka. Still, she and *Agha* were a bit scandalized by how much skin women showed at the beach. Equally shocking to them were the public displays of kissing, hand holding, and hugging among couples. I laughed. By American standards, all we saw was quite modest.

We spent most of our time catching up. There were years of stories to share. I heard about my siblings' weddings and their spouses. Remarkably, we had learned that my brother Behrouz's wife, Parisa, had been imprisoned in Urmia at the same time as Siamak's wife, Jaklin.

Parisa had planned to become a nurse until the government put an end to her university studies. Parisa's father went to prison in October 1981 after guards ransacked the family home and confiscated Bahá'í materials. His death sentence was later commuted to life in prison. Because of his so-called criminal actions, the government took possession of his half of the family home. Parisa's mother was allowed to retain her ownership of the house, but authorities built a particle board wall down the middle of the structure and moved in another family. With that demeaning act finished, Parisa's family assumed the worst was over.

They were wrong.

Revolutionary Guards raided their half of the home again in January 1983. After finding materials they deemed questionable, the guards arrested twenty-three-year-old Parisa, her two sisters (the youngest was sixteen), and two brothers. Her mother, as well as an older brother who wasn't home at the time, were spared. Guards often left one family member free so they would spend their days in anguish over the loss of their loved ones. It was a form of emotional torture.

Parisa and her siblings were placed separately into cement cells so small and narrow that their heads and feet brushed the walls when they were lying prone on the concrete slab. She was blindfolded when guards walked her from the cell into the interrogation room, where she was forced to sit, still blindfolded, with her back to her captors. The men demanded to know who Parisa had voted for in the last Local Spiritual Assembly election. Parisa said she couldn't remember. The frustrated interrogators threatened to whip her bare feet with wire cables. Foot caning is a common and intensely painful torture method often used in Iranian prisons. If Parisa didn't come up with those names within twenty-four hours, she would be flogged. In the end, she wrote down the names of Bahá'ís she knew to be dead or out of the country.

Guards hauled out family-photo albums seized during the home raid and forced Parisa to name everyone in the photographs. Lastly, they asked her to write down everything she knew about the Bahá'í Faith. In her writings, Parisa focused on the faith's acceptance of all people, regardless of religious beliefs, and the doctrine to help others. After two weeks in solitary confinement and grueling hours of questioning, guards released all of the family members, except for Parisa and her twenty-five-year-old brother, who received life sentences.

Parisa was placed into the section of the women's prison that housed the most violent offenders. There were thirty-five inmates in each small cell. Six women slept on each set of bunk beds—three on the top, three on the bottom. They never went outside. On visiting days, Parisa's family would stand outside for hours, enduring freezing cold temperatures or the blazing sun, in the hopes of spending ten minutes with her, her brother, or her father. Often, they were sent away.

It was during her second year in prison, in 1984, that Parisa met Jaklin. When the two women discovered that they were guilty of the same criminal offense—being Bahá'ís—they quickly bonded. Parisa took Jaklin, who was close in age to Parisa's youngest sister, under her wing and protected her as any good big sister would do. Mercifully, Jaklin was sent home after three months in that horrible place. Parisa was behind bars for almost seven years until, in a rare act of clemency, she was freed, along with her brother and father.

Parisa and Behrouz wed in 1989, the same year she was released from prison. She is the great-granddaughter of our great-uncle Heydar, so our families knew each other and arranged the marriage while Parisa was still incarcerated. I marveled at the photographs of their four children and the other nephews and nieces I had yet to meet. My heart ached. I desperately wanted to see my siblings and meet these new family members. I didn't know if it would ever happen.

My parents knew bits and pieces about my time in America and my pilgrimage to Azerbaijan, but now there were endless hours to fill them in on all that I had experienced. I brought postcards of the various cities I had visited, as well as photos of my other families, the Lerners and Kimseys. *Maman* couldn't stop touching my face, my hands, my back. She held tight to my arm wherever we went as if afraid to let go for fear that I would disappear again. I understood her need to anchor us together. Our time together was over sooner than any of us was ready to say goodbye again. This time, our farewells were more optimistic. Now that my parents had passports, they could travel to the United States. When I had left my family in 1988, my destiny was uncertain. None of us knew if I would make it out of Iran alive. Now, I was an American citizen returning to the land of the free to start the next chapter in my life.

– – –

Before committing fully to launching my career in Denver, I entertained potential job prospects in the Midwest, Northeast, and South. I talked to a retiring optometrist in Boardman, Ohio, outside of Youngstown, who was interested in selling his practice. But after nine years in the Midwest— and after seeing the breathtaking beauty of Colorado—I couldn't imagine putting permanent roots down in that small Ohio town. I considered joining optometry practices in Boston and Atlanta. But the Rocky Mountains kept calling.

At the end of June, I stuffed my belongings into my Nissan Sentra and headed west.

Once again, the Kimseys welcomed me into their home. I worked in the optical lab of a Denver eye clinic for several months until I received my Colorado Optometry License and was hired at an eye-surgery center. I stayed there for three years, working alongside ophthalmologists and honing my surgical skills. I moved into different apartments. I stayed close to the Kimseys and became actively involved with the Bahá'í community and the Local Spiritual Assembly. I interviewed to join an optometry practice as an associate and was shocked when the person told me that my accent was a detriment. Patients wouldn't be able to understand me, she said. There was no way they could bring me onto the team. It was one of the first outwardly prejudicial experiences I had in America. Hurt and confused, I didn't know what to do with this feedback except continue to improve my English, which everyone else told me was already exceptionally good.

I took out some of my job frustration on the soccer field, joining an adult league. It was there that I met James Kani, a fellow Persian. James Kani was born into a Muslim family from the Turkish part of Iran, but he no longer followed the Islamic ways. He'd earned his optometry degree from a midwestern university in Illinois. We had so much in common and became fast friends. During one soccer match in October of 1998, my knee twisted in the wrong direction, and I felt a popping sensation. I had torn my anterior cruciate ligament, or ACL. The timing couldn't have been worse. In just a few weeks, I was booked to go on a 10-day pilgrimage offered through the Bahá'í World Centre. I would be visiting Jerusalem, Bethlehem, Haifa, and other holy sites held sacred by Bahá'ís, Christians, Muslims, and Jews. Surgery to repair the tear would have to wait.

As the youngest, and probably the fittest, person in a group of eighty Bahá'ís, I had planned to walk to as many sites as possible. With a bum knee and crutches, I was now relegated to riding in a van with the more senior silver-haired travelers. Despite my mobility issues, I'm thankful every day that I went ahead with that trip. Since my original visit in 1998, I've been back to the region twice. Unfortunately, continual civil discord and fighting have made it too dangerous to access many of the sites I was privileged to see.

When I returned to the United States, it was time to fix my knee injury. Surgery was slated for late December. Few people wanted to undergo eye surgery during the holidays, so it was a good time to take off a couple of weeks to recover. ACL surgery in the 1990s was much more extensive than it is today. Arthroscopic surgery—which uses small incisions and lets a patient go home the same day—was still in its infancy. I underwent a more complicated surgical procedure that involved cutting and removing the patellar tendon from below my kneecap and using it to repair the torn ACL. I had multiple incisions that were several inches long. After spending a night in the hospital, and being shown how to do physical-therapy exercises from bed, the hospital sent me home.

Maneuvering into and out of the taxi, and then into my apartment, left me exhausted and in pain. I was on day two of a six-week recovery period where I wasn't supposed to put any weight on my injured leg. I had absolutely no idea how I was going to manage basic things like grocery shopping, cooking, bathing, or getting to my follow-up doctor appointments. As I sat on my couch, my swollen, throbbing leg propped up on pillows, I realized that now would have been a good time to have a girlfriend. Or my *Maman*. I needed help, so I called the one person who I could always count on: Tofigh. For two weeks, Tofigh shopped, chauffeured, and helped me figure out how to perform tasks while using crutches. In return, I helped him figure out the next steps he needed to take to fulfill his dream of becoming a doctor.

Since earning his bachelor's degree, Tofigh had floated from one meaningless job to another. He had paused his job delivering pizzas to come to Denver and be my caregiver. For a while, he worked for the forestry service, planting trees. In his heart, Tofigh knew he was meant to be a physician. Unfortunately, his poor college marks during his breakup meant no Canadian medical school would consider him. After talking with me, Tofigh had a new plan: He would apply to medical school in the Caribbean. These island schools were eager to take international students. I was certain he would get in.

———

Chapter Thirty-Four
1999

When my knee healed, I headed to Vancouver in April 1999 to visit Tofigh. He was busy applying to medical programs, and I thought it might be my last chance to see him before he moved. As I always did when I visited a city, I went to the Bahá'í Center. While there, I met a stunning young woman. Roza Niazi's family had lived in Canada since 1985, two years after they fled Iran. Our encounter was brief. We talked just long enough to exchange pleasantries and inquire about the areas of Iran we hailed from, and then Roza had to be somewhere else. I couldn't stop thinking about her. Roza was beautiful. Her long, black hair shimmered with shades of caramel. She had fawn-like brown eyes and a flirtatious smile. Her profession as a nurse showed that she was compassionate, a giver. Roza looked to be about twenty-five—much too young to be interested in someone ten years older.

A few weeks after my return to Denver, Tofigh called. I thought it was awfully soon for us to catch up since we had just seen each other. "So, how was your visit to the Bahá'í Center?" Tofigh asked. *What an odd question*, I thought. "Did you meet anyone?"

"What do you mean?" I asked him, my heart racing. I hadn't mentioned Roza to Tofigh. What was he getting at?

"I hear you met a pretty woman named Roza. She's been asking about you."

I couldn't believe it! I tried to control my excitement. "Yes, I met Roza. She seems terrific, but a bit too young for me."

"What are you talking about?" Tofigh asked in surprise. "She's thirty. That's only five years' difference."

Yet again, I was shocked. The age gap between us wasn't nearly as large as I'd feared. Roza's beauty made her look younger.

"She asked my friend Mark what he knew about you," Tofigh said. "If you're interested in talking to her—and it sounds like you are—call Mark to get her number."

I hung up the phone. I debated whether I should wait a day or two to call Mark so I didn't appear too eager. That thought lasted about five seconds before I had Mark on the line. I hadn't thought through what to say, so we exchanged a few pleasantries until I awkwardly asked, "Do you remember Roza?"

"Roza? Sure, I remember Roza. In fact, she's right here," and before I could say anything else, I could hear Mark yelling, "Roza! It's that guy from America, Mansur. He wants to talk to you."

I barely had time to register the fact that I was about to speak to Roza before her tentative "Hello?" touched my ear.

"Hello, Roza! What a surprise! What are you doing there?" I hoped she couldn't sense the conflicting emotions I was experiencing. I was anxious. I wasn't expecting to talk to her right this second. I hadn't prepared anything to say. It turned out, Roza was attending a Bahá'í marriage workshop taking place at the home of Mark and his wife. These types of relationship workshops were commonly held as a way for singles and couples to learn more about the faith's perspectives on commitment and marriage. Not wanting to keep Roza from her class—and completely unprepared to have a meaningful conversation—I asked if I could call her another time at her home. She said yes.

I spent a few days thinking through what I wanted to say. The fact was that I was a 35-year-old bachelor who was ready to settle down and have a family. By this point, all of my siblings, including my youngest brother, Iraj, were married and raising children. Now that I was a doctor, an American citizen, and working in a rewarding, well-paying career, it was time for the next logical step: marriage. If Roza had lived nearby, I would have taken her out a few times, gotten to know her better, and gauged whether she was ready for commitment, too. As it was, we were on the same continent, but living in different countries. I didn't have the luxury of a long, drawn-out courtship. During the first phone call, I laid everything out for Roza. We spoke in English because we both needed the practice.

"I'm not interested in having a girlfriend," I nervously told her. "I'm looking for a life partner, someone who wants to share a life together." To my relief, Roza said that she, too, wasn't interested in casually dating. She was all in for a bigger commitment. Had Roza felt differently, I probably would have wished her the best and ended the phone call within five minutes. As it was, we spoke for three hours that night. These marathon phone conversations became our nightly ritual. I told her about growing up in Harvan and my family's life in Tabriz. I didn't feel comfortable sharing details on the phone about what led to me leaving my family behind in Iran. Today, even though I know nobody is listening to my conversations, I remain a bit paranoid about oversharing information on the phone. That feeling of being watched is a hard one to shake.

I learned that Roza's departure from Iran had gone a bit more smoothly than mine. Still, it wasn't without peril. Roza grew up in Babol, a city located about 140 miles northeast of Tehran, between the northern slopes of the soaring Elburz Mountains and the southern coastal waters of the Caspian Sea. Called the "City of Orange Blossoms," Babol is famous for its orange farms. Although I had never made it that far north while living in Iran, I'd always heard that Babol was one of the country's loveliest cities.

Roza's maternal grandparents were profitable landowners. By Bahá'í standards, the family was quite well-to-do. Roza's parents both worked at the city's health department: her father, Iraj, as a data analyst; her mother, Eshrat, in a vaccination program. Tending to the sick and less fortunate was in the family's blood. Iraj was on the Local Spiritual Assembly, a position that often brought death threats to him and his family.

Roza's grandparents were leery of the changes taking place throughout the country even before Ayatollah Khomeini seized power. Sensing that life would only get harder for Bahá'ís, in the 1970s, they sent the youngest of their four sons to the Philippines, where he studied to become a pharmacist. His subsequent move to Canada helped secure the family's relocation to that country nearly a decade later.

As the family feared, treatment of Bahá'ís worsened after the Islamic Revolution. Roza's uncles, who once held prominent, rewarding careers—as a cardiologist, engineer, and mathematics teacher—were no longer permitted to work in their fields. In 1983, the men paid smugglers to get them to the United Nations Refugee Center in Pakistan. Once settled, they sent for the rest of the family. Roza, her parents, and her siblings, along with an aunt and two younger cousins, left Iran. Her widowed grandmother stayed behind. She wouldn't leave her one daughter who had married a Muslim man and converted to Islam.

From Tehran, the families flew to Zahedan, a city about twenty-five miles south of where the borders of Iran, Afghanistan, and Pakistan meet. In a village on the outskirts of the city, they met the three smugglers tasked with getting them out of the country. Roza was shocked at how young the men looked. Unlike the mountain-hardy, middle-aged Kurdish men who led me out of Iran, these smugglers still had pimples. Their thin arms and slender upper bodies didn't seem strong enough to get the family past any ruffians they might encounter on the journey. By Roza's assessment, she and the smugglers were close to the same age. Roza no longer felt confident about her family's chances, but they were at these smugglers' mercy.

Roza's father and aunt wedged themselves into the cab of a pickup truck with the driver. The rest of the family climbed into the open truck bed with the other pubescent men. Roza remembers drifting in and out of sleep during the drive, her twelve-year-old sister Romina's head resting and bouncing against her shoulder. About four hours into the 500-mile drive to the Pakistan border, Roza was startled awake by her *Maman* pounding on the back of the truck cab. "Stop! Stop!" she shouted.

When the driver pulled over, Eshrat insisted that the smugglers turn back. She claimed to have left valuable jewelry hidden in the village home where the family had spent the previous night. Roza's family needed these valuables to help pay their way to Canada. The smugglers, as well as Roza's father, tried to convince Eshrat that they had covered too much ground. Turning back would take up the rest of the day and further delay the family's escape. Eshrat insisted. She even offered to give some of the jewelry to the smugglers as payment for their trouble. Reluctantly, the driver turned the truck around.

During the return trip, Eshrat tried to look reassuringly at her children, but Roza could tell that her *Maman* was scared. Roza assumed she was worried about the jewelry. If someone else had already found the treasure, how would the family pay for their escape? As the village came into sight and the truck started to slow, Eshrat shouted at the children. "Be-par! Be-par!" Roza didn't understand what was happening, but she and her siblings followed Eshrat and jumped out of the still-moving truck. Eshrat sprinted to one of the homes, shouting for help. As the villagers gathered, Eshrat proclaimed that she'd overheard the two smugglers in the truck bed plotting to kill Roza's father and eleven-year-old brother so they could have their way with the women. No one would be any wiser, they figured, if the family never reached their destination. Bahá'ís went missing all the time in Iran.

Eshrat hadn't left the jewelry. It was a ruse to get her family out of harm's way.

The villagers, who relied on the smuggling operation to support their families, turned on the smugglers. This sort of plotting and deception was not tolerated. Roza and her family were ushered into a home while the village men dealt with the teenagers. The next morning, the family headed out again, this time with older men as their escorts.

With sufficient bribes, the family easily slipped into Pakistan. They traveled by minibus to the United Nations Refugee Center in Quetta, 350 miles away, near the Afghanistan border. From there, the family went to Abbottabad to stay with Roza's uncles, who had been living there for a couple of months. This affluent city outside of the Pakistan capital of Islamabad made history in 2011, when U.S. military forces executed Osama bin Laden, leader of the Islamist terrorist group al-Qaeda, thought to be responsible for the September 11, 2001 attacks, as he hid inside a compound in the city. At the time of Roza's stay, the city was known for its wealth and proximity to one of Pakistan's most revered military academies. Roza and her family stayed in Abbottabad for two years before moving to Canada.

— — —

During one of our many nightly phone calls, I told Roza about how I'd evaded being set up on dates by telling co-workers that I was in love with Princess Diana. Like most of the world, I was crushed when the Princess died in a senseless and tragic car accident. Roza confessed that she had also dodged well-meaning co-workers and friends intent on fixing her up. The next words she said made me smile: "I'm happy in my life and my career. I don't want to settle for just anyone. I'm waiting for the right person with the right qualities and whom I feel is worthy of a lifetime commitment." She didn't say that I was Mr. Right, but I thought it might be implied.

Of course, our late-night phone calls were no substitute for being together. Roza and I had spent less than five minutes in the same room. I hadn't met her family. It was possible we weren't meant to be a couple. Toward the end of May, I flew to Vancouver to see if the spark was really there—for her. I was certain Roza was the one for me. I spent the entire flight thinking through scenarios of what might happen. I considered myself to be a likeable, fairly good-looking guy. I was committed to my faith, family, and medical calling, and I would be fully committed to my wife and the family I'd hoped to have. If there was a connection, I wanted our long-distance courtship to be as short as possible. The decision about how fast the relationship would progress—or whether it progressed at all—wasn't solely up to the couple. The Bahá'í Faith views marriage not just as a union of two people, but as a uniting of two families. For this reason, both sets of parents must give written consent to the Local Spiritual Assembly for a wedding to happen. I knew one couple who'd waited six years before the bride's parents finally gave their blessing. I didn't want to wait that long to marry Roza.

When I arrived at Roza's parents' house, I was so happy to see her. Without thinking, I wrapped her in a hug. She blushed and glanced over her shoulder at her parents standing behind her. They didn't look pleased. I had been in her presence for less than a second, and already I had embarrassed her and offended her parents. There was still time to redeem myself. I asked her parents for permission to court their daughter. They agreed. Roza and I spent our days exploring Vancouver. Meals with her family were delicious and reminded me of home. Unfortunately, my stomach was constantly in knots, so it was hard to enjoy the wonderful food. I so very much wanted her family to like me—for Roza to like me. She was even more beautiful than I remembered. I couldn't believe someone so gorgeous was interested in me. Later in our relationship, Roza shared that one of the things that set me apart from other guys was my reserved manner with her. She was used to men fawning over her. I had hastily decided I was too old for Roza, so I was respectful, not flirtatious (I am not flirtatious by nature, in any case) when we met. Surprisingly, she thought I was playing hard to get!

Roza was also very smart and kind; she had a fantastic sense of humor. I was relieved that our conversations in person were as effortless as they were on the phone. We still had so much to learn about each other—and so much history to catch up on. The days went by much too fast. Toward the end of my visit, Roza and I went to a bookstore. I laughed when I saw her book selection: *Men Are From Mars, Women Are From Venus*. Was she trying to tell me something? I don't remember what book I chose. What sticks in my memory instead is the two of us cozying up together on an overstuffed loveseat in a corner of the store. Roza rested her head on my shoulder and opened her book. Soon, I heard soft snores. She was comfortable enough to have drifted off to sleep. I knew then that I was going to marry her.

Later, I would learn that Roza had her own way of knowing that I was the man for her. Months before I visited the Vancouver Bahá'í Center, Roza dreamt that she would meet her future husband there. When we first met, she felt compelled to learn more about me, partly because of that dream. Our time together was too short, but it confirmed for me that Roza was the person I wanted to spend the rest of my life with.

We made plans for Roza to come to Denver in June. That didn't give me much time to plan a proposal. I enlisted the help of Romina, Roza's younger sister. I had no idea what women wanted in an engagement ring. While out shopping one day, Romina asked Roza to go inside a jewelry store with her to look at some necklaces. Romina slyly drew Roza over to the case with sparkling diamond rings and pointed out the ones that she liked. "What ring do you like, Roza?" she asked. Roza pointed to a white gold band with a dainty round center diamond and tiny sparkling stones on each side. It was part of a set that came with a simple white gold wedding band. As soon as Romina called with the information, I called the jeweler and purchased the rings, which Romina picked up the next day. That part was finished, but I still needed to get the rings to Denver. Once again, Romina came to my rescue.

"You should take a gift to Mansur," she told Roza. I genuinely like wearing suits both professionally and outside of work, too. Roza picked out an exquisite tie, which Romina offered to wrap. She slipped the engagement ring and wedding band in with the tie before wrapping the box. Roza carried that box in her purse, onto the plane, and all the way to Denver, never suspecting what was really inside. When Roza handed the elegantly wrapped present to me, I thanked her and set it aside. I could tell she was hurt that I didn't open it right away, but I didn't want the rings to fall out and ruin my surprise. On Friday, June 18, 1999, Roza and I drove to the mountains and took a carriage ride to a romantic restaurant. I carried a bag with a dozen red roses (Roza thought I had brought sweaters to keep us warm in the chilly mountain air). The engagement ring was wedged into my sock, which was the only safe place I could think of to stow it. I told our server about my plans and asked him to use my camera to snap a few photos when I proposed.

While Roza was looking at the beautiful Rocky Mountains, I fished the ring out of my sock and steered her toward the cozy fireplace. There, I followed the American custom and got down on one knee, held out the ring, and asked that momentous question.

The expressions on Roza's face changed from confusion to disbelief. I was still waiting for a look of joy. For a "Yes! I'll marry you!" Instead, Roza walked away in a bit of a daze, stunned by my proposal, and by the appearance of a ring that had somehow made its way from a Canadian jeweler to a Colorado mountain lodge.

"How did you get this ring?" she exclaimed. "This is the ring I looked at with Romina!" The ring seemed to have stunned her more than the proposal.

While I remained awkwardly down on one knee, ring still nestled in my outstretched hand, our server hovered nearby, camera at the ready, waiting almost as anxiously as me for Roza's answer.

She said yes.

— — —

In July I flew to Vancouver, where Roza and I received her parents' verbal consent to wed. Back in Iran, my parents were elated that I had found someone who completed me. My bride didn't have to be Persian or a Bahá'í, but the fact that we shared these commonalities helped cement our families' bonds. In accordance with Bahá'í law, both sets of parents sent their written consent for our union to the Local Spiritual Assembly in Vancouver, where we planned to wed.

All of Roza's family was in Vancouver. We made plans for an October 16 wedding, which meant that Tofigh, who was set to start medical school in the Caribbean in January, could attend. Afterwards, Roza and I would start our new life in Denver. As a nurse, Roza could work anywhere. It was more complicated for me to get a medical license in Canada and re-establish myself in a different country.

One month before the wedding, while Roza was in Denver for a visit, she suggested that we go to Immigration Services to make sure we had all of the necessary documentation for her move after the wedding. While there, we were shocked to learn that, if we went through with our plans to marry in Canada, Roza would have to stay there for up to two years while the U.S. government processed her request for permanent residency. She wouldn't be allowed to move or visit me in the United States during this time. However, if we changed our plans and got married in America, Roza could apply for permanent residency immediately. She would be free to visit her family in Canada after requesting and receiving what the federal government calls "advance parole." While the term sounds criminal, advance parole is really just a travel document that allows someone to travel abroad while waiting for a Green Card. If a person leaves the country without this travel document while the Green Card is pending, the government automatically invalidates the permanent-residency request. An American wedding meant Roza could freely travel between the U.S. and Canada. We scrapped the Vancouver wedding plans as quickly as we had thrown them together (losing deposit money in the process) and started making plans for a ceremony in Denver.

Six months after we first met, Roza and I wed on October 1, 1999, at the Denver Bahá'í Center. Her parents and sister, as well as Tofigh, attended. My parents listened on the phone, and *Agha* blessed our union with a prayer during the ceremony. It was a day of much love, laughter, and celebration. My only regret was that my family couldn't physically be there to celebrate this momentous day and meet my beautiful bride.

1999—Roza running away after seeing the ring.

———

Chapter Thirty-Five
2000–2008

While the world worried about Y2K and the changing of the calendar to the double aughts, I was the happiest and most hopeful I had ever been. The year 2000 held much promise.

Tofigh was now attending medical school in the Dominican Republic and solidly on his way to earning his MD.

I was in serious discussions with my friend James Kani about a possible business venture. In June, we purchased six metro-Denver optometry practices and vision centers.

My parents received their Green Cards. In July, they traveled to the United States for the first time to meet their daughter-in-law, who was then four months pregnant with our first child. As I drove them to our recently purchased four-bedroom home on the outskirts of Denver, *Agha* and *Maman* commented on how much the topography reminded them of Iran. They understood why I'd put down roots in Colorado.

As a farmer, *Agha* was also a fan of the weather. During summer days, temperatures in Denver often hit well into the nineties—just like in Iran. But from June through August, you could count on late-afternoon, monsoon-fueled thunderstorms to roll over the Front Range and soak the parched earth. It was great farming weather. "America is blessed with so much goodness," *Agha* said. "Even the weather is good."

While Colorado and Iran shared some geographical similarities, people's ways of living were very different. "People
are like rabbits here," *Agha* noted. "Always go, go, go. Where
is everyone going? Why so busy?" I laughed, remembering
that I had the same thought upon my arrival to the United
States. Americans are forever on the move. There's always
somewhere to be, something happening, someplace else
to get to. Without being aware of it, I had become like the
Energizer Bunny myself. In just a few months, I had started
a new business, purchased a new home, and was getting
ready to welcome my first child into the family. There was
little time for rest.

When my parents arrived, I found myself with another
job: interpreter. Residents of Tabriz, like those in Harvan,
speak Azeri. In Babol, where Roza grew up, everyone speaks
Farsi. My parents still had little mastery of Farsi, and Roza
didn't know Azeri. Conversations between my wife and my
parents were a humorous mix of broken Farsi, Azeri, and
miming. It reminded me of my struggles communicating
with the Kurdish-speaking smugglers.

Agha and *Maman* stayed with us for the birth of their
grandson. Their presence was a blessing in many ways.
Ryan Anees made his entry into the world on December
31, 2000. I had long ago discovered that Americans' idea
of ringing in the New Year is nothing like Persian *Nowruz*,
which involves weeks of festivities, family gatherings, and
merriment. Still, when Roza went into labor on New Year's
Eve, I thought we were lucky that our child would be born
on a day that the entire world celebrates.

My parents waited for hours at the hospital to meet their
grandson while Roza labored. I was so proud to introduce

them to Ryan, a ruddy-cheeked baby with a mop of black hair. Ryan entered the world with a fierce wail. As our son nestled sleepily in Roza's arms, I asked *Maman* if she wanted to hold her grandson. I was surprised when she shook her head. "No, he is where he belongs," she said, looking adoringly at Roza and child. *Maman* knew that Roza needed that bonding time with her firstborn. It was too soon to take him out of his mother's arms. Besides, we all thought there would be plenty of time to cuddle and spoil Ryan when he was home.

But within a few hours after his birth, a nurse noticed Ryan having what appeared to be a seizure while he was in the nursery. They quickly moved him into the hospital's neonatal intensive care unit, where fragile babies receive the highest-level medical care. There, doctors gave him phenobarbital, an antiseizure medication. When Roza and I finally saw Ryan again six hours later, he was enclosed in a plastic bubble, with wires taped to his skin. Monitors blinked and beeped. He didn't look sick. He looked peaceful. Healthy. Phenobarbital is a powerful sedative. Ryan barely stayed awake long enough to nurse. He didn't cry or fuss. He was too sleepy to make a sound.

For the first three days, doctors administered various treatments, including infusions of calcium and magnesium. Finally, Roza asked them to try an intravenous nutrition feeding called *total parenteral nutrition* that often helped the elderly patients in her care. The treatment seemed to work, and Ryan's seizures stopped. But Roza and I couldn't celebrate. The doctors were less than encouraging about our son's future. They were concerned that the seizures had deprived Ryan's brain of oxygen, causing brain damage. "You should be prepared for your son never to walk or talk," the doctors told us. "He may need lifelong care."

Roza and I both worked in medical fields. But when it is your child whose life is in jeopardy, none of that medical training matters. We weren't pediatricians or seizure experts. We believed what the doctors told us. We steeled ourselves to take our son home to love and care for him for the rest of our days.

When Roza called her parents with the news about Ryan's condition, they booked the next flight to Denver. Upon laying their eyes on Ryan, sleeping peacefully inside his plastic bubble at the intensive care unit, they couldn't believe that their healthy-looking, dark-haired grandson was unwell. "The doctors are wrong," Eshrat said definitively. She seemed so sure of it. I didn't know what to think.

While Ryan was still in the hospital, I attended a dear friend's memorial service. Archie Evans and I had served together on the Local Spiritual Assembly. He was a man of pure heart. During an eye exam years prior, I saw signs that indicated Archie had diabetes. I advised him to get it checked out, and his doctor later confirmed the diagnosis. At the family's request, I said a prayer at Archie's service. I don't know what compelled me, but I started to silently speak to my departed friend. "Archie," I implored. "You are such a good man. But you have gone to the next world, and Ryan needs your help—your soul and your health—to get well. Please help Ryan get better." It was a foolish gesture that I quickly put out of my mind. I was too embarrassed to mention my pleas to my deceased friend to Roza or anyone else.

After we brought Ryan home, Roza, all four grandparents and I hovered over him nervously, vigilantly watching for signs of a seizure. He seemed like any other baby—crying when he was tired, hungry, or in need of a diaper change. He blew spit bubbles and made crooked smiles at us. Roza and I were worried that a seizure might stop his breathing in the middle of the night even as we slept with him in our bed.

One night in March, several months after Archie Evans' funeral, Roza woke me from a fitful slumber. "Mansur, I had a dream. Archie was in it." This news quickly woke me. I sat up and looked at my wife. Ryan was breathing softly by her side. "Archie said Ryan will be fine. We don't have to worry." Roza looked down at our sleeping baby. "As soon as I woke up, I knew Archie would protect Ryan, and Ryan will be fine." She was so happy, so full of hope. It was only then that I told Roza about my prayerful conversation with Archie on the day of his memorial service. "I believe Ryan will be fine, too," I said.

As Ryan grew and continued to show no signs of seizures, Roza and I enjoyed our son more and worried less. Right along with us, my parents witnessed Ryan hitting all of the expected milestones month after month. He rolled over. Grasped for toys. Held a spoon. Fed himself. Crawled. Pulled himself up. Walked. Said "Dada," and then "Mama." We held our breaths, waiting for Ryan to regress, for another seizure to hit. Practically since birth, Ryan's pediatrician had told us that she didn't see any indications that Ryan was anything but a typical, healthy baby. Still, it took Roza and me a while to accept that Ryan's pediatrician was right and that the doctors at the hospital had been wrong. By the time my parents flew back to Iran in April, we were all confident that Ryan had a bright future ahead of him.

– – –

Amidst all of my worrying about Ryan—and fretting about how Roza was handling the news that our son was sick—I continued to see patients and build up the various practices with my partner. When James Kani and I purchased the vision centers, we vowed to help the less fortunate. Our practices provide free vision services to immigrants who don't have the resources to pay. We also partner with a local women's crisis center to provide complimentary services to survivors of domestic violence.

In the early 2000s, Medicaid reimbursements for vision care were a joke. The subsidy paid $27 for eye exams and $11 for eyeglasses. Many optometrists wouldn't see Medicaid patients. James Kani and I agreed from the onset that, even if it meant losing money (which it did), we would help as many Medicaid patients as possible. At one point, we were seeing thirty people on Medicaid—essentially for free—every week. I am pleased to say that Medicaid has since improved its vision coverage. Still, our eye clinics continue to treat the largest number of Medicaid patients in Colorado.

– – –

On the morning of September 11, 2001, I was knotting my tie, minutes away from heading off to work, when terrorists crashed a plane into the north tower of the World Trade Center in New York City. Nine-month-old Ryan was sitting contentedly in his high chair, picking up pieces of strawberries in his chubby little fists and shoving them into his eager mouth. Pink juice dripped down his chin. Roza sat across from him, offering a spoonful of yogurt, her untouched cup of hot tea perched on the kitchen table safely out of Ryan's reach. The television was tuned to the local morning news.

Roza and I watched in stunned silence as the local news cut away to images of huge billows of black smoke engulfing the upper part of the building. A plane had somehow gotten off course, the broadcasters speculated. It was clear that hundreds of lives had been lost. "How would they get the people in the top part of the tower out?" Roza and I wondered out loud to each other. I should have left for work, but I couldn't pull myself away. Then, less than twenty minutes later, we watched in shock as another plane came into view, made a sharp turn, and slammed into the other tower. Ash and burning debris rained down from both buildings. I will never forget the look of horror in Roza's eyes as her head pivoted from the scenes on TV, to me, and then back to the TV. We knew, along with the rest of the country, that there was no way that planes had accidentally flown into two of the country's most recognized symbols of wealth and greatness.

America was under attack.

"Please don't let it be Hezbollah," I said to Roza. This Shia Islamist militant group was based in Lebanon but had roots in Iran. If Hezbollah were involved, all Iranians living in America would be persecuted, even those of us who weren't Muslim.

My patients were expecting me. I had to go to work. I kissed my wife and son goodbye, wishing fervently that I could turn off the TV, shut out the rest of the world, and spend the rest of the day with my family pretending none of this had happened. I had just pulled into the parking spot at work, my mind consumed with thoughts about everyone who had gone to work that day at the Twin Towers not knowing the horror that awaited them. My heart ached for their loved ones. I wiped away tears and steeled myself to greet the office staff and the first patients of the day when radio newscasters announced that a third plane had struck the Pentagon. The fourth and final hijacked plane crashed in a field in Pennsylvania less than one hour later.

By the end of that awful day, the suspected identity of the terrorist organization behind the attacks was revealed. I confess I breathed a sigh of relief when President George W. Bush uttered the words "al-Qaeda." This radical Islamic militant group, led by Osama bin Laden, had terrorist cells in Afghanistan, Iraq, Pakistan, Sudan, and other countries—but not Iran.

Until the September 11 tragedy, I had never felt the need to address my nationality or religion with patients or anyone else. If someone asked where I was from, I assumed they were curious about my accent. I would either tell them I was from Iran or that I was Persian. Both answers were true. I never felt the need to provide more information. The events of 9/11 changed that forever.

My business partner James Kani and I quickly conferred about how to handle the potential fallout the attacks might have on our professional and personal lives. While we understood that this hateful act was carried out by a small faction who had greatly strayed from the peaceful teachings of Islam, that wouldn't stop many people from placing blame on anyone perceived to be Muslim. James Kani had been raised as a Muslim, although it had been decades since he had been actively involved with the faith.

After 9/11, I continued to answer truthfully when people inquired about my origins—except now I expanded on the answer. To this day, I feel compelled to provide more information that absolves me and my family from any prejudices.

"Actually, I have an interesting story," I tell people. "I escaped religious persecution in Iran." This approach often leads to a larger discussion about the Bahá'í Faith and the injustices still happening today in my homeland. I use it as an opportunity to educate others, and also to honor my family in Iran and the Bahá'ís there who'd unjustly lost their lives.

– – –

Despite the hardships and tragedies that marred 2001, I was optimistic as the year drew to a close. Ryan was a happy, healthy, toddling, babbling one-year-old. He had never shown any signs of seizures. Roza was pregnant with our second child. I was excited about growing our family, and at the prospect of my parents visiting and meeting their new grandchild.

After the trauma of Ryan's seizures and weeklong stay in the hospital, Roza and I were apprehensive about the birth of our second child. We prayed for an uncomplicated delivery and a healthy baby. Roza went into labor on a cloudless, blue-sky Saturday in July. The delivery was too long and too difficult. She lost a lot of blood. The doctors feared for her life and for the life of our unborn baby. Had Roza given birth as my mother had in Harvan—at home, without a doctor or any hospital services, with no tap water or electricity—she and our baby would have died. Thankfully, she was in a well-equipped hospital with a well-trained, fast-acting medical team who brought our son into the world via emergency C-section.

For a few nightmarish seconds after the doctor pulled the baby from the womb, the room was silent. And then Dustin Nabil Nurdel let out a wail that let everyone on the floor know that he had arrived. Roza and I soaked in the sight of our beautiful boy, who looked so much like his older brother: the same mop of black hair, the same birthweight (six pounds, six ounces), the same dark, probing eyes. As the minutes, then hours, then days ticked by, we held our breaths waiting for Dustin to have a seizure or show other signs of trouble. He was fine.

Roza and I had planned to have at least four children. But after the intense and frightful births of both babies, we decided our family was complete. I rejoiced knowing that our sons' childhoods would be filled with a measure of peace and acceptance that Roza and I had never known. They would be able to worship as they pleased, study whatever they wanted, and love freely. I left Iran, in part, because I wanted those gifts of freedom for myself, but more importantly, I wanted them for my children.

With Green Cards in hand, my parents arrived in Denver shortly after Dustin's birth. It was our shared hope that my parents might someday become naturalized citizens. They had worked, struggled, and sacrificed all of their lives. I was now in a position to help them live the rest of their days in comfort and peace. The naturalization process required that they live in the United States for a combined total of thirty months during a five-year timespan. They couldn't be out of the country for more than six months during a twelve-month period. Unfortunately, *Agha* fell ill in 2003 while in Iran. By the time he was well enough to travel, more than half of the year was gone. *Agha* and *Maman* still had their Green Cards, but the time frame for obtaining citizenship was reset.

Around this same time, the Iranian government began issuing passports once again to Bahá'ís of all ages, not just the elderly. This change opened the door for Bahá'ís to legally leave Iran and seek refuge elsewhere. Followers no longer had to bribe smugglers and jeopardize their lives to get out. In 2005, my sister Mahin, along with her husband and their two young children, flew to Istanbul and took a bus to the United Nations center in Ankara. In forty-eight hours, Mahin and her family were granted asylum—a feat that took me nearly two weeks and almost took my life.

My status as a United States citizen meant that I could sponsor Mahin's family. Within a year, I was hugging my sister, brother-in-law, niece, and nephew at the Denver airport. Eighteen years had passed since Mahin clasped that Bahá'í charm around my neck and tearfully bid me farewell. At the time, I didn't know if I would ever see anyone in my family again. There were many times during my early years in America when the feelings of aloneness and longing for family made me ache. Now, I had a wife, two children, a sister and her family, and parents who could visit anytime they wanted. I felt incredibly fortunate.

I would have welcomed all of my family into my home in Denver, but my brothers were reluctant to leave Iran. They had wives and children of their own now. Those wives had roots in Iran, too. Relocating was still a costly and complicated endeavor even if the act of crossing the border was less risky. Despite the hardships and constant threats of arrest, torture, and even death, Iran was home, and my brothers had accepted their fates. The optical lab and eyeglass store I established in Tabriz were still lucrative. Nephews and nieces whom I had never met were now working in the family business. If I couldn't get my family out of that oppressive place, I felt good that I had left them with a productive, honorable way to make a living.

Since my brothers couldn't visit me in America—and I would be imprisoned, if not killed, if I returned to Iran—we made plans to meet up in Turkey in March of 2008. We hadn't seen one another in twenty years. My parents stayed in Iran to look after the family businesses and homes. Mahin and her family remained in Denver—it had been only a few years since she'd left Iran. The trip marked the first time that my sons, then ages six and seven, would meet their uncles. Conversely, it was the first time I would meet my sisters-in-law, nephews, and nieces.

Javad was claustrophobic, which is why he opted to spend three hours in the confines of a plane versus three days in the tight quarters of a train like Behrouz, Iraj, and their families. Both options made Javad sweaty and panicky, but the flight was over with faster. Because Javad flew his family to Istanbul, they arrived first.

With only two years separating us, Javad was both a big brother who I admired and also a friend. We had always been close. To my surprise, I found that I was nervous about seeing him. It had always been his dream to become a doctor. He was so smart. I had no doubt that he would have finished at the top of his medical-school class and gone on to become a brilliant doctor who helped others. If only the government would have allowed it. My dream was to become an architect. But here I was, the only member of our family with a medical degree. I knew Javad was happy that I had escaped Iran and done well for myself in America. Still, a part of me felt guilty that his dream was still unfulfilled.

Over the years, *Maman* had mailed photos of the family to me. I was aware that two decades had passed since I last saw Javad, and he was no longer the young man in his mid-twenties who I had left behind. Still, I was taken aback by the-almost 50-year-old man who embraced me at the airport. Time and worry had etched lines in his face. His once-jet black hair was peppered with gray and starting to thin. I noticed a little more cushion in his midriff when we hugged. But he was unmistakably my brother.

I had a similar experience when we met Behrouz and Iraj at the train station. Behrouz was now in his mid-fifties but looked even older. As the eldest of the family, he had shouldered more of the worry and responsibility of looking after our parents and all of us. Ryan and Dustin weren't sure what to think about their Uncle Behrouz's gruff demeanor and loud voice, but he soon had them laughing as he shared stories about what an annoying little brother I was, always begging to tag along with him and his friends.

Iraj, the baby of the family, was forty-one. I still thought of him as a kid, the teenager whose identity I'd used to get me out of the military service. It was a bit of a shock to see him as a husband, a father, a man.

In total, eighteen members of the Nurdel family reunited in Turkey. We spent two memory-making weeks in Istanbul. It was during this time that I first heard stories about how my departure had affected my family's lives in Iran. It seemed that Javad and Iraj, who were forced to serve in the military after evading the requirement for years, had it the worst.

Any amount of university education earned most military members a higher ranking. But not if you are Bahá'í. Javad was given the lowest rank, despite his having attended medical school. And Iraj, who went as far with his education as the government allowed (high school), was ranked below peers who had dropped out.

Originally, Javad had been assigned to an office job because he was a fast typist. But he was soon removed because the job was deemed too easy for a Bahá'í. Next, he was assigned to drive a water tanker through some of the war-torn desert areas of Iran. But the officer in charge decided he didn't want someone who was *najis* contaminating the water. "It was just like in Harvan," Javad told me. "I wasn't allowed to drink the water, or wash in the water, and then, I wasn't even fit to drive the truck that carried the water."

When my brothers correctly filled out the required documents listing all family members and their whereabouts, my location in America put an even bigger target on them. I listened, with heart in my throat and tears in my eyes, as my brothers told me about the physical and psychological torture they endured. Although Javad and Iraj served in the military at different times, they were both assigned to stand watch all night (literally stand, no sitting allowed), and then complete drills with their units during the day. This would go on for three or four days in a row, with my brothers snatching moments of rest when granted permission to use the bathroom.

They were regularly interrogated by officers about my escape. "Tell us how your brother got out. Who helped him escape? Did you help him escape?" Of course, this questioning was also filled with the usual references to Bahá'ís being filthy dogs and damned to hell. There were numerous visits with mullahs in an attempt to get my brothers to convert. There were threats against our family. Hearing this, I knew I had been right to keep my family in the dark about my escape plans. When Javad and Iraj told the officers that they didn't know how I escaped, they were telling the truth.

For most of their time in the service, my brothers worked as trash collectors during the day and watchmen at night. Picking up trash, and occasionally cleaning up human waste, was the most demeaning and lowest military position there was. The job almost always went to a Bahá'í.

I felt terrible that I was responsible for my brothers' mistreatment. And even worse that I was the only brother who hadn't served. I'd really had no idea what their time in the military was like. My brothers assured me that they would have been subjected to some level of cruelty simply because of their faith. But I knew Behrouz hadn't endured as much abuse during his time in the military. It was clear to me that I was the reason for the intensified scrutiny and torturous actions that fell upon Javad and Iraj.

I had insisted that they tell me about their experiences, but my brothers wouldn't let me dwell on the bad things. After all, I couldn't undo any of it, nor would I have done anything different. It had been too long since we'd been together. This was a happy occasion. I decided not to let the Islamic government ruin my time with my family.

Fourteen days isn't nearly enough when you've been separated from your family for two decades. Still, we squeezed in as many hugs, laughter, and stories as we could. Saying goodbye was a little easier. While the Iranian government could always change their minds and stop Bahá'ís from traveling again, we pushed away such negative thoughts and started making plans for our next get-together. I had a smile on my face for months after that trip. Seeing my brothers and their families happy and thriving soothed a wound in my soul that I hadn't realized existed.

– – –

On a Tuesday in late October, I answered a call from Jenny Lerner in Milwaukee. I knew it had to be important for her to contact me in the middle of a workday. "Gabe is missing," she said. I could feel her panic vibrating through the phone. "Please pray for him."

Gabe, the cherub-faced boy who turned me into a diehard Packers fan, was no longer a kid. After graduating from Georgetown University Law School, Gabe landed a job as a law clerk for a Superior Court judge in St. Thomas, Virgin Islands. I last spoke to Gabe shortly after he'd moved to the island at the beginning of the year. After a lifetime of frigid Wisconsin winters, Gabe was loving the warm rays and relaxing ways of island life.

It was completely out of character for Gabe to shirk any responsibilities. When he didn't show up to work on Tuesday, his supervisor, the judge, reported him missing. Investigators determined that he hadn't come to work the day before, either. The judge was off that day, and co-workers assumed her clerk was off, too. A friend had jogged with Gabe on Saturday morning. Nobody had seen him since. His car was also gone.

I was stunned. I didn't know what to say to my under-standably distraught friend. Bahá'ís went missing all the time in Iran, but not in America. We had no reason to suspect that Gabe's religious beliefs had anything to do with his disappearance, but given my past life experiences, this was where my mind naturally went. Another missing Bahá'í. I offered Jenny some halfhearted reassurances. "He probably got lost on a hike and is waiting for someone to rescue him. I'm sure he's okay. They'll find him." For the rest of the day, I waited for these hopes to solidify into truths, for word that Gabe had been found unharmed. I distractedly tended to my patients, drove home, and wrapped my sons into an embrace so tight that both boys cried out, "Ouch! Too hard, Daddy!" I eased up and then hugged them again.

Jenny called that evening to say that police had found Gabe's car. Two men had been spotted in the car on Tuesday afternoon. When police attempted to pull them over, they sped off, ultimately crashing the vehicle into a police cruiser at a roadblock, and then fled on foot into a nearby wooded area. They evaded capture for two hours. The men, seventeen and twenty-two years in age, weren't saying what happened to Gabe.

I spent Wednesday in a fog. When I hadn't heard from Jenny by the evening, I called, only to learn that the police had been questioning the suspects all day. The family still didn't know Gabe's whereabouts. Aerial search teams, as well as ground teams with scent-tracking dogs, had been scouring the island for days. Gabe's father Jerry was on his way to join in the search. He was confident he would find his boy.

When the phone rang very late that same evening, I was afraid to answer. "He's dead, Mansur," Jenny sobbed. "Gabe's dead." Police had found Gabe's body lying on the edge of a dirt path, a bullet hole in his head. He was twenty-seven years old.

Gabe had been on his way to a weekly meeting where he and other Bahá'ís mentored youth from the community. He often helped the teenagers with their homework. He came upon two young men walking along the road who seemed to need help. To Gabe, I'm sure they looked like the teens he was on his way to meet that day. Most people would have kept on driving. He offered them a ride. At some point, the older man asked Gabe to pull over so he could relieve himself. Gabe obliged. Instead of getting back into the car, the man flashed a gun, demanded Gabe's wallet, and then told Gabe to climb into the trunk of the car.

They made their way to a more wild, remote area of the island, stopped the car, yanked Gabe from the trunk, and forced him at gunpoint down the dirt path. In court proceedings three years later, the younger offender (who would go on to serve ten years of a twenty-year prison sentence and who is now free) said Gabe turned and asked, "Are you going to kill me now?" In response, the older man told Gabe to turn around and then fired at Gabe's head. The man who pulled the trigger is serving life in prison without the possibility of parole.

Jenny told me that she had last talked to Gabe a few days before he was killed. He had called to tell her that he had found the most beautiful part of the island. "Mom," he said, "I've found paradise." It was the very place where his life was taken that day.

Gabe's murder remains a dark spot on my time in America. In Iran, my heart had hardened and scarred over after years of seeing so many bodies riddled with bullet holes. It had been decades since I had borne witness to such a senseless taking of life. My softening heart held a special place for Gabe, who was like my little brother. A rage I hadn't felt in years swelled up inside of me. These men had deprived the world of a kind, intelligent, thoughtful young man all for some pocket change and wheels. Gabe's death made me weep in a way that I hadn't cried since coming to America.

Chapter Thirty-Six

2011

As my parents grew older and frailer, they began to spend more time in Iran and made fewer trips to Colorado. On their last visit to Denver, in 2011, there was a minor incident on my parents' connecting flight from Frankfurt, Germany.

For some reason, the flight attendant mistook my parents for Hispanic. After the flight took off, she asked my parents in Spanish if they were from Mexico. My parents, of course, didn't understand Spanish, but they recognized the word Mexico. *Agha* and *Maman* panicked, thinking the flight was headed to Mexico, and not America. They didn't know anyone in Mexico, and had no idea how they would get in touch with me, or how I would find them.

Agha and *Maman* kept repeating the one word they understood: Mexico. By now, the flight attendant surely knew that the Azeri words coming from my parents' mouths weren't Spanish. While she could tell they were upset, she didn't know exactly why. Fortunately, an Azeri-speaking passenger a few rows back heard the commotion. After speaking to *Agha*, he explained to the flight attendant in English that my parents had mistakenly thought they were on the wrong plane—headed to Mexico. "Oh, no, no!" the flight attendant said in English. "America! Yes, America! We're going to America!"

Hearing the words, "Yes, America!" my parents smiled and relaxed. When *Maman* told me this story after I picked them up at the airport, her distress was still evident. She was shaking. I knew the travel was getting to be too much for them. This would be their last trip to Denver.

— — —

At this point, my family had moved into a spacious home that Roza and I had meticulously designed to capture the Mediterranean feel of the stately houses in Iran that had dazzled us so much during our youth. We had purchased the land in a growing suburb south of Denver in 2003 for its sweeping views of the Rocky Mountains. It had taken six years of painstaking planning before the house was ready.

Never did I allow myself to dream that I could own a home such as this. Persian rugs adorn the gleaming marble floors in the foyer, which showcase a baby grand piano that Ryan and Dustin play. I designed the foyer specifically with the idea of hosting large Bahá'í gatherings there.

It was my parents' first time seeing the home. When I pulled into the circular drive, they looked in wonderment at me, at the house, and at each other, their eyes wide. I had come a long way from my family's one-room, clay-brick house in Harvan. *Maman* reached up and took my face into her hands. She patted my cheeks. I could see tears in both my parents' eyes.

I had been sending money to my brothers in Iran to build a three-story residence, which was completed earlier that same year. Each brother occupied one floor with their families. My parents still lived in the family home I left behind, and I faithfully sent money to help them have the latest technology and comforts of home. *Agha* seemed astonished that I had managed to help my family in Iran while also building the house of my dreams for my family here.

I showed my parents around the main-floor dining room, family room, and kitchen, and then took them upstairs to see the bedrooms and my office. Ryan, then ten, and Dustin, who had just turned nine, gleefully led their grandparents to the basement to show off the theater with its massive film screen and stereo system. "Have a seat," Ryan said as he led his grandfather by the hand to one of the black leather chairs and then pushed the button to glide it back into a reclining position. My father laughed and shook his head. "This room is bigger than Shoá Allah's cellar," he said, referring to the small underground room our family crammed into after fleeing to Tabriz. I pointed out that the recliner was a lot more comfortable than the dirt floor, too. My parents and I laughed while my sons looked on in puzzlement.

Ryan and Dustin knew I had grown up in circumstances much different than theirs, but at their young age, I didn't want to burden them with the reality of my childhood. They were Persians and members of a Bahá'í family. But they were also Americans. To my knowledge, none of their classmates called them "dogs." No one had ever said they were impure or implied that they were going to hell. They were enjoying the kind of innocent childhood I had longed for. It warmed my heart to be able to give that gift to my children.

– – –

My parents were unaware that Roza and I, along with my sister Mahin, had plotted to surprise *Agha* with a birthday celebration. He turned eighty-five that year. Because no one knew his actual date of birth, we picked August 28 for the festivities. When I was a child, Persians didn't celebrate birthdays—at least not the way Americans do. You might get a sweet treat or a small gift of some kind. But we didn't have large gatherings with people showering you with presents, candles aflame on cakes, and a spotlight shining brightly on your special day. Mahin and I felt our father deserved a party in his honor, and Roza heartily agreed.

Roza's parents, Iraj and Eshrat, flew in for the occasion. And Behrouz's son, Hooman, requested time off from the U.S. Air Force to visit with his grandparents. Mahin's family arrived early that Sunday. She joined *Maman*, Roza, and Eshrat in the kitchen to prepare a traditional Persian feast.

Soon, the sounds of laughter and the aromas of my childhood filled the home. My heart swelled. As was customary in Iran, we gathered in the family room before dinner to enjoy freshly brewed Persian tea spiced with cardamon, ginger, and cloves. We nibbled on ghorabieh, a soft, chewy almond cookie that *Maman* had brought from a Tabriz bakery. People often serve ghorabieh at engagement parties, weddings, and other festivities. I associate only happy times with the cookie's almond scent and sweet taste. As I took a bite, I was transported back to my days in Tabriz when *Maman* made the dessert to take to relatives during *Nowruz*. It was one of the few times my brothers and I ever fought to help in the kitchen. Each of us wanted to taste the batter and be the first to sink our teeth into a cookie still warm from the oven.

When the meal was ready, *Agha* and I sat across from each other at the heads of the table. I looked at my father and *Maman* seated to his left. They seemed filled with happiness at being reunited with our families, but there was no denying that they were getting more beaten down by the struggles they faced every day in Iran. I thought back to all that my parents had endured and sacrificed in order to give their children better lives. Despite these efforts, two of their children had felt compelled to leave Iran to forge brighter futures. The Nurdel family was forever splintered. My children might never be able to safely visit the country that Roza and I still fondly thought of as home. I longed to be able to take Ryan and Dustin to Iran, where they could experience the deliciousness of sour cherries and apricots plucked from the trees in an orchard in Harvan, dip their toes in Roza's beloved Caspian Sea, and run around and explore Tabriz with their cousins.

Agha's birthday celebration was to be a happy occasion. And I was so grateful to have my parents with me. When I fled Iran, I struggled with the thought that I might never see any of my family again. I knew I was fortunate to be seated at the table with my parents, my sister, and her family. The fact that Roza's family could also be with us—that they, too, had managed to escape Islamic rule—was also a stroke of good fortune. But a sadness washed over me as I thought about my brothers, sisters-in-laws, nieces, and nephews who couldn't be with us for this celebration. We would never gather around a table like this at the Tabriz homes of Behrouz, Javad, or Iraj, sharing the blessing of good food and reminiscing about our childhoods.

At that moment, I missed my brothers immensely, and an anger bubbled up inside me at the unfairness and injustice of it all. That feeling took me by surprise. I am not one to linger in the past, ruminating about life's missed opportunities and what-ifs. I prefer to focus on what is and what can be—the positive, the future. It was this attitude that helped me get over the treacherous Zagros Mountains more than two decades ago, when many would have given up and perished. It was what propelled me to fulfill my promise to become a successful doctor and allowed me to provide my family here and in Iran with many of life's comforts.

I didn't realize how far into my reflections I had gone until I heard Ryan ask, "Daaadddd! Are you ever going to pass the rice?" I looked sheepishly at Roza, who squeezed my hand. I quickly glanced at Mahin and thought I saw my sister wipe her eyes with a napkin. Perhaps they were lost in similar thoughts, too.

I inhaled the sweet, robust scent of saffron, a spice my parents brought with them whenever they visited. Iran is famous for growing the world's best saffron, and saffron rice is a staple of most Persian meals. I have never found anything comparable in America. I grabbed the dish and began loading up my plate as Ryan and Dustin groaned, waiting impatiently for their chance to dig in.

Roza, Mahin, *Maman*, and Eshrat had outdone themselves. The table was crammed from corner to corner with traditional Persian dishes. I filled a bowl with ghormeh sabzi, a flavorful stew made with lamb, sour Persian limes, kidney beans, and fenugreek—many consider this to be Iran's national dish. It was one of *Maman's* signature meals that I dreamt about as my stomach growled during the arduous trek over the mountains.

Another large bowl brimmed with khoreshte fesenjan, a Persian chicken stew made with walnuts and pomegranate seeds. Each bite of these dishes evoked a childhood memory for me. I was happy to see that, despite my children's penchant for hamburgers and pizza, they, too, were piling their plates high. *Agha* laughed and pointed at Dustin's overflowing plate while *Maman* and Eshrat beamed. My sons had a fondness for Persian dishes made with love by their grandmothers.

When dinner was over, it was time for *Agha's* birthday surprise. I clinked my knife against my glass of apple cider and stood up to toast my father. "*Agha*," I said, surprised to find myself getting choked up. I cleared my throat. "In appreciation for all that you do for your family, we proclaim today to be your day, the day of Aziz!" Everyone grabbed their glasses of cider, held them high, and cheered, "To Aziz! To *Agha*! To *Baba*!"

Agha didn't know what to think as Mahin carefully placed a double-layer, chocolate-frosted birthday cake in front of him, and his grandchildren sang the traditional American "Happy Birthday" song in English. *Agha* understood the song's meaning from watching American television shows. He turned and looked quizzically at *Maman*, who shrugged her shoulders and laughed.

"*Tavalodat mobarak!*" we all shouted as the birthday song ended.

"*Tavalodat mobarak?*" he asked, his eyes bright in wonderment.

Mahin explained that we thought it was time for him—at age eighty-five—to celebrate a birthday. Ryan and Dustin had placed a candle in the shape of the number eight on top of the cake, a leftover from Dustin's birthday the previous year. We couldn't find the number five candle, so the number eight stood alone. The boys eagerly explained to their grandfather that he needed to make a wish and then blow out the candle. "But don't tell anyone what you wish for, or it won't come true," Dustin cautioned.

Agha's shoulders quaked with laughter, and I swear his face took on a look of glee that only a child celebrating a birthday should have. *Agha* looked around the table at the beautiful family he and *Maman* had created. And then to his grandchildren's delight, he blew out the candle.

Mahin sliced the cake, putting the first plate in front of the man of honor, and then passed bigger wedges to her eager sons and nephews. Since my days spent scraping vats of chocolate at Ambrosia, I can't stomach the smell or taste of chocolate. I grabbed another ghorabieh and eagerly took a bite.

No Persian celebration is complete without dancing, and *Agha's* birthday party was no exception. Once the dishes were cleared, we headed to our grand foyer, which Roza and I had designed with dancing in mind. Roza and Eshrat brought out a teapot and plates of fresh melon, grapes, and berries (this is how a Persian dinner would typically end when birthday cake isn't on the menu). My nephew, Hooman, took over as DJ, cranking up dance favorites from Iran like Sakineh Daygezi and Bari Bakh. I'd never seen *Agha* dance, and while *Maman* and Mahin tried their best to pull him from his seat on the chaise lounge, he just shook his head *No* and laughed. As the rest of us danced, twirled, and clapped, I could see *Agha* seated on the couch, his feet tapping rhythmically to the music, a huge smile on his face.

I don't know what *Agha* wished for that day. Perhaps he wished that, one day, his entire family could safely be together again. Or he might have wished for peace for Bahá'ís everywhere. I do know that he greatly enjoyed his first, and only, birthday celebration.

– – –

During the four months that my parents were with us, they saw their grandsons off to school every morning, welcomed them home, and cheered from the sidelines of several soccer matches.

Our former home was within walking distance of my first optometry practice, and *Agha* used to walk to it nearly every day. When he grew bored, he explored the shops in the nearby strip malls. His communication was mostly a friendly nod to the store workers and an occasional tentative attempt at "Hello." But he became a regular customer at TJ Maxx. I worked out an arrangement with the store manager. *Agha* would pick out whatever he wanted—for himself, *Maman*, his children and grandchildren in Iran—and I would stop at the end of my workday to pay for and pick up the purchases. *Agha* shopped there almost daily and could always find something to buy. He was astonished that one store could sell such a variety of items.

He also marveled at the number of people who came to my practice for eye exams and eyeglasses. In Iran, a busy optical store might have four or five customers a day. I was seeing nearly ten times that many patients. In fact, the practice had outgrown its space, and my partner and I were eagerly waiting for construction to finish up on a new building that would house our optical store and six eye-exam rooms. In five years, we had become the largest eye-care center in our community of Highlands Ranch. Eventually, we would become one of the nation's top independently held eye-care centers. The new space was more than twice the size of our old one. But it wasn't close enough for *Agha* to walk to from our home, and there wasn't a TJ Maxx nearby.

I took as much pride showing *Agha* and *Maman* around the practice as I had when showing them my home for the first time. And they were equally speechless. My partner and I employed close to one hundred employees at various optical locations throughout metro-Denver. As I had done in Iran, the business was a family affair. Mahin's husband worked in the optical lab, and later Mahin became an employee, too.

— — —

When it was time to take my parents to the airport, my heart felt as heavy as it had twenty-three years earlier when we hugged goodbye before I fled Iran. I was once again in a position where I didn't know if, or when, I might see my parents again. I knew they would continue to come to America, but I could no longer ask that of them. Instead, I promised that my family would travel to Turkey as often as possible to see them. It still wasn't safe for me to return to Iran, and I doubted that I would ever feel comfortable stepping foot on that soil. Family reunions in Turkey every couple of years would have to do.

I have never second-guessed any of my decisions. I know Roza and I are fortunate to have had the opportunities to build this life together. None of it—our educations, our careers, our legally recognized marriage, our open faith, our beautiful home and family—would have been possible had we stayed in Iran.

While my brothers have found their own sense of peace and happiness in Iran, we'll never know what they could have accomplished had they been given the freedom to forge their own paths without prejudice or fear, as I did in America.

———

Epilogue

October 2022

As I write this message in October of 2022, my sons are both college students, with aspirations to pursue careers in medicine. When Ryan and Dustin each turned fifteen (what our faith considers to be the age of spiritual maturity), they chose to declare their belief in Bahá'u'lláh and become Bahá'ís. They understand that their ability to pursue and achieve their dreams is something still denied to their Bahá'í cousins in Iran. None of us take the promise of their bright futures for granted.

Agha passed away in March of 2022 at the age of ninety-six after suffering a stroke the previous year. *Maman* is eighty-three. You might mistake her for delicate, but she can still tap that powerful force that kept my siblings and me in line when we were unruly children.

When COVID-19 swept across the globe in 2020, the virus hit Iranians hard. It has given me yet another reason to worry about the well-being of my family there. The pandemic, of course, put an indefinite hold on any plans to reunite with my family in Turkey. And sadly, our last visit didn't go as we hoped.

In June 2016, Roza, the boys, and I planned to meet my parents and a nephew in Turkey. I'd passed on my love of soccer to my sons, and my family's vacation centered around attending a few EuroCup soccer matches taking place in

France. The night before we were to catch an early-morning flight from France to Turkey, ISIS terrorists detonated bombs and opened fire at the Istanbul airport. Forty-one people lost their lives, and more than 230 were injured. The airport shut down. Flights were canceled. There was no reunion. I last saw my parents in 2018, when I traveled to Turkey alone.

— — —

Nearly thirty years passed before Siamak and I met again. He flew to the United States to attend a work conference in 2017. After twenty-six years of marriage and two children, Siamak and Jaklin divorced in 2014. Siamak worked for a while as a language translator at an immigration center on Christmas Island off the coast of Australia. He currently works as a computer technician in Queensland, where he lives with his wife and their two children. The family had to cancel their plans to visit the United States in 2020, when the pandemic brought all travel to a halt. We hope to reunite when the crisis ends.

As our lives became busier with work and family, reunions with Tofigh—who achieved his dream of becoming a doctor and worked at an internal-medicine practice in Vancouver—happened less frequently. He married and had two daughters. Because getting our families together was such a challenge, I was very much looking forward to getting together with him and his family in Arizona in January 2017. Ryan and Dustin were playing in soccer tournaments, and the state's warm weather offered a perfect respite from the wintry cold weather in Canada and Colorado. A few days before Tofigh and his family were to arrive in Phoenix, he canceled. "I'm not feeling well," he said. I knew if he was feeling too poorly to make this trip, then something was seriously wrong. I pressed Tofigh for more details—his symptoms, how long he had been ill, whether he had seen a doctor or was doing what so many physicians do: self-diagnosing and treating himself. Tofigh was dodgy with his answers. "We'll talk in a couple of weeks when you're back from Arizona," he said. I wouldn't let it go. Something was wrong, and I needed to know what.

"I have cancer," Tofigh finally said. "Leukemia. And it's aggressive."

I paused long enough to digest this unexpected news: my best friend had a life-threatening disease. Then, I shifted into doctor mode. Like the medical professionals we were, Tofigh and I discussed his diagnosis and treatment options. I was dumbfounded when he admitted he'd known about the cancer for years. Leukemia can lie dormant, inactive, for long periods of time. Something had activated those cancerous cells in Tofigh's body. The cancer was back, and the prognosis wasn't good.

Soccer matches still needed to be played. I kept one eye on my children's games while standing on the sidelines, phone in hand, reading everything I could find online about the latest research and treatments. Tofigh and I were smart people, with solid healthcare backgrounds. Surely, we could find a way for him to beat this, or at the very least give him more time with his family. I reached out to medical experts in Denver and placed numerous phone calls to cancer centers throughout the country. I made plans for my family to go to Vancouver as soon as school let out in May.

I thought we had time.

By April, he was gone.

It was like losing a brother. I had spent more time with Tofigh than my own siblings over the last thirty years. Only he and Siamak truly knew the trials we overcame during that long, perilous trek out of Iran and through Turkey. Only they understood how it felt to be lost in a blizzard while the sounds of machine guns and fierce, barking dogs came at you. It was a collective effort for all three of us to make it out of Iran alive, to start our lives over with nothing. When one of us struggled, the other two stepped in and made sure no man was left behind. I thought of our bond as unbreakable.

I remain in touch with Tofigh's widow, who regularly sends photos of their daughters. The girls were both younger than ten when they lost their father. I made an unspoken promise to my friend that his daughters would know what a courageous, intelligent, compassionate man their father was. The stories in this book belong to them, as well as Ryan and Dustin, and Siamak's children.

Each day, I say a silent, thankful prayer for the blessings I have been given in life: a chance to get an education that enables me to help people; the right to worship as I choose; and the opportunity to raise my sons where so many freedoms are guaranteed. I am grateful that my sister and her family get to enjoy these freedoms, too. I only wish that the Iranian government would grant all Bahá'ís in Iran the same liberties.

America is an extraordinary country. It has an energy and a spirit that allows immigrants like me the opportunity to thrive. My story stands for people all over the world who also dream of living free in such an accepting home. They want to learn, love, prosper, and raise their families without fear. They want safety and justice in their lives.

It is my hope that America will always be the welcoming country that gave me a chance. Our country's greatness grows when we open our hearts to others.

Mansur and his family enjoying a beautiful
Colorado sunset in Fall 2020.

———

Resources

To learn more about the Bahá'í Faith, or to help end the ongoing persecutions happening in Iran and other countries today, contact Bahá'ís of the United States Office of Public Affairs (https://www.bahai.us/public-affairs/).

You can also visit the following websites to support these organizations' missions:

* Bahá'í Faith: https://www.bahai.org/

* Bahá'í Institute for Higher Education (BIHE): http://www.bihe.org/

* Bahá'ís of the United States: https://www.bahai.us/

* Bahá'í International Community: https://www.bic.org/

* Bahá'í House of Worship for North America: https://www.bahai.us/bahai-temple/

* United Nations Refugee Agency: https://www.unhcr.org/

* Virgin Islands Bar Association Gabriel Lerner Scholarship Fund: https://vibar.org/page/GabrielLerner

About the Authors

D r. Nurdel is a board-certified optometrist with offices throughout the Denver Metro Area. In addition to his time spent as a doctor, he is a real estate agent and investor. He currently resides in Castle Pines, Colorado, with his wife and two boys.

Jeannette R. Moninger is a freelance journalist with more than 20 years of experience writing for national magazines, including *Family Circle*, *Parents*, *Women's Health*, *Cure*, and *Redbook*. Her work has won numerous awards, including multiple National Health Information Awards, the Folio Editorial Excellence Award, the Planned Parenthood Maggie Award for Media Excellence, and the Meredith Corporation Creative Excellence Award. Born, raised, and educated in West Virginia, Jeannette now lives in Colorado with her husband, twin sons, and two cats.